Anthony Clavane was born in Leeds in 1960. He started life as a history teacher and is now chief sports writer for the *Sunday Mirror*. He has won Press Gazette Feature Writer of the Year and BT Regional Sportswriter of the Year awards. His previous book *Promised Land* was named Sports Book of the Year by the National Sporting Club and the Radio 2 Book Club. *Does Your Rabbi Know You're Here?* was short-listed for the 2013 British Sports Book Awards.

'An enthralling new book by Anthony Clavane, whose *Promised Land* was the sports book of 2011 by a mile.'

Patrick Barclay, *Evening Standard*

'Part family memoir, past social history, Clavane's book introduces us to a host of footballing Jews . . . and with great warmth and skill weaves their individual sporting stories into the longer arc of English Jewish history.'
Times Literary Supplement

'A poignant and rigorous history.' Simon Briggs, *Daily Telegraph*

'The story of the involvement of Jews as players, administrators and owners in English professional football.'

Richard Williams, *Guardian*, Sports Books of the Year

'A thought-provoking, absorbing exploration.'

Independent on Sunday

'A very entertaining account of a largely unexplored phenomenon with just the right co~~~~~~~~~~~~~~~~~~~~~~~~~~~~~~~~~~~~~ personal auto-
biograph~~~~~~ Toby Young

D0487227

DOES YOUR RABBI KNOW YOU'RE HERE?

The Story of English Football's Forgotten Tribe

Anthony Clavane

Quercus

First published in Great Britain in 2012 by Quercus Editions Ltd

This updated paperback edition published in 2013 by

Quercus Editions Ltd
55 Baker Street
Seventh Floor, South Block
London
W1U 8EW

A CIP catalogue record for this book is available
from the British Library

PB ISBN 978 0 85738 814 8
EBOOK ISBN 978 0 85738 813 1

10 9 8 7 6 5 4 3 2 1

Text and plates designed and typeset by Ellipsis Digital Ltd

Printed and bound in Great Britain by Clays Ltd, St Ives plc

To Mum, Dad and Peter. With love.

Contents

Part 1: The First Age

Part 2: The Golden Age

Part 3: The New Age

Acknowledgements

This book would not have been possible had Jon Riley and I not met for a pint at the Head of Steam, a fine Huddersfield pub. So a big thank you to him for the idea (although my friend Mike Collett had also mentioned a similar one a few months earlier), for his inspiration, for his excellent editing and for his moral support. My friend and literary agent David Luxton has, as always, been there for me, especially when things have not gone as smoothly as expected. Sorry, again, to my family for being in 'cave mode' while finishing the book. Thanks to Josh Ireland for his painstaking work on the text, David Dee, for his groundbreaking academic work on Jewish involvement in British sport, Tony Collins, who was an inspiring pioneer in this field, Danny Lynch from *Kick It Out,* Antony Spencer for his time and brilliant anecdotes, Caitlin Robinson and Nick Stimson for providing peaceful places to write, Josh Abbott for his work on Spurs, Steve Abbott and Sheryl Crown for their great support, Simon Glass for his excellent film *The Last Tribe,* the *Jewish Chronicle* and the *Jewish Telegraph* for their archives, and the London Jewish Museum and Manchester Jewish Museum for theirs. And the British Library for being my second home. Thank you also to William Bowman and Joanne Rosenthal for all their help.

There are a number of interviewees who were extremely helpful, kindly putting me in touch with their friends and contacts. Alex Fynn and Lord Triesman head this list. This has been a sensitive subject for some people, so I particularly appreciated David Pleat's openness and insight. The other interviewees who generously gave up their time include Nathan Abrams, Shaul Adar, David Baddiel, David Bernstein, Henry Bernstein, Tony Bloom, Paul Bobroff, David Buchler, Emile Clavane, George Cohen, Ivan Cohen, Simon Corney, Allan Dein, David Dein, Jeremy Dein, Micky Dulin, Paul Elliott, Edward Freedman, Dean Furman, Peggy Gaunt, Gary Gaunt, Mel Goldberg, Michael Grade, Alex Grime, Alan Harris, Keith Harris, Leila Harris, Barry Hearn, Ernest Hecht, Joe Jacobson, Morris Keston, Mark Lazarus, Joyce Levy, Peter Lorimer, Peter Lush, Edward Marshall, Jeremy Michelson, Izzy Pear, Susan Pleat, Stephen Pollard, Tony Sheldon, Barry Silkman, Leslie Silver, Nick Sonenfield, Antony Spencer, Jonathan Wilson, Brian Winston, Lord Young, Edward Ziff and Michael Ziff.

And a final thanks to The Great Glanville.

'In the highly improbable event of his being asked to nominate the one most un-Jewish thing he could think of, Sefton Goldberg would have been hard pressed to decide between Nature and football. But he would almost certainly have come down finally on the side of football. The game was not Jewish.'

Howard Jacobson, Coming from Behind, 1983

Stewardess: 'Would you like something to read?'
Passenger: 'Do you have anything light?'
Stewardess: 'How about this leaflet, *Famous Jewish Sports Legends*?'

Airplane, 1980

'Mr Football Jew does not exist. He is a misnomer. This is because Mr Football Jew is not Jewish at all. He is just another facet of the collective imagination.'

Nick Lambert,
Jews in Europe in the Twenty-First Century: Thinking Jewish, 2008

Preface

Ariel Friedlander is a devoted Queens Park Rangers fan. In her mid-twenties she landed her dream job as the club's official photographer. When a match at Tottenham was rearranged to take place on Rosh Hashanah, the Jewish New Year, she was faced with a dilemma. After consulting her rabbi, who also happened to be her father, she decided to attend the synagogue service in the morning and then rush over to White Hart Lane. Spurs scored an early goal, it started to rain and then came the inevitable lightning and thunder. God, clearly, was trying to tell her something. When QPR fans started singing 'Does your rabbi know you're here?' she screamed back at them 'Yes, he does, and he said it was my decision.' Not long after this incident she enrolled at the Hebrew Union College and trained to be a rabbi.

Rabbi Friedlander's epiphany – 'I realised God was sending me a personal message' – is one of the many entertaining stories I heard on my never ending tour of shuls, schools, universities, literary festivals, *Chanucah* parties – and the odd barmitzvah – to promote this book. It is funny, poignant and, like the majority of tales unearthed during my research, a previously untold one; part of the secret history of English football's forgotten tribe. Since the book's publication there has been an explosion of interest in the subject. Both the Manchester and London Jewish Museums have organised exhibitions. There have been many newspaper and magazine articles, several radio programmes and an excellent new academic tome from David Dee of De Montfort University.

We are living, as I reflect in the final section, in a new footballing age characterised by a great deal more openness about cultural diversity. Even so, it was a shock to see pictures in the *Jewish Chronicle* of thousands of Orthodox Jews crowding into Leyton Orient's stadium at Brisbane Road. The *Charedim*, it turned out, were congregating for an anti-internet rally; they have a strong anti-football tradition, although I am indebted to Jo Rosenthal at the London Jewish Museum for showing me 'a review of the halakhic opinions from Talmudic to contemporary authorities regarding the permissibility of playing ball on *shabbat* and *yom tov*.' The article's author, Rabbi Saul J. Berman, concluded that 'while contemporary custom is to refrain from playing ball on those days, normative legal opinion holds that such activity is permitted'.

This will have come as a great relief to Nick Blackman who, when he turned out for Reading at Stoke on a cold *shabbat* afternoon in February 2013, became the first English-born Jew to start a Premier League game.

I am not convinced that a combination of the Berman pronunciation and the Blackman breakthrough will open the floodgates. In the twenty-first century, Anglo-Jewry is, predominantly, a middle-class community and English football remains, predominantly, a working-class sport. For a large part of the previous century, however, many Jews took the traditional immigrant route out of the ghetto, becoming footballers, boxers and entertainers. And yet, during my never-ending tour, I have been discovering that the very idea of Jewish footballers continues to make people smile. 'Think back to your schooldays,' a review in *Shabbat Shalom* – 'Synagogue Newsletter of the Year' – began. 'What were your favourite subjects? English? History? Geography? What about PE, or football, or rugby? Exactly, Many of us hated with a vengeance anything which involved the donning of shorts or "pumps". Give us a good old essay on the Wars of the Roses any day. Or ask us to describe and draw an oxbow lake. But sport? No way.'

At the same time, I lost count of the number of people who told me about a relative who had briefly played for Bolton or been given a trial at Liverpool. I was contacted by James Baker, whose father, Arthur, starred for Hackney Junior Schoolboys in the 1930s. 'His place was eventually taken by future England player Eddie Bailey, but his performances earned him a trial with Orient', wrote James. 'However his parents, who were observant Jews, would not allow their son to play football on a Saturday.' As a result of poor records, and an understandable desire to keep their identity under wraps in a hostile environment, we will never know just how many Jewish professionals there were. Or, indeed, are. Several members of the audiences I addressed revealed that their sons, or nephews, were currently plying their trade in the Football League. Vic Shroot, for example, who remembered 'schlepping goalposts across Hackney Marshes on a Sunday morning' mentioned that his son Robin, now at League One side Stevenage, played in an FA Cup tie for Birmingham City at Wolves a few years ago.

Researching the book was initially difficult because key figures refused to speak, some on the grounds that their careers would be jeopardised. Jews tend to be an upwardly-climbing, past-erasing tribe who, following Lot's lead, prefer to look forward rather than back. As the community became more affluent in the latter half of the twentieth-century, the number of footballers dwindled to minis-cule proportions. Since the Second World War, the tribe has made its mark more as supporters than players. One club in particular, Tottenham Hotspur, is identified as *the* Jewish one, hence the chanting that Rabbi Friedlander mistook for a divine revelation. Wolfing down a bowl of *lokshen* soup before popping along to The Lane might, these days, be a halakhically acceptable way of spending the sabbath but, as Rabbi Berman admonishes, 'ball playing on *shabbat* and *yom tov* is a vacuous, pointless activity.' Which instantly brought to mind Woody Allen's famous line about sex without love being an empty experience – 'but, as empty experiences go, it's one of the best.'

Ignoring the fact that their bitter rivals, Arsenal, probably now have a greater number of Yiddisher fans, Tottenham's Jewishness, as a reviewer in the *Wall Street Journal* noted, 'has become an indelible part of the team's identity. It's not uncommon to see Israeli flags flying in the stadium and Tottenham's "top boys" – soccer slang for a club's most aggressive supporters – refer to themselves as the "Spurs Yids."' As a Jewish fan who doesn't support Spurs, this makes me feel very uncomfortable. At the same time, I don't support the Society of Black Lawyers' preposterous threat to report Tottenham to the police. As a club statement pointed out, fans 'adopted the chant as a defence mechanism in order to own the term and thereby deflect anti-Semitic abuse.' In the past year there has, sadly, been a rise in such abuse. In trips to Italy and France, Spurs fans have been attacked by fascist mobs. And whilst the days of English football crowds making massed monkey noises are thankfully gone, the 'oldest hatred' appears to be resurfacing in this country. After one encounter with Spurs, West Ham United issued life bans to supporters who had sung Hitler songs and made hissing noises – in emulation of the gas chambers – whilst offering up Nazi salutes.

It would be ridiculous to suggest that Jews are more obsessed with football than Gentiles. But, from Manchester City to Manchester United, and from Leeds United to Leyton Orient, a number of elderly fans at my talks put forward the reason for their obsession: a desperation to belong, to be accepted, to be part of what they once called the 'host community'. Football was the way my grandparents shed their Old World Yiddishness and became English. And it was the way my parents' generation became part of Leeds: The Rebbe in the morning, Don Revie in the afternoon. To my own, far more integrated, generation there is a lot less significance attached. Many of us are no longer so obsessed, simply enjoying the distracting triviality of twenty two players kicking a ball around like *meshuganahs* on a cold *shabbat* afternoon. Still, as distracting trivialities go, it remains one of the best.

Introduction: The Myth of Absence

'We had been Russians or Poles or something – why split
hairs? – and now we were setting about becoming English.'
Howard Jacobson, *Roots Schmoots*, 1993

In February 2012 the *Sun* newspaper hailed David Bernstein as 'an
avuncular, Old School figure with a touch of a Henley-on-Thames
bank manager about him'. Nothing exceptional in this, you may
think. Bernstein had, after all, just seen off the unpopular Italian
coach Fabio Capello, responsible for England's disastrous 2010 World
Cup campaign in South Africa. Previously, he had stood up to the
all-powerful FIFA president Sepp Blatter, responsible – in English
minds, at least – for myriad crimes against football. A cross between
Dad's Army's Captain Mainwaring and, according to one over-excited
broadsheet columnist, wartime prime minister Winston Churchill,
the chairman of the Football Association was lauded as the archetypal principled, resilient Little Englander unafraid to do battle with
Johnny Foreigner. The Anglophiles who had been so desperate to
'convert' his eastern European Jewish ancestors into Good Englishmen would have been very proud.

A few months later, after anointing Roy Hodgson as Capello's
successor, the new England coach was asked to name his favourite
writer. 'Philip Roth,' replied Hodgson. In the long hours of negotiation over terms and conditions, it would be interesting to know if
Hodgson and Bernstein had discussed one of the literary giant's

favourite themes: the integration of the Jewish outsider into main-stream culture. Or picked over Roth's quote about baseball, which describes the American national game as 'a kind of secular church that reached into every class and religion of the nation . . . a space where the marginal can become central, where the charges of not really belonging, of not being real men, of being interlopers or cheats can be defeated'. Unlike in the States, where novelists, sociologists and politicians have tended to view sport, particularly baseball, as an ideal vehicle for assimilation, Anglo-Jewry has been written out – and has often written itself out – of the history of English sport, particularly English football. Whenever an Anglo-Jewish sporting hero, like the world welterweight champion Jack 'Kid' Berg, the Olympic gold medallist Harold Abrahams or the Wimbledon champion Angela Buxton, has emerged, he or she has tended to be portrayed as the exception that proves the rule. Sometimes, as in the case of Abrahams, whose 100-metre win in the 1924 Olympics was immortalised in the film *Chariots of Fire,* he or she has suggested that being a Good Jew and being a Good Sportsman are incompatible aspirations. In the Oscar-winning movie, Abrahams, a keen Gilbert and Sullivan fan, was portrayed as the classic outsider who overcomes prejudice to become the very model of a thoroughly anglicised Jew. In one of the movie's most memorable scenes, he runs along the beach to the tune of 'He Is an Englishman'.

The argument of this book is that the role of Jews in English football's transformation from a working-class pursuit played in crumbling arenas to a global entertainment industry has been driven by this trope; that English football has, for the past century, been a vehicle for anglicisation, a space where ethnic identity has connected, even become intertwined, with national identity; an arena where Jews have fought the notion that they were invaders who needed to be fended off, newcomers who did not belong. There is always the risk of supplying ammunition to conspiracy theorists, especially those on the far right who continue to fantasise about the existence of a 'kosher nostra', but football history is far too important to be left to the anti-Semites. I have chosen eleven key figures, alongside many other equally intriguing if less important ones, who have all, in their different ways, embodied this trope. Their stories illustrate the different phases of Anglo-Jewry's 100-year evolution, the three stages of integration into English society: the First Age, the Golden Age and the New Age.

The eternal debate about whether Jews are a race, religion, nationality or ethnicity is of little interest here. I have settled on 'tribe' because they have, over the course of a century, formed a distinctive – if often hidden – subculture within the game, sharing not only a common ancestry and culture but also a tribal determination to prove themselves, to be accepted, to belong. In *Books Do Furnish a Room*, the novelist Anthony Powell wrote: 'It is not what happens to people that is significant, but what they think happens to them.' Everyone, Powell elaborated, has a personal myth. He was talking about characters in a novel, but the axiom can be equally applied to insecure migrant communities. The Anglo-Jewish football myth – of absence – is at odds with a long history of passionate involvement in the People's Game. Contrary to the stereotypical outpourings of large sections of both Jewish and non-Jewish opinion, Jews have bodies as well as minds. The culture is as physical as it is cerebral. In fact, today in England, as David Baddiel has observed, 'it is virtually impossible to be Jewish and male and not interested in football'.

The eleven key figures in this book represent a challenge to the myth of absence, a 'first team' of largely forgotten pioneers whose stories dramatise crucial moments in an epic journey from ghetto outsiders to FA insiders. Of course, to stretch the old joke, for every eleven Jews there are always twelve opinions. For this is a fractious and unruly tribe, often populated by non-conformists, dissenters, mavericks. All human life is there, in all its diversity, challenging the enduring stereotype of a narrow, clannish people. There are eastern and central Europeans, working-class East Enders and Sephardic Israelis, American sports moguls and Russian oligarchs. Jews have been players, fans, hangers-on, managers, directors, thinkers, fighters, writers, administrators, owners, showmen and introverts. Anglo-Jewry, in football as elsewhere, has never spoken with a single voice. Very often it hasn't spoken at all, preferring, often as a matter of policy, to blend in, maintain a low profile, not make a fuss. To keep schtum. This has made it difficult to write the definitive book on Jewish involvement in English football. Records have not been kept, sources have been lost, several key figures have simply refused to speak – some on the grounds that their careers may be jeopardised. By their very nature, Jews are an upwardly climbing, past-erasing tribe who, following Lot's lead, prefer to look forward rather than back. This has, however, made the unearthing of so many 'secret' lives all the more exciting and groundbreaking. The great historian Eric Hobsbawm, another distinguished Jewish émigré – and Bolton Wanderers fan – hardly mentions football, let alone Jewish participation in it, in his seminal accounts of the twentieth century. But he nevertheless recognised its national potency when he wrote: 'The *imagined community* of millions seems more real as a team of eleven named people.' My tribe seems, to me, more real as a team of eleven named, gutsy, presumptuous, footballing pioneers.

Becoming English

Since the first Jewish immigrants were brought to medieval England by William the Conqueror in 1070, four years after the Battle of Hastings, most of the tribe's fractious and unruly sections have been committed to a single goal: Becoming English. Integrate, assimilate, anglicise. In footballing terms, this has meant becoming so anglicised that their presence has been barely noted. Hence this book's subtitle: 'English Football's *Forgotten* Tribe'. Despite being a tiny part of the population, never, at any point in its history exceeding 450,000 – less than 1 per cent – it has produced its fair share of footballers, especially when, in the first half of the last century, it was a predominantly working-class tribe. In the second half of the century, as Jews became more acculturated, and more upwardly mobile, as they entered the professions, moved out to the suburbs and became middle class – as they became more English – it was almost as if they had forgotten they had once been footballers.

Just as they had forgotten they had once been boxers. After the Second World War, English Jews, like their American counterparts, quietly buried the public memory of their pugilistic past. And yet, from Samson to Daniel Mendoza, there have always been *schtarkers* – the Yiddish word for strongmen – in the ranks. Mendoza, English champion from 1792 to 1795, invented scientific boxing, which emphasised skill and speed as opposed to brute force, and received the patronage of the Prince of Wales, the future George IV. Towards the end of his career, he toured the country, giving demonstration bouts in front of huge numbers of fans. Such was his fame as a prize-fighter, newspapers reported one of his victories ahead of the storming of the Bastille in 1789. His triumphs, like those of Dutch

Sam, Aby Belasco and Barney Aaron, were credited with reducing attacks on Jews in the late eighteenth century.

Long before the creation of Israel in 1948, the myth of the unphysical Jew was being blown away in the dark, grimy alleyways of Whitechapel, Aldgate and Spitalfields. East End boxers like Kid Lewis and Kid Berg were part of an alternative tradition harking back to the folkloric fables of famous *schtarkers*. They appeared in the Yiddish imagination as a muscular counterpart to spiritual, Talmudic Judaism, protecting defenceless Pale of Settlement *shtetls* against Cossack pogroms. In the 1920s, the Jewish escapologist Harry Houdini and Zishe Breitbart – who could tear chains with his bare hands, break coins between his fingers and lift huge weights with his teeth – both competed for the billing of the 'strongest man in the world'. In the Jewish-American underworld so fascinatingly documented in Rick Cohen's *Tough Jews*, a gangster generation flourished. Lewis and Berg were the last of the great Yiddisher fighters to punch their way out of East End poverty. They personified the necessity of Jewish toughness in a threatening world. In the Devonshire and Blackfriars arenas, Jews would sit downstairs and Gentiles would perch in the balconies. When their heroes fought non-Jews, the roar of the crowd would split in half. A succession of spindly assassins raised their fists against prejudice, refusing to perpetuate the role of victim. Anshel Young Joseph, an exceptionally clever boxer, won the British welterweight championship. The little scrapper Cockney Cohen held his own in four bouts with ex-world bantamweight champion Pedlar Palmer. They were followed by Matt Wells, Harry Mason – an English and European lightweight champion – Johnny Brown, Jack Broomfield – the British middleweight and British Empire light-heavyweight champion – and Harry Mizler. In the late 1930s, a few years after becoming English welterweight champion, Mizler fought one of Oswald

Mosley's Nazi henchmen, delaying the knockout punch until he had inflicted as much damage as possible.

The greatest fighters of this golden age were the two 'Kids', who racked up almost every major British and American championship belt before the war. Lewis, who like Mendoza hailed from Aldgate, was known as the 'Yiddish Wonderman'. With a Star of David sewn on his shorts and *tefillin* – small black leather boxes containing scrolls with verses from the Torah – on his arms, he shamelessly whipped up local support. He became the first Englishman to win a world boxing title in the United States before returning home to claim six British and European gongs. By the time he retired, in 1929, he had blown all his riches and two years later, astonishingly, became Mosley's bodyguard. On discovering the British Union of Fascists were virulently anti-Semitic, however, he beat up Mosley and two of his cronies.

Jack 'Kid' Berg recalls:

My gang was mainly from my street. Sam Bibbikraut was the leader. Then there was Gussie, Sammy Front, Morrie Greenberg, maybe one or two others, younger brothers. We grew up together. I could lick Sam – I could lick any of them. I was fighting every day, to survive. I had to fight, it was my way, you see. When I was in the street, if anybody hit somebody I knew, I used to shield that person. I never wanted people to take liberties with me. What's right is right, but I never wanted people to take liberties. I always landed the first punch, whatever happened. I'd get in first. If I'm right or wrong, I'm going to hit you, I'm not going to wait until you bang me one. Gangs of Gentiles used to sing bad things to us on the streets, often in front of old Jewish people, and when we kids used to hear that, well, we didn't like it. Our spirits used to be on fire, we'd burn. We would make a dash for them. We were always fighting. You had to fight. It was part of my nature.'

'In the old days,' said Michael Grade, whose father and uncles set up a showbusiness dynasty after the war, 'there were a lot of Jewish prize-fighters. Which is unusual, I'm surprised their mothers let them. They fought their way out. My family chose the other way out, the stage, bless 'em. It was their way out of the ghetto, to go on the stage and dance. Rather than, say, box.'

During the First Age, of integration, from just before the First World War to the 1953 England–Hungary game, football also performed this role of escape route. After Louis Bookman became the first Jew to play in the First Division thousands of immigrant children took to the streets, playgrounds and muddy pitches, fantasising about a life of glory and impossible glamour. This fantasy life was encouraged by communal leaders, anxious that young immigrants should quickly adopt English values such as fair play and sportsmanship. Anglicisation implanted fervent allegiances, from the East End to north London, from inner-city Leeds to inner-city Manchester. Jews became fierce and passionate players, using tough muscles and sharp brains to escape their claustrophobic enclaves. The Gentiles had their Saturday football – which second-generation Jews, often without telling their parents, would sneak off to watch after going to the synagogue – and the Jews had their Sunday football. When players broke through into the former, however, no mention would be made of their ethnicity. This is because Anglo-Jewry has never wished to be regarded as an ethnic minority. Communal leaders have always been threatened by such a description and have strongly opposed being identified on the national census in this way. The Jewish Establishment has always wanted its primary identity to be English.

It is not difficult to understand why, especially at the end of the First Age, anglicisers chose to adopt such a narrow definition of their identity. During the Second World War, let us not forget, only twenty miles of salt sea separated the community from extinction. Insecurity, particularly the fear of exclusion, expulsion – even elimination – is part of the tribal folk memory. In the third century, the principle known as *dina de-malchuta dina* was established in the Jewish diaspora, which, translated from the Hebrew, meant an acceptance of the law of the land in which you live. Throughout the twentieth century, embracing humility as an assimilationist strategy, the Anglo-Jewish mantra was *minhag Anglia* – the tradition of England. British Jews have always taken this strategy to great extremes, showing exaggerated respect to their host country, enlisting for military service – from the Napoleonic wars to the two great twentieth-century conflicts – in disproportionate numbers, forever fearful of anti-patriotic slights. As a young boy, I always wondered why it was felt necessary to include an oath of allegiance to the Queen in Saturday services at the synagogue. And why, for that matter, had we all changed our names? My family used to be called Clavinsky, my grandmother was a Tompowsky, and most of my relatives worked in a factory owned by Montague Ossinsky – better known as Montague Burton. In researching this book I interviewed the eighty-two-year-old widow of Leslie Goldberg, a Leeds United player of the 1930s. After the war, she told me, he had been transferred to Reading and, in order to fit in, had changed his name to Gaunt.

And then I remembered how proud I felt reading an extract from Tony Blair's 2006 speech at Bevis Marks Synagogue in the City of London. 'As the oldest minority faith community in this country,' the then prime minister told the packed congregation, 'you show how identity through faith can be combined with a deep loyalty to our nation.'

Loyalty – or, to put it another way, blending in, maintaining a low profile, not making a fuss, keeping schtum – has been the cornerstone of Anglo-Jewish policy since 1656, when the Jews were re-admitted to England. In 1290, the 2,500-strong community had been expelled by Edward I and did not return, officially at least, for another 366 years. The Edict of Expulsion had been the culmination of a long process of demonisation; clerics and popes had routinely stirred up ill feeling against the 'Christ-killers' and in 1144, East Anglian Jews had been accused of murdering a young boy, William of Norwich, to use his blood in a religious ritual. Although charges were dropped through the intervention of the Crown, similar blood libels were to occur throughout British history. When Richard the Lionheart joined the Third Crusade in 1190, anti-Semitic rioting erupted throughout the realm. Thousands of Jews in Bury St Edmunds, Colchester, Thetford and London were robbed, beaten, forcibly baptised, hung or burned to death. York's small community fled to the royal castle for protection. When help did not arrive, most killed themselves or perished in flames rather than face forced conversion. The mob massacred the few who survived. In the early 1200s, many Jews were expelled from their homes and required to wear identifying badges, an eerie precursor of the Nazi yellow stars.

Despite being banished, a small number returned clandestinely over the following centuries. These included Spanish and Portuguese Jews who had embraced Christianity – *Marranos* – Tudor court musicians and, during the reign of Charles I, Jewish merchants disguised as Spaniards. The first Jewish families to come to London in 1656, after Menasseh ben Israel of Amsterdam persuaded Oliver Cromwell to readmit the community, on biblical grounds, were also Sephardim; of Mediterranean as opposed to north European – Ashkenazi – origin, they had enjoyed five centuries of cultural and intellectual splendour until the Inquisition forced them to convert, flee or be put to death. Primarily from the Iberian Peninsula, but including some second-generation emigrants from central and western Europe as well, they assimilated quickly into English society, being accustomed both to hiding their Jewish identity and to inter-acting with non-Jewish communities. Although officially recognised by Cromwell, who allowed them to establish a synagogue, they faced repeated assaults. 'Political instability and changes of regime gave Christian fanatics and business competitors opportunities to demand their expulsion,' wrote David Cesarani. 'As a consequence, their leaders feared that any infraction of the law or provocation could be used against them.'

Intermarriage and conversion were common in London, and were attractive because they offered access and membership to English institutions. During the eighteenth century receiving a university education, gaining a place at the Inns of Court and obtaining a seat in parliament were all denied to non-Anglicans. In 1701, the Sephardi Jews set up a congregation at Bevis Marks, the first purpose-built synagogue in Britain since medieval times. By the 1730s, the Jewish population, which now included Ashkenazi settlers attracted by the prospect of religious freedom, had grown to 6,000 – larger than in the Middle Ages. By the end of the century it numbered 20,000. When George III came to the throne in 1760, the Sephardi elders presented him with a petition of loyalty on behalf of Jews belonging to 'the Portuguese nation'; the Ashkenazi congregations objected and, eventually, both communities formed a joint committee called the Board of Deputies, the first representative body of Jews in Britain.

The Jewish Naturalisation Act of 1753 – known as The Jew Bill – had, briefly, granted the community English citizenship, but it was repealed after widespread protests. The vast majority of Ashkenazi immigrants crowded into London's East End. As they grew in number, their European Hebrew pronunciation, prayer forms

and language, Yiddish, supplanted the area's original Sephardic character. They established cemeteries, synagogues, religious schools and
ritual bath houses and were self-supporting; they fed their hungry,
provided dowries for needy brides, cared for widows and orphans
and buried their poor. Streets thronged with peddlers hawking rags,
used clothing, shoe buckles, watch chains, rings, snuff boxes and
buttons. Tailors recycled frayed jackets into serviceable children's
wear, and cobblers stitched up shoes good as new. Their poverty
was exacerbated by overcrowding, inadequate sanitation and disease.

By 1830, there were about 20,000 Jews living in London and
another 10,000 in the provinces. It was at this point that the
complexion of the migratory flow became more middle-class. Some
of the newcomers were political refugees, like Karl Marx, but most
were German merchants and clerks attracted to England because
of its unrivalled mercantile and industrial pre-eminence. They
opened offices and warehouses in Bradford, Leeds, Manchester and
Nottingham to buy goods for export to the Continent. Although
there was a small trickle of impoverished, lower-class Jews from
eastern Europe, the embourgeoisement of the community continued
unabated during the mid-Victorian era. Material success, economic
mobility and acculturation sparked a shift in self-definition; a more
intimate identification with Englishness reflected by the increasing
demand for secular education. The spread of secondary education
encouraged middle-class Jews, in Todd Endelman's words, 'to think
of themselves as English, as well as Jewish, as rooted in the life of
the country rather than tossed on to its shores by circumstance'. In
industrial centres outside London, particularly Manchester, Liverpool
and Leeds, the new professional classes became involved in literary
and philosophical societies, dining clubs, musical societies, Masonic
lodges, choral groups and mechanics institutes. These institutions,
independent of church and chapel, and located in areas where landed

upper-class influence was weak, provided a space for the integration of successful Jewish businessmen into local society. Meanwhile,
the wealthiest families, like the Rothschilds, acquired country estates,
pursued rural pleasures and entertained the political elite.

This assimilation into Gentile society spawned demands for emancipation: the removal of barriers to full civic equality and the right
to participate in public affairs. Unlike in Napoleonic France or the
Russian Empire, Christian advocates of Jewish suffrage did not make
their support conditional; Napoleon, for example, called on French
Jews to repudiate separatism and Russian liberals insisted on the
abandonment of orthodox beliefs and habits. Jews were eventually
admitted to parliament because they were viewed as hard-working,
loyal citizens and they had anglicised their synagogue services, modi-
fying them to reflect middle-class notions of decorum and gentility.
During his forty-five-year tenure as chief rabbi, from 1845 to 1890,
as more Jews absorbed English tastes and identified their fate with
their adoptive country, Nathan Adler encouraged a new type of
non-European, pastoral religious leader to emerge – and urged
rabbis to preach in English, even if they were natives of Germany
and Poland.

The assassination of Tsar Alexander II in 1881 provoked a mass
migration to the West. Blamed for the murder, two million Jews
fled the subsequent pogroms – Cossack attacks on their villages –
which took place in the Russian Pale of Settlement, an area they
had been restricted to in the eighteenth century following the parti-
tioning of Poland. Previously, when the Russian army had captured
a Polish town, its entire Jewish population had been put to death;
on this occasion, Catherine the Great opted for ethnic containment
rather than cleansing. Most refugees went to America, but thousands ended up in Britain. By 1919, the Anglo-Jewish population
had increased from 46,000 in 1880 to about 250,000. There was a

huge gulf between the impoverished eastern European refugees and the 'aristocrats' of the anglicised Establishment. 'A remark that would have brought a blush to the cheek of a Young Person in Mr Podsnap's household,' noted Stephen Brook, 'would have had the same effect in the drawing rooms of the Mocattas or Montefiores or any of the other Jewish grandees of the time.' The middle-class leaders were horrified by the old-world religious practices of the new arrivals. Having intensely pursued Englishness for the best part of two centuries, they suddenly saw all their good work being undermined by this invasion of ill-kempt foreigners, who were both conspicuous in their appearance and indecorous in their worship.

The Jewish Board of Guardians took an active part in repatriating thousands of undesirable immigrants. Advertisements were placed in eastern European Jewish newspapers discouraging them from emigrating. But they just kept on coming; by the end of the nineteenth century, the population of some parts of the East End was one-third immigrant. The Jewish population of Leeds, located in one of the city's worst slums – the Leylands – trebled between 1888 and 1902. Strangeways and Red Bank in Manchester also had vibrant communities, and smaller ones flourished in industrial regions such as south Wales and the north-east. Most immigrants entered the British economy as workers in sweated industries. Hundreds of small workshops sprang up in immigrant districts, housed in garrets, cellars, backrooms, stables, disused sheds and crumbling warehouses. The majority were overcrowded, dimly lit, poorly ventilated and littered with rubbish. Inspectors discovered floors smeared with faeces. Tailors who toiled fourteen- to eighteen-hour days contracted respiratory diseases from working in these tiny, damp, overheated spaces. Education was then, as now, seen as the way out of the ghetto. The Education Act of 1870 had established state-financed, nondenominational primary schools – and it was here that first- and second-generation immigrants were reshaped as English citizens. As a scholarship boy at a Whitechapel school revealed, 'The unspoken but quite clear message was: "Now, if you accept what we have to offer, we might, after several years of concentrated endeavour, turn you out as a passable imitation of an educated member of the English middle class."'

During the First Age, anti-Semitism was part of the public discourse. This had first become apparent during the debates on prime minister Benjamin Disraeli's policy towards Turkey. A converted Jew who flaunted his Jewish roots – having been baptised he was able to enter parliament in 1837, twenty-one years before the first official Jewish MP, Lionel de Rothschild, was allowed to take his seat – Disraeli's handling of the Eastern Question sparked an explosion of anti-Jewish feeling. During the Boer War, from 1899 to 1902, Jews were accused of manipulating British foreign policy. The eastern European exodus was the final straw, provoking a moral panic. 'Aliens' were blamed for urban squalor, unemployment, disease and crime. A witness told the 1903 Royal Commission on Alien Immigration that 'the feeling is that there is nothing but the English going out and the Jews coming in.' In Whitechapel, a social worker noted that 'the English visitor feels himself one of a subject race in the presence of dominant and overwhelming invaders'. The newcomers were, on the whole, regarded as filthy, clannish, indecent and subversive. 'They worked on Sundays,' wrote Endelman, 'slept outside on hot summer nights, ate herring and black bread and read Yiddish newspapers. The fundamental grievance, of course, was that the immigrants were not English.' To the anglicised leaders, they were the wrong kind of Jews.

The great fear was that their overtly Yiddish behaviour would fuel anti-Semitism. The Establishment had done its best to blend in with the host culture, but the *Ostjuden* stood out, reminding

them of their own lowly, foreign origins. When xenophobic journalists whipped up public opinion against the 'foreign invaders', the
Balfour administration introduced the 1905 Aliens Act, which severely
restricted immigration. Subsequent acts in 1914 and 1919 empow-
ered the state to deport aliens who engaged in political or industrial 'subversion'; dozens of non-naturalised Jews were kicked out
of the country during the 1920s. Official discrimination was accompanied by everyday racism and sporadic anti-Jewish violence from
right-wing groups.

Anglo-Jewry's answer was to adopt a policy of radical assimilation.
The foreignness of the newcomers would be erased as every available
resource – lay, ecclesiastical, educational and sporting – was mobilised
for a crash course in Englishness. At Jewish schools, children were
taught English literature, the glories of the Empire and songs celebrating the bulldog spirit. And they were encouraged to play indigenous sports, such as football and cricket. The Jewish Lads Brigade,
which was set up to emulate the British Scouts, adopted the motto
of 'a good Jew and a good Englishman', with particular emphasis on
the latter. According to its founder, Colonel Albert Goldsmid, the
organisation would 'iron out the ghetto bend' and produce 'Englishmen
of the Mosaic persuasion'. Algernon Lesser, who ran the JLB annual
summer camps, argued that sport was a powerful catalyst in turning
'the child of the alien into a good English citizen. Probably the most
curious feature which strikes the communal worker, when he first
starts work in the East End of London, is the enormous difference
in so many ways between the alien parent and the English-born child.
What are the causes which bring about this remarkable change in
one generation? Firstly, no doubt, is the influence of the school [but]
the encouragement which the clubs give to athletic sports of all description, and the enthusiasm with which the members take up these
sports, are powerful helps towards anglicisation.'

Staying Jewish

In the late 1960s, at the Selig Brodetsky Jewish Day School in Leeds, my friends and I would spend every minute of our spare time kicking a football around the playground. The joys of unrestrained youth. Except we were soon to be restrained. One morning our headmaster, Mr Abrahamson, summoned us to his tiny, tobacco-scented office. After confiscating our ball he proceeded to lecture us for about half an hour on why Jews were people of the book not people of the penalty kick. The next morning, at break-time, we played with a tennis ball. When he confiscated that, we switched to an apple core. Then, when he banned the apple core, we decided to use a banana skin. Finally we took to dribbling, flicking and back-heeling orange peels around the school grounds – until receiving, once again, the inevitable summons. 'What chutzpah,' Abie spluttered, before launching into another tirade, this one culminating in a caning. After administering our punishment, and thoughtfully sucking on his pipe for a few seconds, he then issued what he called the Eleventh Commandment: 'Football is not for a Yiddisher boy!'

I have always enjoyed a well-taken penalty kick as much as a good book. Torres and the Torah are, for me, subjects equally worthy of Talmudic discourse. Mr Abrahamson had actually taught my dad physical education at a Leeds secondary modern during the war. So what did he mean, exactly? Was it a religious or cultural thing? Were we simply no good at playing the beautiful game? Was it too rough for us? Abie, as my dad remembered, had once been a zealous inte-grationist, desperate for the Jewish kids to fit in at their Church of England school. Being good at games had seemed the best way to do this. He had been especially proud of young Les Goldberg, the first Jewish boy to play for Leeds United, and the first to play for

England Schoolboys. Our Les had been a portent of the assimilation to come. Next Year In Jerusalem.

My school was named after the Zionist leader Selig Brodetsky,
who lived near the Headingley rugby league ground in Leeds. Between
the wars, Brodetsky warned that 'thousands of boys' were growing
up in complete ignorance of 'Jewish learning, life and thought'. On
Saturdays, he would watch in horror as they walked towards the
ground and away from the synagogue. With *shul* attendance in sharp
decline, youngsters in particular preferring a trip to their local temple
of sport on *shabbat*, such apostasy was a great worry to orthodox
leaders. 'The English game,' Abie warned us, would eventually swallow
us up. Which is why, at school, we learned Hebrew, studied the
5,000-year history of our tribe and were banned from back-heeling
bits of orange peel around at break and lunchtime.

While the longstanding strategy of Anglo-Jewry has been to
pursue Englishness, there has always been an alternative, contradictory narrative lurking just beneath the surface: staying Jewish. The
fear here, as expressed most strongly by eastern European immigrants
at the turn of the twentieth century and revived during the anti-
integrationist backlash of the 1960s and '70s, is that the diaspora would
be assimilated to the point of non-existence. Playing football, particularly on a Saturday, was – like eating non-kosher food or marrying
out – a dangerous symptom of secularisation. Moreover, in its essence,
as Sefton Goldberg, Howard Jacobson's narrator in *Coming from Behind*
argued, soccer was 'un-Jewish'. The sense of there being two parallel
universes – the Jewish and the English, the Yiddisher world and the
football world of, as Goldberg put it, 'beer, bikies, mud and physical
pain' – was a feature of this Golden Age, an era when my father's,
and my own, generation began to ride high on a wave of post-war
social mobility.

And yet Jews have been kicking balls around on muddy pitches, and pieces of rotting fruit around on school playgrounds, ever since Norwood Jews Orphanage thrashed Endearment 11–1 in January 1901, one of the first ever matches played in the Sunday Football League – a competition set up by the Jewish Athletic Association to increase interest in the game. And they have been following football, with a rare fervour, ever since thousands of Yiddisher boys caught the train from Whitechapel to White Hart Lane, to be greeted with the refrain: 'Does your rabbi know you're here?'

Part 1

The First Age

To Be an Englishman

'Go away from your land, from your birthplace, and from your father's house, to the land that I will show you.'

Genesis 12.1

The First Age began with a political assassination and ended with a footballing one. It was marked by two European Jewish invasions: the sudden influx from eastern Europe, triggered by Tsar Alexander II's murder in 1881, and the central European flight from the Nazis. The first invasion differed greatly from the second: the invaders were more religious, spoke Yiddish and were crowded into inner-city, working-class areas. The Continental émigrés, on the other hand, tended to be secular, multilingual and middle-class. But they were both conspicuously foreign and, as such, a great source of worry to Anglo-Jewish leaders. Since being readmitted by Cromwell, the community had developed a deep sense of its own transience. Driven by fear of expulsion, insecure about its vulnerability as the oldest non-Christian minority in Britain and desperate to emulate the mores of the host nation, it had quietly, unfussily blended into mainstream society, becoming 'Englishmen of the Mosaic persuasion'.

*

With increasing hostility and bigotry, as evidenced by the anti-immigration campaign and, in the 1930s, the threat posed by Oswald Mosley and his British Union of Fascists, sporting arenas became sites of anglicisation. Whether elite or proletarian – both football

3

and boxing were taken up in great numbers – competitive games, Jewish leaders argued, would transform 'alien' children into Englishmen and women. Taking part in these games was one of the best ways of countering charges of physical weakness, separateness and 'Otherness'. Organisations such as the JLB and the JAA, whose membership grew enormously between the wars, led a crusade to anglicise the new arrivals through sport. Football, as the historian David Dee has argued, 'acted as a powerful force in the erosion and re-construction of Jewish ethnicity'. Unlike later non-white immigrant groups, Jews could play competitive games without really standing out too much. To be on the safe side, the newcomers were encouraged to change their names, be unassertive and – if outed – swallow slights. Whilst sporting success was viewed as a way of combating anti-Semitism, it wasn't considered wise to be too successful. In the 1930s, for example, the Jewish Lads Brigade withdrew all of their boxers from tournaments after winning the Prince of Wales' Shield twelve times. In a decade when Hitler was conquering the world, it was felt that Mosley's 'Jewish conspiracy' propaganda might be given some credence.

But the main thing was not to look too Jewish; the sight of a sturdy, athletic footballer heading a football into a net would, it was argued, go a long way to undermining the image of the devout, long-bearded ghetto-dweller draped in a yarmulke and prayer shawl.

Sporting legends like Buxton, Berg and Abrahams were gratefully seized upon as role models. They were indeed, as the famous *Airplane* joke would have it, few and far between. But this was as much down to exclusion as it was to self-imposed religious and cultural restraints. When Buxton, as a teenager, tried to join the prestigious Cumberland Lawn Tennis Club in north-west London, her application was turned down. 'You'll never make it,' a coach at the club informed her. 'You're perfectly good, but you're Jewish. We don't take Jews here.' Two years before she won the French Open and Wimbledon Ladies' doubles, in 1956, a local journalist had to act as her hitting partner before a tournament in Southport because club members refused to practise with a Jew. Despite her success at Wimbledon – she also reached the Ladies' singles final – she was placed on a waiting list for membership of the All England Tennis Club. Abrahams, the son of a Polish Jewish immigrant, argued that the best way to be accepted into an elite sport, like tennis, golf or athletics, was to become more English than the English. Observing the Sabbath, he argued, was an important block on success; a Jewish sportsman wanting to reach the top had to assimilate as quickly as possible. The answer to the discrimination that he, Buxton and others faced was not only to become less strict in one's religious observance, but also to keep one's Jewishness hidden from view.

1

The Outsiders:
When Abraham Made the Sacrifice

'When a schoolboy of today selects a picturesque career
he no longer plumps for pirate, engine driver or cowboy
chief . . . No, every spirited youth now wants to be a cellu-
loid comedian with his feet at three o'clock, like Charlie
Chaplin, or a professional footballer like Andrew Wilson
or Jack Cock . . . Their parents are wondering: "Is Football
a suitable career for our Bill?"'

Louis Bookman, *Leighton Buzzard Observer*, 1921

Louis Bookman: The Lithuanian-Jewish-Irishman

In 1912, at the end of his first season with First Division side Bradford City, Louis Bookman returned to Ireland. Bradford were then one of England's biggest teams. In the 1910–11 season, they had won the FA Cup and finished fifth in the league. There had been high hopes for 'Abraham', as his City team-mates had immediately dubbed him on his arrival at Valley Parade, but he had failed to shine at outside-left. In fact, towards the end of the campaign he had hardly played at all. The Yorkshire side finished up mid-table, and Bookman became the scapegoat. Fans attacked the board for wasting hundreds of pounds on an unknown Lithuanian-Jewish-Irishman. Back in Ireland, Bookman felt as alienated from his orthodox, Yiddish-speaking, eastern European immigrant family as from the grey, depressing, Yorkshire skies. In 'the *Heym*', the old country – his parents told him – no one had even heard of 'this English game', let alone played it. Turning out for a shul team on a Sunday was one thing, playing for a *goyishe* mob on *shabbat* quite another. All this nonsense had to stop. Besides, it was his religious duty to keep the Sabbath holy. In continuing with this heathen activity, he was trading his birthright, his ancestry, his Jewishness for ... for what? Is this what he wanted to do? To sacrifice his culture? To cut himself off from his family, his roots, his religion?

*

Bookman's passion for sport – he played cricket for Ireland as well as football for Bradford, West Bromwich Albion, Luton Town and Port Vale – was deemed by his parents to be fundamentally un-Jewish. For Mathias and Jane Bookman, and thousands of other impoverished families from eastern Europe, status was achieved by Talmudic learning and observance. For the middle-class, assimilated leaders who ran the youth clubs that Louis – and thousands of other sports-mad youngsters – joined, it was underwritten by integration. 'Louis' choice' – should I stay in Ireland or should I go back to Bradford? – dramatised a crisis for the immigrants who had fled persecution and sought refuge in the British Isles, which Dublin was then a part of. Bookman had grown up watching his parents re-create the *shtetl* world they had left behind. They weren't interested in him becoming a good English citizen. To them, Englishness and Jewishness were mutually contradictory: the former all stiff-upper-lip reticence, pointless etiquette and meaningful silence, the latter none of those things. Recreation, exercise, moral and cultural improvement weren't as important to them as tradition, the Torah and being a Good Jew. They wanted Louis to stay Jewish, not become English. They thought Englishness would squeeze all the Jewishness out of him. At the very least, they wanted him to stay Irish-Jewish.

There was a culture clash between 'the English game', as my old headmaster called it, and the religious mores of the 120,000 or so refugees who emigrated to Britain between 1881 and 1914. Ripped out of their *shtetls*, hungry and poor, they were strangers in a strange land, ghetto outcasts, living a hand-to-mouth existence, either on or below the poverty line. 'In this spot, with the holy name Whitechapel, a piece of Israel existed,' wrote Jacob P. Adler. 'There we would have to sink or swim, survive or go under, find bread, or if we could not, find death.' Finding a football match to play in, even if they had been of a less devout disposition, was hardly a priority. Even finding a football match to play in on a non-holy day was deemed contrary to the spirit of Judaism, an affront to the religion's traditional emphasis on Talmudic learning. For the past hundred years the game has deeply penetrated Anglo-Jewish society, but most first-generation immigrants viewed it as a heathen activity.

The physical world paled into insignificance besides the life of the mind. According to the Jewish émigré Sigmund Freud: 'The harmonious development of spiritual and bodily activity, as achieved by the Greeks, was denied to the Jews.' This was as much down to exclusion as theology; in the Middle Ages, for example, they weren't allowed to bear arms, ride horses, duel, joust or arch competitively. Rabbi Yosef Caro of Palestine, in a typically protracted debate with Rabbi Moses Isserles of Cracow, went so far as to denounce all ball games. 'Footbollick,' the East End writer Ralph Finn recalled his eastern European grandfather spitting at him in the 1920s. 'Grown men running around like *meshuga*, nothing with nothing.' As Lipa Tepper's parents, also during that decade, warned him: 'A Jewish boy does not play with stupid things and does not do things which all other boys do because he is Jewish and therefore he has got duties to perform and things to do which are unlike anybody else's.'

Today, in our multicultural society, when the anglicisers' forward-looking secularity appears to have triumphed, such narrow-minded tribalism is seen as anachronistic. But in the First Age, when society was monocultural and Englishness was a club with sharp restrictions on its membership, the pressure on talented young sportsmen from within the community, never mind from without, was intense. Playing football was not only about desecrating the Sabbath, which was bad enough, it was about rejecting the separateness, the us-and-themness – the *frummers* would say the very survival – of the Jewish religion. Orthodox families like the Bookmans were steeped in a rabbinic culture that downgraded toughness. Fighting, duelling, wrestling, hunting and sport? Not for the Jews. Of course, Jews had been excluded from many of these masculine activities in the *Heym*, but they followed a traditional Yiddish code called *menschilkayt* which, in its extreme form, rejected the competitive ethos of what they disparagingly called *goyim nachas* – pleasure for the Gentiles.

It has always amused me that Tottenham Hostspur are deemed to be a Jewish club, because their stadium lies on the doorstep of an ultra-orthodox community which scorns integration and favours the pale, physically frail scholar who studies indoors above the secular, football-obsessed 'heretic' who shares the aggressive values of the Jews' oppressors. In Israel, the *Haredi* refuse to fight in the army on the grounds that, in the words of journalist Phoebe Greenwood, their 'right to study rather than serve represents a battle for the preservation of the Jewish people, pitting the value of the body against the worth of the soul.'

This is a familiar anxiety for all children of immigrant parents. Grandchildren and great-grandchildren too. When I passed the eleven-plus at my Jewish primary school, in 1971, I had a big row with my parents about the secondary school I should go to. Passing the exam, I argued, didn't mean that I had to actually attend the rugby-playing grammar school I had gained entry to. The other school up the road, Allerton Grange – famous for its football teams – would be far better suited to my needs. I felt vindicated twenty or so years later, when ex-Allerton Grange pupils Brian Deane and David Batty starred for Leeds United at Elland Road. But I was not really in a position to choose. I was, after all, only eleven years old. And so they won the argument, and a potentially brilliant football career was over before it even had a chance to blossom.

Of course, I wasn't that good really. But I was desperate to play for a team, to be spotted by a scout, to make it. Each one of the eleven trailblazers featured in this book displayed that obsession, that desperation. And each one has had to confront, to varying degrees, their own, internalised version of the Tebbit test. Shall I pursue my dream, and 'become English', or stay loyal to my family, my roots, my religion?

Louis Bookman was the quintessential wandering Jew, travelling as a young boy with his parents on the long, arduous journey from Lithuania to Cork, then going on to Dublin, then Belfast, across the sea to England – where he played for several football and cricket clubs – and back again to Ireland. He had been born in Zagaren, a small Lithuanian town renowned for its cherries, in 1890. His America-bound family, then called Buchalter, arrived in Cork by mistake; distracted by heavy gales, they thought the ship's captain had shouted out 'New York'. Like many of their co-religionists, they saw their stay in Britain as the last stopping-off point in the Old World before their voyage to the New World. Along with their nine children – two of their sons continued on to America – the Buchalters moved to Dublin, changed their name to Bookman and joined the Adelaide Road synagogue.

As with his fictional compatriot Leopold Bloom, the anti-hero of James Joyce's *Ulysses*, he was excluded by one group after another because of his perceived 'Otherness'. Asked why he'd made Bloom Jewish, Joyce – who wrote the classic novel between 1914 and 1921 – said: 'Because only a foreigner would do. The Jews were foreigners at that time in Dublin. There was no hostility towards them, but contempt, yes the contempt people always show for the unknown.' Bloom is asked by a rabid nationalist: 'What is your nation?' He replies: 'Ireland . . . I was born here. Ireland.' Bloom's questioner then threatens to 'brain that jewman'. Louis was involved in a similar incident in 1921, while taking a short holiday in Dublin just before playing in an international match. As reported in a Luton newspaper, 'the popular Town footballer was walking along Parliament Street, which was quite busy at the time, when he saw a civilian held up by two plain-clothed men, who were obviously "Black and Tans."' These, the paper explained, were British soldiers employed to make Ireland 'hell for the rebels to live in'. One of them 'pointed a revolver at him and stripped him of his money and valuables'.

Bookman told the paper: 'The assailant asked me who the h— I was, and ordered me to put up my hands quickly. I told him. He asked me if I were an Irishman and I said that I was. With an oath he then called me "a fine Irishman", pulled a revolver from his pocket and putting the muzzle to the small of my back, he ordered me to march.'

To Bookman's parents, that mugging would have confirmed all their fears about the non-Jewish, *goyishe*, world. Like Bloom, Louis was excluded from the notion of Ireland and Irishness and, up until his move to Luton, he was treated as an alien in the English sporting world. In the late Victorian and Edwardian eras, Jews were openly blackballed in upper- and middle-class sports like golf, tennis and horse racing. In 1894, *Golf* magazine revealed that a Manchester club 'excludes all Jews from membership'. *Golf Illustrated* argued that their 'win-at-all-costs mentality' was alien to the British sporting ethos and published cartoons and fictional stories depicting Jewish golfers, talking in broken English, as foreign, flashy and untrust- worthy. Neither were foreigners welcomed in football changing rooms. In 1892 the Canadian Walter Bowman had become the first non-Englishman to play in the Football League, signing for Accrington Stanley, but only another five – Max Seeburg, Hussein Hegazi, Nils Middleboe, Eugene Langenove and Gerry Keizer – managed to slip through the net before the FA effectively banned overseas recruits, in 1931, by introducing a two-year residency rule for alien players.

Bookman, however, was proud of his Irishness. He had made his mark with Belfast Celtic before moving to Bradford in 1912. He had won his first Irish cap against Wales in 1914 and was a recip- ient of one of the gold watches presented to each member of the team that won the Triple Crown that year. 'There is not a Luton supporter who will not congratulate the Town's outside left on this honour,' commented the *Leighton Buzzard Observer* in 1921, after he had again been selected for Ireland. 'We all hope he will be as successful as he was when he formed one of the Irish team that broke all previous records and won the International championship.' The delight Luton fans took in his success – it was deemed a great honour for a Third Division club to have an international in their ranks – confirmed the assimilationists' argument that Jews could eradicate their foreignness by embracing a new national identity.

In 1908, when Louis helped Adelaide become the first Jewish team to win the All Ireland Under-18 Football Cup, 4,000 Jews were living in the Emerald Isle, over half of them in the capital. Bookman tended to play up his Irishness and play down his Jewishness; if he was perceived to be different, it was better to be seen as the former. Until the early 1880s, there had been no more than about 350 Jews in Dublin. The community came into existence between 1880 and 1901 with the arrival of Ashkenazim from the Lithuanian village of Akmene. Having fled Tsarist pogroms, they quickly found an economic niche in an era of depression and developed a surprisingly vibrant web of institutions – which included several sporting organisations. Louis was a member of the Jewish Athletic Association, which had a twofold mission: to improve the physical condition of young Jews and, by organising sporting fixtures against Gentile teams, integrate them into mainstream society. Anglo-Jewish leaders – one of whom, Lord Rothschild, had served on the Royal Commission on Aliens which reported to the Balfour government – tried to make a distinction between Good Aliens and Bad Aliens. Bert Goodman was consigned to the latter category after being sentenced to twelve months at the Old Bailey for theft. A year after starring in the Tottenham team that won the Second Division title in 1920, 'Kosher' – as his Spurs team-mates had immediately dubbed him – was transferred to Charlton Athletic. He played in the Addicks' first ever

Football League match, a 1–0 Third Division victory over Exeter City, and, after switching to centre-forward, scored one of the goals in their famous giant-killing FA Cup triumph at Manchester City in 1923. Bookman, on the other hand, was presented in the Jewish press as both a Good Alien and a Good Sport.

The non-Jewish press had not always been convinced. In a *Bradford Daily Argus* probe into how he became the first Jewish immigrant to play in the top flight, the reporter wrote: 'There is no doubt the signing of Abraham Bookman by Bradford City was one of the biggest mysteries in football.' The paper described his strange, Houdini-like disappearance in 1911, when Belfast Celtic, who had signed him as an amateur, had been approached by City. In the end, the FA Cup holders had to pay Adelaide – who'd got wind of the deal and immediately signed him up as a professional – for his services. His eligibility to play for Ireland was questioned throughout his career, even though his family had been naturalised. When he had helped his adoptive country win the British Home Championship, at England's expense, in 1914, he earned a lucrative move to West Bromwich Albion. After the First World War, however, he fell out with Albion officials, who refused to allow him to leave. Somehow, again ever so mysteriously, he ended up back in Ireland, playing for Glentoran and then Shelbourne. When he was transferred from Luton to Port Vale for £250, his story about being mugged in Dublin was contested by several newspapers. One questioned his claim that two Black and Tans had robbed him.

At Luton, however, the pacey outside-left had quickly won over the doubters. Colonel Goldsmid, the Jewish Lads Brigade founder, was delighted to read an article hailing him as 'one of the few Jews to have climbed to the top of the football tree'. When he signed for the south Bedfordshire side, in the same year as Goodman's Spurs were promoted, he was praised in the *Leighton Buzzard Observer* for his fair play as well as his athleticism. 'Abe Bookman is a human streak of lightning in his speed,' raved one of their reporters after watching him single-handedly destroy Birmingham City in a 1921 FA Cup match. 'How many times has a great outside-forward won a Cup-tie? Countless! Add one more to the list. Reduced to essentials, it was Bookman, the Irish international outside-left, versus Birmingham – and Bookman won.'

And yet there was still something 'of the night' about Abe. He was often described as 'exotic' and 'mysterious' in match reports. In newspaper cartoons, he was attributed the supposed physiognomic characteristics of his tribe: dark eyes, big nose and swarthy face. During the Victorian and Edwardian eras, surveys of cranial types and hair and skin colour were all the rage – although racial theories were often confounded by the low percentage of blond-haired, blue-eyed Aryans and the high percentage of Nordic-looking Jews. In some of these cartoons, Bookman's Biblical heritage would be alluded to:

> Interviewer: 'Does your brother play, Mr Bookman?'
> Bookman: 'Well, he is able.'
> Interviewer: 'Did you say his name is Abel?'
> Bookman: 'No! I say he can play the game.'

In August 1921, a few months after his Cup heroics against Birmingham, and not long after he played a key role in Ireland's famous 1–1 draw with England at Windsor Park, *The Times* presented conclusive proof that the *Protocols of the Elders of Zion* was a forgery. This infamous tract, which had claimed there was an international Jewish conspiracy, had triggered a spate of caricatures depicting dishonest, greedy, crooked-nosed immigrants speaking Pidgin English. Distinguished literary figures like Hilaire Belloc,

H. G. Wells and G. K. Chesterton warned of a Hebrew threat to the British way of life. In novels, newspapers and the theatre, malicious or crude images were common fare. Jews were viewed as a subversive presence lurking within the national body and caricatured as effete cowards in popular boys' novels. In *Play Up Kings*, for example, a public schoolboy called Marmaduke Howard – scented, bejewelled and expensively dressed – was exposed as a nouveau-riche foreigner after opposing a team entering the house football cup. 'I don't hold with soccer,' he declared. 'It is a vulgar game for the lower classes.' The school magazine duly outed Howard as the descendant of a Jewish old clothes salesman-cum-pawnbroker called Mosieski.

Not only did Bookman hold with soccer, he was, as an *Observer* interview made clear, something of an evangelist for the sport. 'The character of one's team-mates and opponents, in my view, forms a distinct asset in favour of the game,' he argued. 'The pay is also good. A place in a high-class team carries a weekly wage of £9 a week, and a bonus of £2 for a win and £1 for a draw . . . some of the most successful men in the country have passed their apprenticeship in the exacting school of football.' Bookman aligned himself with the 'thousands of straight-limbed, stout-hearted British boys who think they may possess the skill, speed, character and stamina that will compel success in this arena'. This failed to deflect the abuse, especially away from home, although not all of it was anti-Semitic; according to his daughter Joyce, 'he was often mistaken for an Italian and called an "Eyetie"'.

Joyce has only a vague memory of her father, who died in 1943, when she was a young girl. By then, his English football career had been over for twenty years; he had retired at Port Vale. Although he had turned his back on his Irish family's obdurate orthodoxy to earn a living in a hostile English world, he had ended up marrying Rebecca Sirota – who was from an even more religious family. His father-in-law Joseph, a cantor for seventeen years in Manchester's Jewish Quarter, was equally indisposed towards football. After Bookman's death, his wife banned all talk of his sporting life. But, after Rebecca herself had passed away, Joyce made a discovery: hundreds of letters of condolence, from officials and fans of all the teams he had ever played for, had been secretly stashed away in a locked cupboard.

Joyce recalls:

'My mother, well, she was very well educated and she always thought the Sirotas were "royalty". She never forgave me for marrying out of "royalty" either. Her family were from Russia, but when she lived in Manchester she only spoke English – although I remember her often speaking to a rabbi in Russian. Her brother arranged music for the Hallé orchestra. They thought they were a cut above, if you know what I mean. She felt football was an English game. I was very religiously brought up when my father died. It wasn't just her, it was my uncles – my father's brothers – who all thought that playing football was not the *tachlas* [thing to do].'

Bookman was a trailblazer because, in defying the religious and cultural restrictions of his parents' old-world Judaism, he gave hope to all Yiddisher boys who were *meshuga* for the game. My generation had Mark Lazarus, whose winning goal for QPR in the 1967 League Cup Final was celebrated by Selig Brodetsky pupils as if it had brought the trophy to Leeds, not west London. My grandfather's generation had Bookman, Goldberg and Swindon Town's legendary goalscorer Harry Morris. Their exploits encouraged first- and second-generation Jews to defy the 'Eleventh Commandment' by sneaking off, behind their parents' backs, to play football on *shabbat.* It wasn't until the 1960s that the FA officially recognised Sunday football; so, for the first two generations of East European immigrants who wanted to play in Gentile leagues, it was Saturday or nothing. In memoirs written about their childhoods during the 1920s, two writers recalled fiercely contested matches taking place on Saturdays – usually far away from their own streets so as to avoid detection by *frum* neighbours. 'If there was no ball available,' wrote Ralph Finn, 'we made one of paper and string and kicked that around. We played with footballs, tennis balls, little tiny balls, even with glass pebbles. Anything that resembled a ball, however vaguely, was game enough for a game.' As Abraham Goldstone recalls:

I had to get my football boots out on a Saturday afternoon and I had to throw them through the cellar window to some-body who was waiting and then walk out. [My father] says to me: *'Wo gehst du?'* That means 'Where are you going?' And I says: 'I'm only going to the park.' And he says: 'Okay, then, be back in time.' And we used to go and play football. None of our parents knew that we were playing football. We used to wash our jerseys ourselves. I used to send mine to the laundry as a matter of fact. It used to cost me about threepence, three pence in those days, anyway.

But while Harry Morris remains, to this day, a Swindon great – holding the record for the most goals in a League match, most goals in a season and most goals in a career – Bookman is a forgotten figure. When an article appeared in the *Jewish Chronicle* in the mid-1930s, celebrating Goldberg as 'the first Jew to play in the First Division', a correspondent felt obliged to rectify the anomaly. Bookman, he wrote, had got there first:

Louis Bookman, now resident in Dublin, played in First Division football for several years in England, namely, Bradford City 1911–14, West Bromwich 1914–15. He later on played for Luton Town 1919–22 and Port Vale 1924–25. He had the honour to represent Ireland in soccer against Wales in 1913, Scotland 1921 and England 1922. Mr Bookman also has had the distinction of playing international cricket for Ireland for fifteen successive seasons, having played against MCC at Leeds, also against Scotland and Wales. With such a record to his credit, I feel sure that a grave injustice will have been done to a great Jewish sportsman if his records are so soon forgotten.

A Somebody in a Small Place

Harry Morris was a Brady boy, the first of the youth club's soccer-mad youngsters to make it as a professional. Like the other working-class lads who went to the club, he played chess, read books and took part in political discussions. But Brady's declared mission was to achieve integration through sport. At first they had difficulty finding pitches, as the FA had outlawed the playing of football on the Christian Sabbath, but they were eventually allowed access to a private ground at Walthamstow. Matches soon became regular events, most of them played against other Jewish youth clubs and organisations such as the Jews' Hospital, the Norwood Orphanage for Young Jews and Belle Athletic FC. As Brady's annual report in 1896–7 noted, the contest with Belle:

. . . resulted in a well-earned victory for the Brady Street boys by three goals to one. The winning team, captained by Mr F. Fletcher, was made up as follows: A. Goldwater (goal), E. Toff and E. Goldstein (backs), B. Boas, Mr Fletcher and H. Woodwick (half-backs), M. Randall, A. Greenberg, A. Moscow (centre), M. Moses and P. Berlyn (forwards). A word of thanks is due to Messrs. A. S. Joseph and F. Fletcher for their invaluable help in so energetically coaching the boys and evolving out of an undisciplined rabble a team that now shows every promise of becoming a homogeneous and well balanced entity. It may be added that the game was played during very inclement weather and on a sodden ground.

Morris was born in Brick Lane in 1897. This street, like many East End neighbourhoods of the time, hummed with the sound of the rag-trade sweatshops at work. Most of the shop signs were written in Yiddish and English. He went to the Jews' Free School, which had been set up by middle-class Jewish philanthropists to educate the new immigrant working classes. More importantly, given the direction his life would take, he played for the Brady Street Boys Club. Perhaps the biggest anglicising influence of all, this youth organisation was established in 1886 for the children of eastern European immigrants with the aim of cultivating a robust physique through the playing of indigenous sport. 'My father, Mick, grew up in Brady Street mansions,' said David Triesman. 'The youth club was very important to him. It was a very colourful area, full of incredible characters. Brady Street Mansions was a very Jewish area; the people of the mansions lived all down one side of the street. There were loads of tiny flats, with one toilet between six flats. You got a sense that they'd all be together indoors, and then they'd all be together outdoors as well. And the club produced so many good footballers.' Mick Triesman was a journalist on *The Weekly Sporting Review and Show Business*, a magazine about boxing and showbiz. 'In London it was a big magazine,' explained his son, the first Jewish chairman of the English Football Association.

The overlap between the two was so great – and both were routes out for people to belong. A long time ago, doing economics research as a university lecturer, I studied gate-keeping. People might have a desire to get into a profession, they may be even qualified to get in, but that doesn't neces-sarily get them in. The most interesting thing is what opens or closes gates. The gate-keeping thing has often struck me about the things that Jewish people got into. I have no doubt that many of them would have loved to get into other things, but they've found it really hard.

At first, being religiously observant, Morris refused to play foot-ball on a Saturday, turning out for Brady the following day. But on his return from the trenches of the Great War in 1919 he read a story about Bookman's 'brilliant career' and immediately signed on for a team called Vicar of Wakefield. Fulham spotted him and sold him to Brentford, where he scored twenty-nine times in fifty-nine games. After moving to Millwall, Swansea bought him for £110. His first season for the Welsh club – forty-seven goals in forty-one appear-ances – was his best; he scored a hat-trick on his debut at home to Southend, following it up with another three goals against Exeter two days later.

But it was at Swindon where he made his mark, banging in an astonishing number of goals over a six-year period. Signed for £110 in 1926, he scored 228 times in 279 League and Cup appearances and was top scorer for each of the seven seasons he spent with the club. In his first season he scored forty-seven times; in an eleven-match run between October 1926 and January 1927 he hit nine-teen goals and was on target in every game. In another incredible sequence he scored a hat-trick at Newport, four goals against Crystal Palace and then five in a win over Queens Park Rangers – the first

Swindon player to achieve such a feat. After scoring a hat-trick against Southend in his first match for the club, a newspaper headline raved: 'Morris Leads Attack With Rare Skill. New Centre Forward's Brilliant Debut'. Two days later, after claiming another hat-trick against Exeter City, a different paper reported that: 'The Swindon crowd had a new hero and, as soon as the Town gained possession, the cry "Give it to Morris" would ring out from a crowd hungry for goals.' An adulatory profile, written by 'Wellwisher', then appeared in the *Swindon Advertiser*:

> Shrewd judges of football consider that Morris is the best centre-forward Swindon have had since the war and his brilliant play last Saturday and Monday certainly stamps him as a footballer of class, and fitted in every way to make a successful leader of the Swindon attack. Of sturdy build and fine physique, Morris seems to be just made for his job and by the look of him one would take him to be capable of standing the hurly burly of the most strenuous football. He has already shown that he can infuse any amount of dash into his play, but with that dash is blended skill and intelligence, denoting that he has made a thorough study of the game. There is method in his every move and, what is more, he can shoot, as witnessed by his bag of six goals in two matches. Great things are hoped of Morris this season and as long as keeps fit, he can be relied upon to fulfil the expectations of his many admirers.

Also known as 'Abe' by this time, he was the beneficiary of an important change in the offside law. In 1925 FIFA relaxed the rule so that only two, rather than three, players were now required to play an opponent onside, giving forwards more room to move and manipulate space. In an article written at the end of the 1928–9 season, in which he'd scored twenty-six times in thirty-eight games, *Jewish World* proudly noted that 'Morris, formerly a member of the Jews' Free School Old Boys' Club, plays at centre-forward and is a great goalscorer.' The newspaper then went on to claim that Town's David-versus-Goliath clash with the mighty Arsenal had given birth to the innovatory third-back system. In fact, the Gunners' manager, Herbert Chapman, had made the change three seasons earlier after his team had been clobbered 7–0 by Newcastle. Yet, although the use of a deep-lying centre-half was not uncommon by the time Swindon held Arsenal to a goalless draw in February 1929, it could be argued that Chapman's instruction to his gangling wing-half Herbie Roberts to 'police Morris' during the replay, which the north Londoners won 1–0, established a template for the following decade's dominance; under their more advanced third-back system – a 3-4-3 formation, with the attack shaped like a W and the defence an M – Arsenal won the FA Cup in 1930 and the League five times. Chapman had been at the fourth-round games between Swindon and Burnley and seen the havoc wreaked by the freewheeling Morris, whose header eventually put Town through. He had also read reports of Swindon's giant-killing third-round defeat of Newcastle, one of England's best teams. As *Athletic News* pointed out, Morris had even outshone Hughie Gallacher, one of the Magpies' greatest ever players. The fêted forward capped a brilliant display by scoring what he described as 'the best goal of my career . . . I was right on the goal line but realised the wind was with me and shot for goal, and a gust of wind took it into the roof of the net'. *Athletic News* reported:

What a match-winner this Morris, of Swindon, is. For the most part he was shadowed and crowded out by his opponents by sheer force of numbers, yet he never ceased trying and was more dangerous whenever he had a chance than any other forward on the field. There is no doubt that Morris, with his strength, pertinacity and splendid enthusiasm, is a great asset to the Swindon forward line.

An injury prevented him from having a trial for England and in 1933 he was given a free transfer to Clapton Orient. He ended his career with Cheltenham Town before becoming a coach at Swedish club Gothenburg just before the Second World War. He, his wife Edith and son Jack were trapped there after the German invasion of Norway in 1940. Morris took up a job with the British Consulate and helped escaped prisoners get back home. His family emigrated to the US after the war, and he worked in New York for the British Information Service until his retirement. He died, of a heart attack, in California in 1985. Asked in later life why he had never gone to a big club, he replied: 'I could have gone to many First Division clubs but I was happy at Swindon. It is better to be somebody in a small place than nobody in a big place.'

2

The Disappeared:
When Goldberg Became Gaunt

CLAVANE'S CIGARETTES

L. GOLDBERG (LEEDS UNITED)

'Fine defensive work for England by Goldberg of Leeds, who earned the distinction of being the first Jewish boy to play in an international. Goldberg held up the nippy Welsh forwards time and time again. The crowd enjoyed the tussles of the distinctive Day with the wily Goldberg.'

England v. Wales Schoolboys International,

Daily Mail, 6 April 1932

Leslie Goldberg: The Insentient Viking

In the summer of 1948, Leslie Goldberg changed his name to Les Gaunt. Ten months earlier, after two British soldiers were murdered in Mandate Palestine, anti-Jewish rioting had spread across the country. As post-war rationing was extended, and the popular stereotype of money-grubbing black marketeers resurfaced in the media, Foreign Secretary Ernest Bevin accused 'Israelites' of 'pushing to the front of the queue'.

*

'Mr Football Jew' is not a figment of anyone's imagination. From Bookman to Bernstein, he has appeared in a range of gripping, real-life dramas which have illuminated the anxieties and struggles, the comedy and the tragedy, the lows and the ultimate triumphs of the modern Anglo-Jewish experience. But, for most of the First Age, he was hidden. He was an outsider trying not to draw attention to his outsiderness, a European adopting the outward trappings of Englishness, a Goldberg trying to become a Gaunt. In private he drew solace from his tribe's presence as a vibrant, life-affirming, distinctive sub-culture – but in public he adopted the reticent manners of a stereotypical Englishman. So much so that, when my primary school headmaster issued his Eleventh Commandment – 'Football is not for a Yiddisher boy' – I initially believed him, possessing no evidence to the contrary. Of course, my friends and I – like my father's generation – were obsessed with the game. But, until Lazarus raised QPR from the dead at Wembley in 1967, English football appeared to be *Judenfrei*.

My discovery that Goldberg had not only played for Leeds United but had been on the verge of playing for England, which came out during a discussion with my dad just after the Selig Brodetsky Jewish

Day School Orange Peel Incident, was close to revelatory. Dad remembered Abie, who was then his PT teacher, singing the praises of Our Les just after the war. He dusted off an old scrapbook to produce two crucial bits of evidence that flew in the face of the Commandment. The first was the 1946–7 team picture that adorns the front cover of this book. Goldberg is the one with his hair parted down the middle in the obsolete fashion of the 1930s footballer. He looks like a steep-jawed, insentient Viking who just happened to be born into the wrong tribe. The second was a small card bearing the legend:

Churchman's Cigarettes. 16. L. Goldberg (LEEDS UNITED). Leslie Goldberg has been associated with Leeds United since 1932, when, as a schoolboy, he played against Wales and Scotland. He attended the Elland Road ground to train for these internationals and afterwards he signed amateur forms for the club. In 1934 he joined the ground staff and the following season became a professional. Today, he is one of the regular backs for the Leeds United club.

These cigarette cards came free with a packet of fags and were the most popular collectors' items for fans in the interwar years and after.

Like Bookman's and Morris' exploits, Goldberg's emergence appeared to repudiate not only the myth of absence but also the myth of physical inferiority. In New York, Morris had turned down a lucrative offer from Hakoah New York to come out of retirement. The Jewish club, which had adopted Max Nordau's ethos of 'muscular Judaism', was particularly impressed with his sturdy physique. As in Britain, there was a great deal of insecurity about the Jews' status as fully-fledged citizens. In 1914, the American sociologist Edward A. Ross had argued that the ghetto environment of eastern Europe was responsible for stunting the physical development of immigrants. 'Not only are they undersized and weak-muscled,' he wrote, 'but they shun bodily acitivity and are extremely sensitive to pain.' In 1899, the anthropologist study *The Races of Europe* had influenced thinking on both sides of the pond. According to its author, William Z. Ripley, Jews preferred to live by brain rather than brawn and were 'distinctly inferior to Christians in lung capacity'. During the 1905 Aliens Act debate, Conservative MP Harry Lawson even argued that 'the Jewish invasion' of Britain had resulted in 'a backwards march to physical deterioration'. Liberal MP Henry Norman agreed, pointing out that 'it would not be long before the quality of our own people was seriously impaired'.

It is a myth that has retained its power to this day. In an *Independent* article in 2010, Howard Jacobson defined the word 'cultured' as 'the opposite to whatever it is the Chelsea pairing of Lampard and Terry exudes. Blood, sweat, sentimentality and swearing . . . why must football as the English play it be so plebeian? Elsewhere it has moved on from its roots in deprived communities.' The novelist has Sefton Goldberg, his football-hating anti-hero in *Coming From Behind* – he deliberately gives him an obviously-Jewish name – declare: '[The game] owed its origins to working-class culture that was shaped when the Jews were somewhere else . . . it was played on Saturdays – the day of rest [and] it was a violent game, demanding of its players sinew and brawn.'

Yet, contrary to what Jacobson argued, as early as 1900 young Jews were playing with conspicuous enthusiasm in the newly created leagues. Since physical activity on a Saturday was frowned upon, Norwood Jews Orphanage manager Solomon Weinstein suggested 'a Sunday Jewish Cricket and Football League should be formed, with the object of promoting a healthy competition among the Jewish lads all over London'. As Weinstein pointed out, 'the only day available for practice at present is Sunday, which fact necessitates the possession of a private ground. This should not be difficult to obtain, as today three Jewish clubs, the managers of which work unceasingly to promote a love of healthy British sport among the boys under their charge, possess grounds where, Sunday after Sunday, the working lads from different parts of London participate in games of cricket in summer and football in winter.' The league began with only six teams but, by 1907, it had expanded to thirty-six clubs in six divisions. In its first season, the *Jewish Chronicle* reported that a full card of January Sunday fixtures had gone ahead despite 'hurricanes, continual downpours and frozen grounds'. On New Year's Day 1903, a league team held a church side to a goalless draw in the first ever 'official' match between Jews and Gentiles. Brady Street, like West Central, Victoria and Stepney, then decided to affiliate to the predominantly-Gentile London Federation of Working Lad's Clubs, and Victoria became the first Jewish organisation to be presented with the Scott Trophy, awarded for gaining the most prizes over a year's worth of sporting competitions. As the Jewish Athletic Association chairman Frank Morley argued, this achievement meant 'the reproach that Jews did not take part in the national game might be removed'.

The JAA had been founded in 1899 to unite, under one umbrella organisation, the sporting activities of all youth clubs and schools. After changing its name to the Association of Jewish Youth, its highly successful league established itself as a conveyor belt of footballing talent, producing a long line of players, professional as well as amateur. Some, like David Dein and Irving Scholar, went on to become key movers and shakers off the pitch, but many others disappeared from public memory. In the 1920s an all-Jewish team called The Judeans tried, and failed, to join the Football League. Hardly anything remains about them in the football records. According to the historian Tony Collins, they had frequent problems getting a full team to turn out on a Saturday. There is a mixture of reasons for such 'disappearances' from the archives. Some players hid their identity, or were simply not identified as Jewish. And, from Goldberg's debut in the 1930s to Spurs star Micky Dulin's retirement in the 1950s, there appeared to be a glass ceiling in football, reflecting the lack of opportunity in society as a whole; the doors of many occupations remained closed, and Jews continued to be kept out of golf clubs, the Civil Service and the upper echelons of political representation.

Any visible sign of sporting success was hungrily seized upon by the Jewish press. 'It has often been said that Jews have produced very few athletes of note,' noted the *Jewish World* in 1927. 'It is on the track that the Jewish community can look with pride at the wonderful successes of one of its own sons, Harold M. Abrahams, who has rightly been described as one of the "greatest all-round athletes who has ever represented Cambridge University". No English team of athletes would be complete without him.' It was only a matter of time, the paper concluded, before a member of the community turned out for the national football team. There had been high hopes for Monty Berman, who played in goal for Clapton Orient – until he retired to become head of his father's theatrical costumiers. And there was Jack Rosenfield, a junior from Grove House Club, who played for Manchester United but was released after only a year. 'He played most of his games in United's reserve team', according to his son Harvey, 'but he did have a few games in the first team. However, when he met my mother, who came from a Shabbat observance family, he gave it up, as his future father-in-law wasn't happy with a daughter going out with a boy who played football on shabbat.' There were also a couple of up-and-coming Spurs players: Frank Okim, whose career petered out just before the war, and David Levene, who started at Hutchinson House Jewish Boys Club before joining the club's nursery team. Levene's greatest moment came in the 6–0 mauling of Oldham Athletic in the 1933 FA Cup. 'The lads at Tottenham have always treated me with respect,' he told the *Jewish Chronicle*, just before joining Crystal Palace, two years later, never to be seen again.

Goldberg, a player of immense promise, seemed the incarnation of the hopes of those commentators looking for a muscular rebuttal of beliefs about Jewish physical inferiority, and when the *Swindon Advertiser* noted, in 1927, how boxing in the army had built up Morris' strength and fitness, and admired the way he scored goals by shoulder-charging defenders – sometimes even the goalkeeper – the *Jewish Chronicle*'s letters' pages fluttered with relief. Morris and Goldberg were, its editor reflected, 'a living negation of the physical stigma which has long disfigured our race'. They had both nailed the myth of the stunted, pallid Jew of the ghetto – and the notion that football was not a suitable career for a nice Yiddisher boy.

'And we introduce, on the left, Leslie Goldberg, right-back,' a plummy voice announced in a 1938 British Pathé newsreel clip featuring Leeds United. 'A footballer, first of all, must be fit, and PT and shadow boxing both help to that end.' It was the first of a series called 'Famous Football Teams in Training' and it is still an odd sensation, watching the clip on YouTube some seventy-three years on, hearing this most Jewish of names alongside the Ainsleys, Milburns, Holleys and Brownes. Goldberg's widow Peggy, who is not Jewish, met Leslie when he was a PT instructor stationed in Kent during the war. 'He did not conform to this ridiculous image of the Jewish weakling,' she said. 'When we first met, he believed that the more Jews exercised, the more they would be accepted. But later on he didn't think in those terms any more. He didn't really think about being Jewish even. When he came from Russia, his grandfather couldn't speak English. The chaps at customs couldn't speak Yiddish. So they gave them the name Goldberg. It sounded Jewish. It was easy, they could spell it. Their actual name was Gidanansky, which they couldn't spell.'

Sixty years later, in *The Definitive Reading FC*, authors David Downs and Leigh Edwards inserted a note on players' name changes. There are two. 'Goodman changed his name to Getgood in the 1920–21 season,' they inform us, and 'Goldberg changed his name to Gaunt in the 1948 season.' The note provoked the following exchange in a Reading fans' chat room:

> I'm intrigued as to why Gaunt changed his name – Goldberg is a name which might of [sic] aroused anti-semitic feeling, that's the only thing which springs to mind . . .

> No, nothing to do with the move [from Leeds]. I remember him here as Goldberg before the name change.

> I have just had the honour of speaking with club historian David Downes. So overawed was I at speaking with the great man, that I forgot to ask about Les Goldberg/Gaunt's mysterious name change.

There was no great mystery. It was, indeed, as one of the fans surmised, a reaction against anti-Semitism. Many first- and second-generation Jewish immigrants anglicised their names upon arrival in Britain. Buchalter became Bookman, Moshe Osinsky became Montague Burton, Gidanansky became Goldberg. What's in a name anyway? 'If a Cohen wanted to change his name to Cornwallis,' wrote Howard Jacobson in *The Mighty Waltzer*, 'that was his affair. It was no mystery to any of us how come Hyman Kravtchik could go to bed one night as himself and the next morning, wake up as Henry Kay De Ville Chadwick. Enough with the ringlets and fringes. Enough with the medieval magic.' Name-changing was especially prevalent among those who sought advancement outside the clothing industry. For Jews who entered the glamorous worlds of sport and entertainment in the interwar years, it was virtually compulsory. British boxing world champions like 'Kid' Lewis, born Gershon Mendeloff, and 'Kid' Berg – previously Judah Bergman – adopted English names. The most surprising example of all, perhaps, is film star Leslie Howard, who specialised in portraying stiff-upper-lip English aristocrats; the son of Jewish-Hungarian émigrés, he had previously been known as Lesley Steiner.

But what made Leslie Goldberg wake up one morning as Les Gaunt? For Goldberg's generation, football had been one of the ways of escaping the old ghetto, a slum just outside the city centre, and becoming part of Leeds. Seeing one of their own rise to the top had given great *nachas* to the city's Russian-Jewish immigrants, most of whom were employed as tailors. Like the London and Manchester rag trades, they had lived and worked in a squalid New World *shtetl*, suffering the appalling conditions and poor pay of the notorious sweated workshops. Sport had always offered immigrants and racial minorities not just a way out but, more importantly, a way of gaining acceptance. In his performances for Leeds and, at various levels, England, Goldberg had become the repository of his rapidly integrating community's dream of belonging.

Leslie was born in 1918, a year after a notorious mini-pogrom in Leeds; a 3,000-strong mob rampaged through the Jewish ghetto, smashing windows, looting shops and beating up anyone who got in their way. The mob had been fired up by a newspaper article accusing sharp-suited 'Hebrews' of parading in the town centre while brave young Loiners laid down their lives in France. The ghetto-dwellers, in fact, were a patriotic lot, a higher percentage of Jews than Gentiles actually enlisting. And nothing gave them more pride than Goldberg's brilliant career. In becoming the first Jew to play for England Schoolboys, he joined a growing canon of Famous Jewish Sports Legends: Lewis, Berg, Abrahams, amateur golfer Lionel Leonard Cohen, England rugby union international John Raphael and Nathan Rothschild, who played county cricket for Northamptonshire.

The son of an immigrant boot riveter, Goldberg went to Lovell Road School and joined the Leeds Jewish Institute. The declared aim of both institutions was to disprove the charges of disloyalty, cowardice and unmanliness that were the stock-in-trade of anti-Semites. Jewish youths were inducted into the world of sport and taught to admire the host country's imperial grandeur. Max Freeman, who went to school with Goldberg, recalls it promoting 'PT', as the Pathé newsreel announcer had called it, as a pathway to integration. At Lovell Road, as at the Brady Boys Club and the Free School in London and the Jews' School in Manchester, physical recreation of all kinds became an integral part of the pupils' daily life. Goldberg's much-loved sports master Nat Collins, who became his mentor, urged pupils to shed their parents' Old World habits and attitudes – but also taught them to stand up for themselves and fight back if they were attacked. Freeman recalls: 'When the talkies came out, our parents would take us to the cinema with them because they couldn't understand English. All you'd hear in a cinema was "What's he saying?" The cinema was full of Jewish parents with kids. It's like some Asian families today. We went to school at nine, came back at four and then went off to *cheder*, Hebrew school, till seven. Non-Jewish lads used to wait for us outside the school. We used to scrap to get in. I thought it was part of the religion to get into a fight to get into Hebrew school.'

Collins' influence on Goldberg was described by another school friend, Izzy Pear, as:

quite astonishing really . . . he coached him from the start, taught him everything he knew. He was a nice fella, a good teacher, stern and strict. Mr Collins was a good lad, no question about it. He was Jewish and he wanted the school, which was ninety-five per cent Jewish, to make a good impression on the outside world. So he entered us for the Leeds Schools' Cup.

We were virtually a one-man team. I was on the left wing and on the right wing was a lad called Monty Fineberg. I were right quick. We used to get the ball down and then it was 'Pass it to Les.' And Les was such a very good footballer. Exceptional. He had no need to be near the goalposts. He could aim the ball from thirty or even forty yards out and score goals. And that's how we progressed. But we were a team of *holtzhackers* [a derogatory Yiddish term for a hewer of wood]. The lowest of the low. We were unskilled. We were labourers compared to a skilled man. But Les could do everything with the ball. Mr Collins just used to say, 'Give it to Les, send it to Les.' Which is how we got through to the final. Les played centre-half, which was midfield back then. As soon as me or Monty got the ball, Leslie knew we were going down the wing and he knew the ball was coming into the centre because we just kicked it into the centre. 'Send it to Les.' That's how we played.

Astonishingly, Lovell Road reached the Leeds Schools Cup final for the first, and only, time in 1933, attracting a huge crowd. Word had spread that 'the great Goldberg, an England international' – according to the fliers – would be playing.

Izzy Pear continues:

But what happened was Les got ill, didn't he. He didn't turn up. We were devastated. No Les, what could we do? It was a bombshell. We were shattered. We got thrashed 6–1. And the crowd booed. I was on the left wing and I heard them shout, 'Get back to Palestine,' and things like that. When they saw that we were outplayed, they were furious. It was a joke really. There was only one non-Jew in the team, Palmer. The rest were Jewish boys. Ten Jewish boys and Ken Palmer. There was Benny Viner, Myer Landy, Solly Goldman, Nat Forman, Billy Brosgall. But without Les we were just *holtzhackers*. Some of the people in the crowd accused the organisers of lying about Les. Said he couldn't have been a good footballer anyway, not with a name like Goldberg.

Goldberg made his first appearance for Leeds, who were then in the top flight, in 1937, replacing the England full-back Bert Sproston. He was strongly tipped to replace Sproston at international level, having already represented the Three Lions at schoolboy level, making his debut at Wembley in 1932 against Wales. A reporter at that match described him as possessing a 'very brainy game, depending upon clever anticipation, sure tackling and strong volleying'. As a columnist in a Jewish newspaper wrote: 'It is the sincerest hope of Leeds fans, and I have no doubt Jewish football followers throughout the country share this wish, that Leslie Goldberg will one day play for Leeds United and England, and if this does happen may he serve as magnificently as a man as he did as a schoolboy international.'

The Second World War changed everything. The Football League was suspended, with Goldberg having made twenty-one League appearances. During the conflict he guested for Arsenal and saw service in India before being stationed at Hythe, where he met Peggy. When the League began again after the war, he played a few games for Leeds but, with Jim Milburn and Eddie Bannister now the favoured full-back pairing, he was transferred to Reading in 1947. He changed his name to Gaunt a year later. Such an act of reinvention, as George Orwell had wryly observed in his 1945 essay 'Anti-Semitism in Britain', was easier than undertaking speech therapy or removing an unwanted mark on your skin. 'It is generally admitted that anti-Semitism is on the increase,' wrote Orwell, 'that it has been greatly exacerbated by the war, and that humane and enlightened people are not immune to it. It does not take violent forms (English people are almost invariably gentle and law-abiding), but it is ill-natured enough, and in favourable circumstances it could have political results.' At public school, Orwell remembered, a Jew could 'live down his Jewishness if he was exceptionally charming or athletic, but it was an initial disability comparable to a stammer or a birthmark. Wealthy Jews tended to disguise themselves under aristocratic English or Scottish names, and to the average person it seemed quite natural that they should do this, just as it seems natural for a criminal to change his identity if possible.'

When Goldberg played for Leeds, he had been insulated by a tight-knit, insular community; located in one of the biggest cities outside London, it numbered around 30,000 in the 1930s. At Reading, a town populated by only a handful of his co-religionists, he and Peggy felt painfully exposed. He had tried his best, all his life, to fit in, to not be different. Peggy revealed that he had once turned away a group of rabbis from the Elland Road training ground – they had been asking for a contribution to their charity – because he didn't want his team-mates to see him as 'not one of us'. In Leeds, he had been fêted as the latest in a line of local-Jews-made-good: first Michael Marks, then Montague Burton and now

Our Les. He had been the first to play for England Schoolboys, to captain Yorkshire Schools, to play for Leeds United, to appear on a cigarette card and feature in a British Pathé newsreel. He also played for a club, Leeds United, who were formed in 1919, after a false start by Leeds City, in the offices of a Jewish solicitor, Alf Masser, and were keen to attract the then predominantly rugby-supporting Jewish community to their stadium. In 1932, a *Yorkshire Evening News* reporter wrote: 'The United would dearly like to have in their first team a member of Leslie's faith who was an outstanding performer. Such a player, opine the Peacocks, would increase the gates at Elland Road by several thousands every game.' His old headmaster at Lovell Road agreed: 'A couple of thousand extra supporters will go down to see Lesley play,' predicted Collins. 'He is extremely popular.'

But on leaving Leeds to do his army service, Leslie would find himself exposed to several uncomfortable encounters with anti-Semitism. Peggy Gaunt describes such an incident:

I met Leslie during the war in a dance hall, where we all met our boyfriends in those days. He was attached to the 5th Wilts in Hythe, as an army physical training instructor. He wasn't there for long, but during that time we fell in love. I remember one night, it was most embarrassing. We went to quite an exclusive club to dance. These two sergeants kept asking me to dance. They could see I was with Les, but they kept taking it in turns to ask me. I said, 'You are obviously anti-Semitic.' One of them, a Scottish chap, said, 'You know he's a Jew so why do you go with him?' I said, 'Well, if you're an example of a Scottish gentleman, give me a Jew every time.' And I refused to dance with them. So they stopped. You have to put them down verbally. Leslie said: 'Ask your parents if they mind you going out with

me.' I said, 'Why?' He said because he's Jewish. And I said, 'So?'
We'd known each other for about three weeks or so, and then
he told me. He'd had an unfortunate experience from where
he was stationed before. He took a young girl dancing, and her
father met him at the front gate one evening and said: 'I don't
want my daughter going out with a Jew.'

When he and Peggy moved to Reading they began, for the first time
in their marriage, to experience anti-Semitism on a regular basis.
'The manager of one shop used to shout loudly every time I came
in: "Good morning, Mrs Goldberg,"' said Peggy. 'Every time I came
in – and everyone turned around to see who this foreigner was. He
never said anybody else's name. And there were other, worse, incidents. And in games Les started being verbally abused.'

In 1950, after seventy-one League appearances for Reading,
Goldberg's career came to a premature end when he broke his leg
in a match against Norwich. 'They went for him deliberately,' said
Peggy, 'or so I was told. It was a bad break. His friend, up in the
stand, heard the bone break. There was anti-Semitism involved.' In
his column in the *Jewish Gazette*, my great-uncle, Louis Saipe, remembered how Leslie had been hailed as a shining example of modern
Judaism. As a schoolboy he had been a sporting all-rounder,
excelling at swimming, cricket and athletics. Being a good sport,
my uncle warned, was admirable – as long as you didn't, in the
process, shed your identity. When I read this column in my research
for the book, I began to understand why Goldberg was no longer
talked about when I was a child. My old headmaster Abie, like the
rest of the community, had either forgotten him or else deliberately
chosen to ignore his career.

I tracked down Leila Harris, Goldberg's niece, who described her
uncle's drift from the faith: 'My father, his brother Hymie, used to

follow him all around the country when he played for Leeds – with his other brother Nat and brother-in-law Louis. When he went to Reading he mixed with a clique of people who were very British, you know English. I don't think he wanted them to know he was Jewish. A bit upper-class, some of them. Met a lot of dignitaries, I think. He used to have quite a good social life. So obviously he was invited to all these receptions and whatever. It's a shame, but it's one of those things.'

The brothers had been close and had lovingly documented his rise in a scrapbook of cuttings. The scrapbook includes a reference to the one goal he scored in seven FA Cup ties for Reading, as well as covering his management of non-League team Newbury Town. He went on to scout for Reading and Oxford United and then returned to the Berkshire club in 1969 as an administrative and technical assistant to the manager, Jack Mansell.

As Peggy Gaunt puts it:

He moved away from Jewishness when we moved away from Leeds. He'd been in the army for six years. So he lived amongst non-Jewish people. That was his world. The football world was the same. He never wanted to go back. He was a good scout. He discovered Stephen Death, who played more games for Reading than anyone. And he looked after the third team and was scouting as well. He could sort out a good player immediately. The thing is, he'd lived in the 'English' world more than his other brothers. When we moved to Reading there were no Jews. Well, a few young Jewish men chased him up – but they, like him, married out and drifted from the faith.

When his scouting days were over, Goldberg worked his way up through the ranks of Crimpy Crisps, becoming their London and south-east area manager. Then he moved to the Fuller-Kunzle company, which made cakes, and ran a restaurant in a casino for a while, mixing with an upper-middle-class social set. 'They didn't know about his footballing past,' said Peggy. 'One of them turned out to be a crook, but we had some marvellous times with them. We went to very posh dinner dances with them. We weren't following any religion then. We didn't really fit in.'

Goldberg died, aged sixty-seven, in 1985, the same year that Harry Morris passed away.

The Backlash

The old, sceptical view on 'footbollick' – as expressed by the Bookmans and other first-generation families – returned with a vengeance in the post-war years, the era that formed Howard Jacobson. Those footballers who 'made it' were no longer paraded in the Jewish press, and the Jewish leadership's attitude towards professional sport changed; the trauma of the Holocaust brought into sharp relief the need to prioritise Staying Jewish over Becoming English. Assimilation might have created opportunities that would not have existed in their grandparents' day, but it was fast turning into a nightmare. The community reached its numerical peak in the immediate post-war years, reaching around 450,000, but since 1945 there has been a gradual decline in religious adherence. The Goldberg and Abrahams stories were only the tip of the iceberg. In *Lost Jews: The Struggle for Identity Today*, Emma Klein revealed that in the 1940s 100,000 British Jews were unaccounted for in statistical charts; their mysterious 'disappearance' suggested a shrinking population in terms of self-identification. Abrahams, the son of a Polish immigrant, had been a successful public-school athlete and had eventually gained access to an exclusive social and cultural environment, a sport dominated by middle- and upper-class amateurs. Before *Chariots of Fire* came out in 1981, little had been made of his Jewishness. This is because both the sporting and Jewish establishments had, for many years, simply ignored it. Even in 1973 an article in *Athletics Weekly* had celebrated his 1924 Olympic triumph without mentioning his ethnic roots. The sprinter himself argued that being 'too Semitic' in one's personal and sporting life was incompatible with reaching the highest levels of sporting achievement. 'One must make it clear that a strict adherence to Judaism would prevent one from participating in Saturday competitions,' he wrote in a 1920s newspaper article, 'and, as a result, the strict Jews could never hope to attain recognition.' This was a view shared by Arnold Siegel, who played for Orient for two years after the war. According to his daughter Carol, he hated any reference to his ethnicity. 'My father was very English,' she said. 'He was very patriotic. His parents, who were from Romania, spoke Yiddish to each other in the home, but he used to get very cross if there were people wearing *kippot* in public. He was very conscious of Jews not being seen as different.'

This period was the beginning of a backlash against integration which was partly a reaction to the interwar decline in Jewish practice but also a reflection of a political shift that had taken place in the Anglo-Jewish leadership. The Board of Deputies, the main representative body of British Jews, had long been the preserve of the assimilated, middle-class, pre-1880s community. But this old establishment was beginning to lose its grip as a new eastern European cohort, particularly aroused by the issue of a Jewish state, challenged their strategy. A *coup d'état* during the war brought the Zionist Selig Brodetsky, from an East End Russian-Jewish family, to the presidency. When he moved to Leeds, to take up a lectureship at the university, he was shocked by the community's unbridled passion for sport. Every Saturday he would look through his window and see a stream of Jews heading for the rugby league ground rather than the synagogue. In one of his talks, just after the war, he warned young boys against following the Goldberg route and 'disappearing' into football. The game, he argued, was an insecure profession that could not provide a stable income. Why, for the sake of short-term glory, put your long-term financial security at risk? Even Albert Morris, a Leeds fan, and a future club chairman, agreed: 'Jewish parents will not encourage their sons to enter football seriously, even if the ability is there, as they prefer their sons to go into a secure business.' As did chairman of the all-Jewish club Wingate, Maurice Abbey, who noted that 'many of the Jewish boys take their footballing careers to a certain stage, but they are not prepared to make the sacrifice of time in order to continue to make progress as footballers. Many boys prefer to continue with their academic work, rather than turn to the insecurity of football, and you can't really blame them.'

Several players became professionals but their careers were often short lived. Harry Gilberg controversially replaced the legendary Eddie Bailey as Spurs inside-forward for the 1949 FA Cup tie against Arsenal at Highbury; following a humiliating 3–0 defeat he made a swift return to the obscurity of non-League football. So did Mickey Barnard, who ended up at Southern League side Chelmsford City after a promising start at Portsmouth. Tottenham were desperate to sign Leon Joseph, a clever, fast and incisive winger, but, after a handful of games, he chose to spend the rest of his career at Isthmian League side Leytonstone. Jack Koffman, who had appeared twice for Bolton Wanderers during the war, was signed by Manchester United just after it, played in the 3–2 defeat at Huddersfield and then, after brief stays with Congleton Town, Oldham and Hull City, went back to being a hairdresser. Stan Pollock, a towering goalkeeper who earned himself a considerable reputation playing for Wingate, refused professional forms for Sheffield Wednesday, preferring to stay in the Jewish League and continue his successful business career. And then there was Abe Rosenthal, a clever inside-forward who weighed fourteen stone and had been a paratrooper in the war – but was far more interested in running his ice-cream business. Every summer he moved on a free transfer either from Tranmere Rovers to Bradford City or from Bradford City to Tranmere Rovers. 'All done for tax reasons,' revealed Brian Glanville, who has a simple theory about why there were more second-generation boxers than footballers: 'Jewish boys from Stepney went out and fought for a few shillings because their families were starving, and because if they stuck to it there was big money to be made. By contrast, professional footballers were pegged till 1961 to the ludicrous maximum wage.' And even when the salary restrictions were abolished, it remained a highly unappealing career option. As Glanville remarked, 'There were, by now [1961], vast sums to be earned by the successful player, but the risks were so great, the career so brief, that it remained unattractive to a now chiefly middle-class community.'

The careers of the last two maximum-wage-era Jewish footballers to make it – Miles Spector and Micky Dulin – had a familiar trope. While still at Hendon Grammar School, Spector played truant to turn out for Chelsea's reserve team in an Eastern Counties League Cup game against Spurs. He missed a penalty and had a poor first half but, luckily for him, the Blues' manager, Ted Drake, arrived at the interval. In the second period, the sixth-former scored a fine goal. When he was called into the headmaster's study the morning after the game, he feared the worst. Instead of being punished, however, he was told he'd been picked to play for the Chelsea first team. He made his debut, as an eighteen-year-old schoolboy, in a 3–2 win over Sunderland at Stamford Bridge. For each of the six times he played during the

1952–3 season, Drake had to telephone the school in advance to get the head's permission. Spector's best performance was in the FA Cup fourth round win against West Bromwich Albion. With the score goalless at half-time, he came on to set up three of his team's four goals. At the end of the 1950s, however, he was offloaded to Hendon. When the non-League club's historian wrote a profile of him for a magazine, Spector requested that all references to his Jewishness be removed.

Dulin was also snapped up as a schoolboy – by Tottenham – and also preferred to downplay his background. A skilful, pacey right winger, he made his debut against Burnley in 1955, scoring twice in the eleven matches he played that season. But an horrific injury against Birmingham, two years later, forced him out of the game, and he became a fire brigade welfare officer. 'The strange thing about me is that when I played for Tottenham they didn't really know I was Jewish,' he said. 'They thought I was Turkish or Greek. You could be all things to all people. I was dark-skinned. With Jews, we don't go out of our way to broadcast. We keep quiet and let other people get into it. You meld into the background. Things are said that's not right. You think "What do I do here?" You turn away. If there are three or four of you, though, it's a different story. In my era, and just before my era, Jews couldn't be this and they couldn't be that. In my era, if you were Jewish, you weren't welcomed into tennis clubs or golf clubs.' So, like Goldberg and Spector, he ignored his ethnicity, quietly and unfussily integrating – some would say disappearing – into the mainstream. 'We all just kept schtum,' he said. 'That was the way it was in those days.'

3

The Europeans:
When Big Moses Attacked Little England

'I had come to this country filled with the awe I had always felt for English football, and you know how painful it is when one has to part with the favourite dream of one's youth.'

Willy Meisl, *Soccer Revolution*, 1956

Willy Meisl: The British Foreigner

In 1953, the Hungarians turned the football world upside down by beating England 6–3 at Wembley. It was the national team's first defeat to Continental opposition on home soil. This should have been a watershed moment in the domestic game; Gustav Sebes' 'Golden Squad', in the middle of a long, unbeaten run, taught a team which included Stanley Matthews, Stan Mortensen, Billy Wright and Alf Ramsey a footballing lesson. Just before the match, Willy Meisl met Brian Glanville at a Fleet Street coffee house and predicted that Little England would perish as a leading football nation – unless it shed its Little Englandness.

*

When Meisl, a journalist whose brother Hugo had created the great Austrian 'Wonder Team' of the 1930s, wrote about the decline of the English game in his 1956 book *Soccer Revolution*, he was dismissed by several offended football writers as another of those 'clever Continentals'. This tells you a great deal about the post-war game's insularity. The national team might have been walloped, twice in two years, by the Hungarians, but an empire-shedding, Suez-bruised, Austerity England was in no mood to be lectured. And certainly not by a foreigner. In fact Meisl, like so many of the central Europeans who fled the Nazis, was a confirmed Anglophile. Describing himself in the book as a 'British foreigner', he eventually became a naturalised citizen and spent the last thirty-five years of his life in London. 'Whatever terrible things Hitler has done to me, he also did me one great favour,' he wrote. 'He made me move to the homeland of sport, where I would be able to see British soccer, the world's best, to my heart's content . . . I came, I watched and I began to disbelieve my eyes and ears.' When I first read his magnum opus, it occurred to me that he had broken one of George Mikes' golden rules. His fellow émigré had published a famous trilogy of *How to Be* books in the post-war years that poked gentle fun at the English and their relationship with foreigners. Mikes dealt with such important topics as the weather, tea, queuing and sex – 'Continental people have sex lives: the English have hot water bottles' – and noted that being clever was considered bad manners. His advice on 'how to be a naturalised citizen' was: eat porridge for breakfast and allege that you like it.

By the early 1950s, Meisl could no longer claim that he liked English football. The country, he warned, had to stop deluding itself that it was the best football nation in the world. He used to be 'a profound admirer, not to say an addict, of British soccer' but, in his prophetic programme notes for 1953's England v. Rest of the World clash – staged a month before the Hungarian thrashing – he declared: 'We must free our soccer youth from the shackles of playing to order, along rails as it were. We must give them ideas and encourage them to develop their own.' Almost sixty years later, our soccer youth remains shackled. Technically, English football is still lagging way behind the other major footballing nations. The flaws Meisl identified have gone uncorrected – which only serves to underline the enduring resonance of his minor masterpiece.

He was born to a wealthy family in 1895 and grew up in Anglophile Vienna, where 'the English game', introduced at the turn of the century, cast a magical spell on young Jews wishing to assimilate into Austrian life. He was a sporting polymath from a young age, a member of the Austrian water polo team as well as a champion swimmer, boxer and tennis player. After a brief spell as Austria's goalkeeper in 1920, he played and coached in Sweden before returning to Vienna. He became Germany's most famous sportswriter in the 1920s, editing Berlin's *Vossische Zeitung*, the country's leading newspaper, until the Nazi takeover in 1933. A few months after writing an article repudiating the notion of Jewish physical inferiority, he was forced to emigrate to England. In 1936, he joined the staff of *World Journalist*, the official publication of the British Olympic Committee. After a three-year spell in the army he served at the British Foreign Office.

In 1956, two years after British weekly *World Sports* named him 'the World's No. 1 Soccer Critic', he published one of the most prescient football books ever written. Although he credited Chapman with introducing a third back – Herbie Roberts, playing in that role, had been instructed to 'police Morris' in a 1929 FA Cup tie – he dismissed the Arsenal manager's innovation as a 'safety first' system. By blindly aping it, coaches were denying their players the room for self-expression. The 3-2-2-3, or W-M, formation might work at home, but it would expose English teams as technical novices abroad. This was one of the mistakes, he argued, which led to England's 1953 humbling. He was strongly in favour of improving the technical ability of English players and promoted the concept of the 'whirl': players constantly swapping positions, drawing their markers all over the pitch, passing the ball intricately around until their opponents' heads started to spin. His criticisms, inevitably, went down badly. Even now, in a post-*Fever Pitch* England, it remains unfashionable to theorise about the game; wearing rimless glasses is normally all that's required to be thought of as some kind of football intellectual. But in interwar central Europe the two worlds of soccer and culture, deemed to be mutually exclusive in Britain, had become intertwined. In their home cities, the émigrés had discussed tactics and formations in coffee houses; in London, where most of them settled, such matters tended not to be aired in tea or public houses.

The central Europeans who sought refuge from the Nazis were, on the whole, middle-class and assimilated rather than, as with the

Ostjuden, impoverished and observant. Whilst making a television documentary on the filmmaker Emeric Pressburger, his grandson Kevin Macdonald was stunned to discover the Hungarian's fervent support for Arsenal. Macdonald asked Ernest Hecht, one of the talking heads, how a violin-playing, crossword-compiling sophisticate like his grandfather could feel so strongly about the working man's game. 'In central Europe,' the publisher corrected him, 'football wasn't working-class. It was not professional. If you were a good player you'd get a job. If I was running a club I'd hire a good centre-forward to do our packing or something.' As Jonathan Wilson explains:

> In Willy Meisl's Vienna, and Sebes' Budapest, they would get out bits of paper, start drawing diagrams and discuss terms and formations. They gave football a language. There, football was discussed sitting down – not, as in England, in the pub standing up – so you could draw diagrams. The coffee-house culture of Danubian cities and the large Jewish populations was a happy coincidence that produced the first intellectualisation of football. The class that takes up football in Austria is not an uneducated working class but a very educated middle class whose natural mode is to theorise and discuss. And there was a very strong Jewish element in that class.

The émigrés did not dismiss the game as the province of proletarian ruffians. They were new, not old, Europeans. They crossed national borders without any cultural misgiving, and a small minority followed 'foreign' ideologies like communism and Zionism. Sometimes the two ideologies overlapped: the pro-communist historian Eric Hobsbawm, who was a schoolboy in Berlin when Hitler came to power, and grew up in Vienna, recalled his affection for

Hakoah, a Zionist club, who 'faced my father and Uncle Sidney with a problem of conflicting loyalties' when playing Bolton Wanderers.

Founded in 1909 by a librettist and dentist, and coached by two Britons – Billy Hunter and Arthur Barr – Hakoah recruited the best Jewish players from Vienna and Budapest. They were the greatest Jewish sports team of the twentieth century, the blue-and-white-clad embodiment of Nordau's 'muscular Judaism'. In 1923, after being held to a shock 1–1 draw by Hakoah in Vienna, West Ham asked for a rematch to restore their honour. Forty thousand people crammed into the Boleyn Ground to witness a 5–0 rout of the home side – only a few months after the Hammers had played in the FA Cup final. After the game, the Londoners' star, George Kaye, marched into the visitors' dressing room and declared: 'You are the best team I have ever seen, and believe me I have seen hundreds of games of football.' The *Daily Mirror* congratulated them on their 'scientific football . . . no exhibition of brute force, no kick and rush – they had no time for that. Instead their players worked tremendously well together without relying on long passes. They passed the ball smoothly and made good use of space. They were able to control the moving ball; unlike them, the West Ham players had feet of lead.' The team's triumphs around the world helped build up Jewish self-esteem in the face of discrimination and hostility. 'An entire movement of Jews,' wrote Franklin Foer, 'believed that soccer, and sport more generally, would liberate them from the violence and tyranny of anti-Semitism.' Hakoah's *Schtarkers* fought off Jew-haters in the streets of Vienna and their off-the-pitch toughness was held up as a model to emulate. 'So much is heard of the voice of Jacob that we are sometimes apt to forget his limbs are as flexible as his mind,' wrote J. R. Myrtle in the *Jewish Chronicle*. 'That, all things being equal, he can be a match in the sporting field. For if life is but a sport, where is there an older, or better trained, sportsman than the Jew, who for so long had to use all his ingenuity and supple-ness to hold his own against a whole world of opponents.'

In 1924 Hakoah won the Austrian title and then defeated the Egyptian national team during a tour of the Middle East. The following season they vanquished leading clubs in Belguim and Holland before winning fifteen matches in Poland, Latvia, Lithuania, Czechoslovakia and Hungary. They were closed down by the Nazis after Austria was annexed into the Third Reich, on 12 March 1938, their training grounds appropriated by the German army. Several Hakoah players perished in Hitler's death camps, including their captain Max Scheuer and outside-left József Eisenhoffer. Árpád Weisz, who played for the great 1920s Hungary side before coaching Ambrosiana Inter and Bologna to League titles in the mid-1930s, was forced to leave Italy after the introduction of racial laws in 1938 and took refuge in Holland; following the German occupation he was arrested and deported to Auschwitz, where he died with the rest of his family. Two Hakoah players managed to escape to England – Norbert Katz and Theodor 'Tibi' Wegner – but they both ended up outside football. Most British teams were against relaxing the rules about alien players; when Arsenal tried to sign a Dutchman, Football League secretary Arthur Sutcliffe spluttered: 'This is repul-sive to the clubs, offensive to British players and a terrible confes-sion of weakness.' Katz, who scored Hakoah's final goal in the 1923 hammering of West Ham, became a successful businessman. Wegner invented an anti-perspirant device worn around the wrist that, with tennis star Fred Perry's help, was transformed into the sweatband. His follow-up ideas – the iconic Fred Perry shirt and a brand of sporting clothes called 'Wimbledon' – made him a millionaire.

It would be another forty years, when football finally began to shed its insularity, before Jewish outsiders were allowed to bring a new vision, a fresh slant, to the game. And so it was in the publishing

– rather than, to its great loss, the footballing – world that émigrés reinvigorated post-war life, injecting into English parochialism the exquisite elixir of cosmopolitanism. Ernest Hecht's Souvenir Press immediately made its mark and, sixty years later, is still, as Hecht put it, 'selling books that challenge dominant thinking'. His eclectic list has included five Nobel laureates and many esoteric bestsellers, but it is football that has always consumed him. When, in the 1960s, a conglomerate proposed rolling Souvenir into its empire and putting him in charge, he declined on the grounds that he 'could no longer go off on the drop of a hat to Madrid or Brazil to watch a game'. He watched his beloved Arsenal for the first time in 1941, two years after travelling alone from Czechoslovakia on the *Kindertransport*, the humanitarian trains that rescued 10,000 Jewish children on the eve of war.

Hecht describes the game:

It was against Swindon in 1941 and we won 6–1. It took me three hours to get there from the Wiltshire village I'd been evacuated to. I was twelve years old. The last match I had seen before that was in Prague before I left. It was a local derby. Slavia won 2–1; I dragged my poor mother to see it. It was a great goal scored by the inside-left. Forty years later I had Bill Shankly in my office to present our 'sword of honour' to Kevin Keegan when he was at Hamburg. When I mentioned that goal he said: 'Aye, curly-haired, gypsy-looking lad called Bisan, Hungarian.' I asked Bill how on earth he knew that. 'I played for Preston in Prague in 1938. We lost 4–1, and he was the inside-right, and I was the right-half, and he scored a hat-trick.'

Although Spurs, then as now, had a renowned Jewish following, it was their north London rivals who attracted the support of a small number of soccer-mad intellectuals. 'Arsenal were the émigré's club,' noted Hecht. 'Emeric Pressburger and I both passionately supported them. I came over in 1939. Who, in Europe before the war, would have known any other team? Arsenal won everything in the 1930s. It was the only team we'd heard of. If you are a stranger in a strange land you've got to hang on to something, to support somebody.' Hecht's prestigious 'Sword of Honour' was awarded each year by the *International Football Book*, a legendary Souvenir title which opened up a whole new world to thousands of young English football fans. 'Nobody had ever done that before,' said Hecht. 'We didn't talk down to readers. We would use writers like Glanville and Meisl and have articles that quoted poets like Yeats. Before that we did the *Real Madrid Book of Football*. When we began, you could actually sell a guide to Scunthorpe United more easily than a book on Puskas or Pele. International football was not on the agenda of the average book buyer. We changed that. From 1958 onwards we decided to give an award and we did it for thirty-five years. The football "Sword of Honour", the same as Her Majesty gets, was made by Wilkinsons with a scabbard. It went to Matt Busby, Pele, Keegan. Willy Meisl was one of the early ones. *Soccer Revolution* was ahead of its time.'

Meisl's own book was a lament for a God that failed. He idealised his adopted country, praising its traders, seafarers, engineers, teachers and tourists for spreading the game across the globe. But its amateur elite looked askance at international competition, only deciding to take part in the World Cup as late as 1950. Those clubs who ventured 'abroad' reported that the unobliging natives stubbornly refused to follow the laws of the game. In some parts of central Europe, they even had the temerity to tear them up and start again. In Vienna, Willy's brother Hugo, aided by the forward-thinking English coach Jimmy Hogan, modified the

2-3-5 formation, the standard British line-up since the 1890s. In Budapest, the Hungarian coach Márton Bukovi went even further, inverting Chapman's WM pyramid into the WW used by Sebes' team in 1953. The Meisl brothers, Bukovi, Sebes, Bela Guttmann and Dori Kurschner – who fled to Rio and helped lay the foundations of Brazil's beautiful game – were all part of a cadre of Jewish football revolutionaries who, as Wilson wrote, were 'as comfortable with planning in the abstract as they were with reacting on the field and, crucially, suffered none of the distrust of intellectualism that was to be found in Britain.'

When I first started to read Meisl and Glanville, and in more recent times the likes of David Goldblatt, David Winner, Simon Kuper and David Conn, I never thought of them as Jewish writers. But their perspective, I came to notice, was often that of the discerning outsider looking in, expressing a passion for, but still not quite becoming part of, English football. As the Jewish-Hungarian film director Alexander Korda put it: 'An outsider often makes the best job of a national film. He is not cumbered with excessively detailed knowledge and associations. He gets a fresh slant on things.' In films like *The Private Life of Henry VIII*, *A Canterbury Tale*, *The Life and Death of Colonel Blimp* and the Ealing Comedies, Korda, Pressburger and Michael Balcon – born in Birmingham, but from an East-European family – anatomised the meaning of Englishness from an assimilated Jewish perspective. In many ways, they were more English than the English, revering the country's freedom, composure and tolerance. But they retained, as Winder noted in *Bloody Foreigners*, 'a foreign sensibility [that] might easily see us more vividly and in bolder outline than we see ourselves . . . only those equipped with the means of comparison can discern the outline of our national character.'

The European Englishman

Even after the war, the chinless elite who ran England's public schools included many pro-Nazi sympathisers. 'I had such a time of it at Charterhouse,' wrote Glanville, who has offered a reliably cosmopolitan take on English football throughout his career. 'I went there as a kid, 5 foot 2 and a half, 632 Nazis against you. They used to play a satirical anti-Jewish record over and over in the Long Room. Jew this, Jew that, Jew the other. You never knew where it was coming from, who was going to pop out of the woodwork and insult you next. It was like Auschwitz without the chimneys. The horrific news of the death camps was only just beginning to percolate, but it made no difference.' It is hard to think of any football writer who has exerted anything close to Glanville's influence over the last sixty years. Now in his early eighties, he has been described by the American journalist Paul Zimmerman as 'the greatest football writer of all time'. In his youth he was a reluctant Jew – 'I was barmitzvah, although I found it boring, oppressive and tedious' – and, after being racially bullied at Charterhouse, for many years preferred not to speak of his ethnicity. 'I went around for years being anonymous and not telling anyone about it,' he said.

He first bumped into Hecht at White Hart Lane in 1952. Both young men, like the independent fanzine sellers of the late 1980s, were zealously flogging copies of their books. After opening for business the year before, in a bedroom at his parents' flat, Hecht had borrowed £120 from them to publish *Football: My Life*, the autobiography of former Tottenham captain Ron Burgess, which he sold direct to the Spurs supporters club. Glanville had borrowed £400 from his father to ghost-write the autobiography of Arsenal striker Cliff Bastin. They bonded as Arsenal fans, both idolising

Bastin's old team-mate Eddie Hapgood. 'At the time, many foot-ballers were writing their autobiographies, so I wrote to Bastin,' said Glanville. '"I had plenty of chutzpah. The first one [to release an autobiography] was Hapgood with *Football Ambassador*. He was my hero and I wrote him fan letters.' Hecht had used Football Ambassador as an instruction manual for the teams he managed at Hull University. 'I imposed Arsenal methods on them,' he said. 'They were all taken from the Hapgood book, which I carried religiously around with me.' Glanville's next bit of chutzpah was to march into the *Corriere dello Sport* office, while holidaying in Rome, and ask for a job. 'I didn't speak a word of Italian but I had a file of cuttings.'

He was delighted to see many of his articles translated into Italian for *Corriere Dello Sport* and moved to Rome and then Florence, where he befriended several managers, including Jesse Carver – who enjoyed success at Juventus, Torino and Roma – and Bela Guttman. The latter was a Hungarian Jew who experienced one of the most peripatetic coaching careers of all time, leading Hakoah to the Austrian title before managing teams in Holland, Hungary and Greece. Glanville got the scoop the day after Guttman was fired by AC Milan, despite the team topping the Italian league. 'I have been sacked even though I am neither a criminal nor a homosexual,' said Guttman, who in São Paulo popularised Kurschner's 4-2-4 forma-tion – which was then adopted by Brazil on their way to winning the 1958 World Cup. His greatest triumph was in Portugal, where he led Benfica to back-to-back European Cups. Throughout his long, illustrious, nomadic career he was only ever approached by one English club: Third Division Port Vale.

Glanville, I suppose, is a bit of a one-off in British sports jour-nalism. It would be difficult to envisage any other 'hack' working on the satirical BBC programme *That Was The Week That Was* – where he wrote the song 'Bert the Inert' about FA boss Bert Millichip

– let alone penning more than twenty novels, five collections of short stories, nearly thirty football books and several plays. He was first introduced to the joys of Bognor Regis Town by his father (who had changed his name from Goldberg) but acquired a European sensibility during his years in Italy. When I first attended press conferences as a *Sunday Mirror* football journalist, I noticed how much he irritated colleagues by addressing managers like Claudio Ranieri, Gianluca Vialli and Gianfranco Zola in their native language.

They say you should never meet your heroes, certainly not while sitting next to them in a draughty old ground while they try to dictate copy over the phone. But my first encounter with the great man, at Southampton's old stadium at the Dell, was not a disappointment. In between Glanville sporadically improvising a flawless 800-word match report, I told him how much books like *Goalkeepers Are Crazy*, *The Rise of Gerry Logan* and *The Story of the World Cup* meant to me. His short stories and novels, too, especially *The King of Hackney Marshes*. On the train ride back to London he displayed his breathtaking knowledge of the world game and told me the story of a tubercular Jewish public schoolboy who abandoned a career in law to pursue his passion. He was particularly grateful to Meisl, who became his mentor. Shortly before the 1953 Hungary game, he had begun work on his own titanic call to arms, *Soccer Nemesis*. 'Its theme,' he said, 'was the gradual decline of the British game as it was steadily overtaken by European and South American football . . . Willy helped me a lot on the book. It was published in the same year as his own. I talked to him a lot about European football. About Hugo and the Jewish teams. And Bela Gutmann.'

Glanville remembered, as if it were yesterday, Meisl holding court at the Kardomah café in Fleet Street, railing against English arrogance.

Willy was a rather handsome-looking man, highly intelligent, highly original – but highly didactic. I liked him immensely, but he'd sit in the press box and say, 'Foul, foul, foul,' in that strong Viennese accent he had. He was always right, displaying the typical attitude of those rather bright, Jewish, *Mittel*-European refugees. The Arsenal goalkeeper Jack Kelsey once played two games in the same day, for Wales against England at Villa Park and then for Arsenal in the evening, which was a great double event. 'This is nothing,' Willy said. 'I remember when I was playing goalkeeper for Vienna and first of all for Fussball Austria then I played three games of tennis and water polo; after that I ran in a cross-country race and that evening I *schtupped* my wife five times.' These Viennese refugees were always right about everything. They were so – a lovely Yiddish expression this – *moishe gross*, which means a small man with a big name, a 'big Moses'. Willy never did belong. He was a very opinionated, deeply foreign figure. A bit of a know-all. The way he spoke, the way he looked, his whole attitude to things. He was ageing at that time. Rather dark, specs. Roundish face. I can still see him in my mind's eye. He took me under his wing. He saw me as his protégé. I was very happy to sit at his feet because he could tell me a lot of things that were important for me to know. And he knew them because he had mostly been there when they happened.

The Kardomah was possibly the closest English football came to the coffee-house culture that had witnessed, at close hand, a series of outstanding central European teams, including many of the Jewish football clubs that had sprouted in Vienna, Budapest, Berlin, Prague, Innsbruck and Linz. And it was in this café that Meisl, Glanville and other European-minded football writers would dissect the domestic game.

At the end of the First Age, just after the war, this small offshoot of the Jewish cadre of English football's revolutionaries challenged inherent conservatism. It would be wrong to call them a movement, being small in number and maverick in temperament. Several other leading critics of 'the English style' – an over-reliance on sweat, grit and the long ball – were Anglo-Saxon Protestants. But Meisl, Glanville and Hecht inserted a European sensibility into the national discourse, displaying an appreciation for the neat, inter-passing continental style forged by foreign coaches in Budapest, Prague and Vienna. These central European capitals had experienced a far deeper integration of Jewish immigrants than British cities, but instead of disappearing into the host culture, like the Goldberg generation, they had openly shaped it, creating the conditions for the rise of Jewish sides like Hakoah Vienna and MTK Budapest and the national teams of Austria and Hungary. The magnificent Magyars, unbeaten in three years when they came to Wembley in 1953, were built around an astonishing generation of talented players – Puskas, Hidegkuti, Kocsis and Czibor – but also a trio of Jewish coaches: Sebes, Guttman and Marton Bukovi, a holy triumvirate of gurus who, arguably, had more influence on the tactical side of the modern game than anyone else. Sebes introduced callisthenics, art and theatre to Hungarian football. He developed Chapman's WM system by stopping wingers clinging to the touchline, allowing centre-forwards to drop back and encouraging midfielders and wing-halves to press forward into empty spaces. Every player pulled equal weight and could play in any position. This system, a precursor of the Total Football made famous by Rinus Michels' Ajax in the 1970s, provided a tremendous amount of flexibility. In the 1953 international, forwards Puskas and Sándor Kocsis continually swapped positions, completely confusing the home defence. England's humiliation by Sebes' great Hungary side dramatised a cultural clash between domestic intro-version and foreign innovation. It was, admitted defender Syd Owen, 'like playing people from outer space'.

When the Swastika Flew above White Hart Lane

To understand why this 'soccer revolution', as Meisl called it, failed to spread to the home of football, it is useful to recall an earlier England international: the 1935 friendly against Germany. This game was a perfect example of the myopia that insulated the English against the new ideas emanating from Europe. It also illustrated the extent to which an attenuated Anglo-Jewish establishment was content to mirror the host nation's suspicion of Johnny Foreigner. Between 1933 and the outbreak of war in 1939, around 55,000 central European refugees came to Britain. If the *Ostjuden* had been an unpleasant reminder of their lowly origins, this new influx tended to draw attention to its leaders' submerged cosmopolitanism: to the way diaspora intellectuals transcended national boundaries, promoting 'un-English' ideas about politics, culture and sport. Just as the children of the eastern Europeans were becoming Englishmen, and the ghetto bend was being ironed out, this new invasion threat-ened to 're-Judaise' the tribe. The Board of Deputies, who had striven so hard to anglicise the community, were alarmed at the prospect of all their good work unravelling. The international was played at White Hart Lane, virtually a second home to many north London Jewish fans, and the swastika was flown above the ground. What worried the board was not the propaganda possibilities for the Nazis, but a potential Jewish presence outside the Spurs stadium. The *Jewish Chronicle* warned their readers against supporting any protests, 'to shun, like the plague, any disorderly move. Let them stay away from the match. Violence or disturbance would only play the Nazi game: it would bring discredit on the Jews and alienate the very sympathies it sought to enlist.' As thousands of 'invisible' Jews inside the stadium watched England cruise to a 3–0 victory, hundreds stood outside, handing out leaflets about a Polish goalkeeper murdered in Silesia. At the beginning of the year, during a match in Ratisbon, German spectators had discovered the ethnicity of the player and assaulted him with stones; he died on the way to hospital. Meanwhile, a group of refugees from the Nazis shepherded 10,000 German fans around London's tourist attractions, acting as guides and interpreters. This separation, between 'football lovers' on the inside and 'intellectual foreigners' on the outside confirmed, for Meisl, the soccer–culture divide – and brought home the reality of Anglo-Jewry's long-nourished investment in silence.

Despite the *Chronicle*'s exhortations, there were two incidents, one before and the other during the game, which threatened to draw attention to Jewish protests. Special Branch cautioned a '40-year-old Jew of foreign extraction' after he had threatened to 'fly overhead and make the game in more than one way unpleasant and damaging'. Visiting him at his home, officers discovered that he possessed neither a pilot's licence nor a plane. Midway through the first half, a Spurs fan, Ernest Wooley, climbed on to the roof above the grandstand and ran down the swastika flag. He was charged with doing three shillings and sixpence worth of damage. An outraged Herbert Dunnico, chairman of the Counties Association of Football Clubs, condemned Wooley for 'despoiling the high traditions of British sportsmanship'. Wooley's lone act of defiance went unreported by the *Chronicle* and most national newspapers. Instead they published articles about the foreign Jews who had acted as guides to the visiting party. The former were depicted as otherworldly, unsporting intellectuals who preferred chaperoning 'true fans' around the capital to standing next to them on the terraces. The reason they were refugees in the first place appears to have been forgotten, as was the fact that one of the first things Hitler had done on coming to power, two years before the White Hart Lane friendly, was to Aryanise German sport, removing all Jews from positions of influence.

The Foreign Office, committed to its policy of appeasing Hitler, was also desperate not to provoke a hostile German reaction. Sir John Simon, the home secretary, told a TUC deputation: 'I think that we have to keep up in our country a tradition that [this] sporting fixture is carried through without any regard to politics at all.' Simon's argument was somewhat undermined by the fact that all sporting contact with Germany had been cut off after the First World War; the FA, like its counterparts in Ireland, Scotland and Wales, had refused to play German teams at club and national level for several years after the conflict. The night before the game, the Anglo-German Fellowship had held a dinner in honour of Hans von Tschammer und Osten, the sadistic president of the German Olympic Council. Von Tschammer, described by English socialite 'Bunny' Tattersall as 'a man of outstanding ability, besides possessing extremely good looks', advocated a march in support of staging the game through the Jewish residential areas of Stamford Hill and Stoke Newington. It was called off, at the last minute, for 'public safety' reasons.

Despite Tottenham's high concentration of Jewish supporters, club officials advised the FA to ignore all protests. Coincidentally, the match took place in the same month as Abrahams' condemnation of an Olympic boycott – in fact, he ended up going to the following year's Berlin Games as a BBC commentator – arguing it was not 'ultimately in the best interests of world sport and better world relationships'. The 1935 friendly was clearly a test bed for Nazi diplomacy.

One newspaper report of the game chose to contrast England and Germany's 'pluck and resolve' with the 'pretty-pretty but ineffective' continental football of the Austrian national team, who had played West Ham at Upton Park a few days earlier. In Aryanising German football, the Nazis took this separation to extremes, inventing a distinction between the manliness of the Third Reich sportsman and the cowardly cosmopolitanism of Jewish outsiders. After the following year's Anschluss, Austria was integrated into a German team that had been *Judenfrei* for three years. On Hitler's orders, the German FA had declared in *Kicker* magazine that 'members of the Jewish race' were 'unacceptable in leading positions in regional organisations and clubs, who are urged to initiate appropriate measures, if they have not yet been taken'. Hugo Reiss and Kurt Landauer, two high-profile administrators, had been kicked out of Eintracht Frankfurt and Bayern Munich respectively. The latter were denounced as a *Judenklub*. One of their co-founders, Benno Elkan, emigrated to London and became a prominent sculptor: on commission from Parliament, he built a seven-branched menorah. Landauer, the son of a wealthy Jewish businessman, fled to Switzerland after thirty-three days in the Dachau concentration camp; during a wartime friendly against Switzerland in Zurich, the Bayern players defiantly lined up to wave at him in the stands. In pre-Nazi Germany Bayern had been a club of Jewish visionaries; in the 1960s and 1970s, however, they were marketed as a blue-chip brand, representatives of West Germany's new, golden, Franz-Beckenbauer-led era. Club publications briefly referred to Landauer leaving the country on 'political-racial grounds', assiduously avoiding the word 'Jew'. Vice-president Fritz Scherer admitted they did not want to emphasise their Jewish roots for fear of 'negative reactions'.

Kicker, Germany's most influential football magazine, had been founded by Landauer's friend Walther Bensemann, the unacknowledged godfather of German football. Landauer rejected the notion of *Kampfgeist* – spirit of struggle – seeing it instead as a game of creativity, artistry and joy. A secular Jew, he pushed soccer in grammar schools against strong nationalist opposition. He formed the Karlsruher Kickers, a select team modelled on the English Corinthians, and organised France–Germany matches in Paris. Like Meisl, he was a devout Anglophile – after living in Britain for thirteen years as a sports and language teacher he immediately recruited English coaches on his return to Germany. He died, in exile, unnoticed and penniless, a year before the White Hart Lane friendly; by then the DFB had removed all references to him from their records. Key players like Julius Hirsch and Gottfried Fuchs, the fearsome strikeforce who propelled Karlsruher to their only ever championship in 1910, were also erased from the archives. Hirsch, the first Jewish player to represent the national team, died at Auschwitz in 1945 – but Fuchs, whose feat of scoring ten goals against Russia in 1912 still stands as a record to this day, managed to get out in 1937.

Just over eight years after Wooley had been arrested for trying to pull down the swastika at White Hart Lane, Leon Greenman, a thirty-four-year-old Londoner, was force-marched by the Nazis from Auschwitz-Birkenau to southern Poland and then, in an open cattle truck, transported to Buchenwald. On 11 April 1945, Greenman was liberated by the US army. His wife and young son had been gassed; of the 700 people sent to the camp, he was one of only two survivors. Greenman was born in Whitechapel in 1910 and got married at Stepney Green Synagogue twenty-five years later. His Dutch-Jewish grandparents wanted to spend their last years in the Netherlands, which is how he ended up at Westerbork, the Dutch internment camp from where the trains left for Poland. He was a passionate sportsman in his youth and, at the age of ninety, he looked back on his sporting life with Simon Kuper. 'He still sees himself lying in the grass in Kattenburg and accidentally stopping a certain goal that his brother Morry had shot,' wrote Kuper. At Auschwitz-Birkenau, he recognised two other prisoners: one a European boxing champion, the other a popular Dutch footballer called Eddy Hamel.

Leon takes up the story:

Inside the barracks were wooden bunks, three high; some with a few wooden boards to act as a mattress, some with none at all. I shared a bunk with Eddie Hamel. He had been a well-known professional footballer in Amsterdam, playing for Ajax. We could not believe healthy women and children were gassed to death. It was so absurd you just didn't believe it. It's weird how things turned out. It could have been everybody, but Eddy and I ended up sharing the top berth. There was more fresh air up there, and if the camp guards passed by, you were out of their range of vision. If he had been a better right-winger, or if he'd played for Ajax more recently, maybe he would have had a chance of getting sent to Theresienstadt instead of Auschwitz-Birkenau. Theresienstadt was known as the 'luxury camp' for rich, famous or protected Jews. In the beginning there were eight of us, sleeping on the shelves of the upper berth. But more and more people were selected and taken away. At a certain point, there were three of us left. Lying there together made it hard to get some sleep. Eddy and I used to rub our backs against one another. His body was very warm, you see. He must have had good circulation. The others were very, very cold. We did not get selected for such a long time. Not because, as athletes, we had more strength than the others. I think it was just luck. On the day of the Great Selection, from early in the morning 'til late in the evening, all they did was inspect your body. We were forced to undress and line up. Eddy Hamel was right behind me, because his name started with H and mine with G. He said to me: 'Leon, what will happen to me? I've got an abscess in my mouth.' I took a look. It looked swollen, indeed. We were forced to walk past two desks. At every desk sat an SS officer. If you were declared fit, they directed you to the right. If you weren't, you went left. I walked past those tables. They pointed to the right. Eddy followed, I looked around and saw them sending him to the left. The unfortunate moment. I thought they'd send him to hospital, but I never saw him again. It took me several months before I realised they were actually gassing people.

The Limbs of Jacob

Some central European footballers who survived came to England and helped galvanise grass roots football. In Manchester, just after the war, many of the founders of a new Sunday league were émigrés. As a young boy growing up in Vienna, Herbert Elliott's head had been turned by Hugo Meisl's 'Wonder team'. 'For an international between Austria and Hungary,' Elliot recalled, 'there was always a curtain raiser, then something in between and then the main match. So you got four hours' entertainment.' One of the six to eight thousand émigrés who reached Manchester, he played for Preston North End's youth team during the war. When he moved to Manchester he founded, and captained, Springfield, a team composed entirely of refugees. In the competition's first year they won the League and Cup double.

'In Vienna, I went regularly to football matches,' Elliott recounts.

On Sundays, when I was ten, I went every week to watch or play football. I could watch three matches on a Sunday. There would be matches going on at a local ground from 10 a.m. to 7 p.m. You could go home and come back again during the day. At grammar school, I always organised the class games and was the sports captain. I was always on the class team picked by the teacher . . . We played a lot of football [and] we played a lot with balls. We made a ball out of paper and string. I was picked on by the bigger boys in my neighbourhood. There would be two or three of them, and I would get black eyes. They would call me 'dirty Jew' and spit. One day the local boys passed through the park and made some anti-Semitic remarks. The non-Jewish boys were beaten up badly. That was long before Hitler came in. I was at school on the day when people were saying that Hitler was going to do something in Austria. There were hordes walking past wearing armbands. I was thirteen-and-a-half and I turned around on hearing that schools were stopping and Jewish schools were being closed and said, 'Thank God I don't have to do homework.' I thought nothing about it. By coincidence, after Hitler, the only park where Jews were allowed to congregate was the park I played in. On one occasion youngsters of the Hitler Youth walked in and ordered the Jews to gather and marched them off for physical exercises. Two other boys and myself jumped over the parapet in order to escape. I later found out that seventy Jews were marched to the Danube, where they had to do two hours' physical exercises. Resistance might have brought out the Gestapo. Going to school, I saw Jews with their *tallesim* scrubbing the pavement with their toothbrushes and the rabble making fun of them.

Elliott's mother died in 1938, just before Germany annexed Austria, and his father survived Theresienstadt concentration camp, ending up in a Displaced Persons camp. Like Hecht, he arrived in Britain on the *Kindertransport*. 'When we arrived [at the Jewish Community Centre] there was a queue like at a football match,' he said. 'In front of me was another boy from my class, and he said he wanted to go to Holland. When I was asked I also replied "Holland" but my father said "England". I was annoyed with my father, but he told me I was safer there with water between me and them. I was annoyed at the time. I since found out my friend went to Holland and didn't survive the war.'

In 1945, 732 teenage survivors of the concentration camps, known as 'The Boys' – despite a fair few being girls – were brought over and were taught sport, art and drama at the Primrose Club, in London, by Paul 'Yogi' Mayer. Mayer had studied all three subjects at Berlin and Frankfurt Universities until Jews were expelled from higher education. He trained hard for the pentathlon event at the 1936 Olympics, but when Jews were excluded he became a newspaper reporter and witnessed Jesse Owens winning all four of his gold medals. He escaped, with his wife, in May 1939, enrolled in the British army and served with the Special Operations Executive, teaching agents to speak fluent German before they parachuted behind enemy lines. After the war, as Islington Council youth officer, he persuaded the local authority to install floodlighting and Astro Turf on council estate football pitches. He then went on to manage the Brady boys' team, which included the future Manchester City player Barry Silkman. 'I can still remember with affection his voice,' a former Brady member wrote in an obituary, 'shouting out at a camp in Freshwater, Isle of Wight: "Tent Twenty Plays Tent Twenty-one at Wollyball."'

The Primrose Club became one of the most competitive teams in the Association of Jewish Youth League, winning many trophies. When Mayer was asked by the FA to produce the boys' birth certificates, which he 'was obviously unable to do', he pleaded that 'their special circumstances should be taken into consideration. After all, they had been robbed of playing games at a time when boys in this country played on its pastures green.' After he rebuked one of them for fighting after a match, the lad replied: 'I've lost so much that I cannot keep on losing.' The boys were frequently involved in fierce battles with the locals. 'It was over the local girls,' explained Maurice Vegh. 'These girls just clung to us. They loved us. We played soccer with the local boys. They never won one game. Every time they lost a game they would start a fight. They couldn't beat us on the soccer field, they couldn't beat us with the girls. They just gave up. After what we had been through, we had to excel. We just had to excel.'

Part 2

The Golden Age

We Were and We Weren't

'Then Moses stretched out his hand over the sea, and the
Lord drove the sea back by a strong east wind all night
and made the sea dry land, and the waters were divided.'

Exodus 14:21

In the First Age, when mass immigration from eastern Europe coincided with football's emergence as the national game, young,
working-class, second-generation Jews developed a passion for the
sport – but faced economic, cultural and, at times, self-imposed,
religious barriers to their entry. In the Golden Age, which roughly
dates from the early 1960s to the mid-to-late 1970s, the Jewish
community began to seriously integrate into mainstream society.
Upward mobility was their, indeed British society's, mantra. Football
was one of the areas that began to open up to outsiders – and
aspects of a previously hidden Yiddisher sub-culture began to rub
off on 'the English game'. From Spurs' self-styled super fan Morris
Keston to the club's first Jewish manager, from the tough extroverts
who were proud of their differences to the self-conscious introverts
who still preferred to hide them, these outsiders' energy, drive and
determination to start afresh allowed 'Mr Football Jew' to come in
from the cold.

I grew up in this era. My primary school, the Selig Brodetsky,
was named after the Zionist who had infiltrated the Jewish establishment and which was now keen to stem the tide of secularisation.

Football, or at least football played with Gentiles, was now viewed as a threat rather than a vehicle of emancipation. But the more my headmaster told me to stop playing, the more I wanted to play it. At my secondary school, which was predominantly Gentile, there were frequent Jews v. Christians matches which, strangely enough, bonded rather than divided my year group. I became the first Jew to play in the newly established Roundhay 'soccer' team. It had been a rugby-playing grammar school but introduced the ruffians' sport as soon as it morphed into a comprehensive, and, to the disapproval of some of my Brodetsky friends, I shamefully turned out on Yom Kippur, the Day of Atonement – the holiest day of the year – rushing straight from the muddy pitch to the synagogue. I felt a keen sense of 'in-betweenness' during these formative years, torn, like Bookman, between being a Good Jew and a Good Sportsman. Writing about his Manchester schooldays in the 1950s, Howard Jacobson wrote: 'We were and we weren't. We were getting somewhere and we weren't. We were free of the ghetto and we weren't. We were philosophers now and not pedlars, and we weren't.'

In my home city of Leeds, in the 1960s and '70s, the Jewish community became overwhelmingly suburban. As in Manchester and London, the old ghettoes, which were often close to football stadiums, disappeared – or else the Jews moved out of them. As the Jewish community migrated to middle-class suburbs like Moortown, Prestwich and Golders Green, they became even less involved in playing the game professionally– it remained a resolutely prole-tarian sport – but the passion only intensified, as Jews found other ways to connect, as fans, hangers-on, confidants, directors and owners. As British society ostensibly became more egalitarian, there was a corresponding levelling in the football world. In the Golden Age, unfashionable teams like Orient and Luton played in the top flight, and the top stars still rubbed shoulders with 'the man on the

street'. In 1961, at the beginning of an era of change and transformation, both on and off the pitch – social mobility, greater tolerance, cultural miscegenation, a sense of possibility – the maximum
wage for players was abolished, Leeds United appointed three Jewish
directors, and Tottenham, renowned for its strong Jewish support,
became the first team in the twentieth century to do the League
and Cup double.

Whilst for Jews in eastern and central Europe, status had been
achieved by Jewish learning and observance; in Leeds, London,
Manchester and elsewhere it was achieved through integration. This
integration, however, which took place in most areas of popular
culture, the economy and sport, eventually provoked a backlash –
from the British, as well as the Jewish, establishments. The latter,
so desperate at the beginning of the century to pursue a policy of
radical assimilation, worried about the shedding of a distinct ethnic
identity. In attempting to escape the stigma of 'Otherness', the third
generation were also becoming indifferent to ritual and worship,
threatening the demographic health of the community. In 1945,
Anglo-Jewry numbered 450,000; today it is 270,000 and falling.
'There is a greater emphasis on football than there is on religious
education,' Nigel Gordon, secretary of a Manchester synagogue
complained to the *Jewish Chronicle* in 1975. 'Our children cannot
read properly. It is a struggle getting them to recite *maftir* and *haftara*.'
At the same time, there was a resurgence of anti-Semitism towards
the end of what became known as The Long Sixties. There were
frequent references to a so-called 'kosher nostra' and it was not just
the National Front who 'outed' Jews in high places and complained
about conspiracies. When Harold Wilson published his resignation
honours list in 1976, several right-wing, and the odd left-wing, newspaper columnists drew attention to the disproportionate number
of Jewish businessmen and financiers on it. Just as the increasingly

secularised children and grandchildren of eastern European immigrants were playing a bigger role in mainstream culture, the old tropes of anti-Semitism – manipulating national economies, running the press, promoting religious conflict, controlling events behind the scenes – appeared to be making a comeback.

4

The Fans:
When Morry Changed His Religion

'Everywhere I go people say "there's Morris Keston of Spurs."'

Morris Keston, *The Glory Game*, 1972

Morris Keston: The Superfan

In 1962, Mark Lazarus left Wolves for QPR, Harry Zussman celebrated Orient's first ever promotion to the First Division, David Pleat joined his home club, Nottingham Forest, as a seventeen-year-old schoolboy, and Spurs manager Bill Nicholson arranged a tour of Egypt ahead of a vital European game. Morris Keston, a successful businessman in the rag trade, couldn't wait to join the players on the trip. He had been stationed in Cairo during his army days and wanted to show them around his old stomping ground. There was just one snag. Being Jewish, Spurs' biggest fan was not allowed into the country.

*

Keston's solution was simple. He applied for an entry visa and, when it arrived, wrote 'C of E' in the box marked 'Religion'. 'At breakfast in our Cairo hotel, I told Jimmy Greaves and Bobby Smith all about my little white lie,' he wrote. 'They started saying "Shalom Morry" to me as a wind-up. Bill Nicholson got worried, telling them not to upset the Egyptians, which made them do it even more. Each morning I was greeted with an ever-louder chorus of "Shalom" from the players. Bill thought they were going to cause a diplomatic incident. It was a very sensitive time in the Middle East.' When the team returned to London, a newspaper got wind of the story and ran it under the headline 'Jew Defies Nasser to See Spurs'. The Egyptian president might have led a revolution, nationalised the Suez Canal and given the British government a damned good kicking, but he was no match for the King of the Lane.

As Morry was taking on Nasser, Glanville was writing *The Rise of Gerry Logan*, a novel based on the rise of Spurs captain Danny Blanchflower. One of the minor characters, a hanger-on called Sam

Cowan, was inspired by Keston. 'At that time Jews were just strange to me,' Logan says. 'I'd known very few of them in Glasgow and none at all in Jarrow, but now in London I found a lot of them I liked. They were individuals and they had this vitality about them and this generosity . . . here were people like Sam coming along and spending pounds and pounds on parties for the players.'

Keston's wild, lavish, after-match parties were the stuff of legend. Jimmy Greaves, known for liking a drink or two, once arrived at a barmitzvah with a coachload of thirsty team-mates. Keston recounts:

> I had said to Jimmy, 'So, do you fancy coming along to a barmitzvah?' and he said, 'Is there a bar at the mitzvah?' and I said I'm sure, so he said, 'Count me in.' In fact he brought all the other Spurs players, and they were clapped and cheered as they got off the coach and were led to their seats. At each table the host put a case of Scotch, one bottle for each of the fourteen players . . . but the players wanted beer instead. I put their request to the host, and ten minutes later a crate of Goldstar beer was brought to each table. Before long, the players were out of their seats dancing along to the sound of the Beach Boys.

Ten years after *Gerry Logan*, Keston again appeared in a best-selling football book, this time as himself. In *The Glory Game*, Hunter Davies devoted an entire chapter to him. 'Every big club has a fan like Morris,' noted Davies, 'but few have them as big as Morris.' Keston, whose parents had fled Poland to escape anti-Jewish riots, was renowned for his love of shoulder-rubbing. In the 1960s, he could get any Spurs star to turn up at one of his Jewish charity functions at the drop of the hat. 'Wherever the team stays, no matter where it is in the world,' explained Davies, 'Morris Keston stays.' In the Golden Age, before agents, well-connected fans like Morry would sometimes act as unofficial middle-men between players and management. 'No matter where and when we played he was there,' said Greaves. 'He was always there to help and advise if a player ever got into bother; and he knew more about what was going on at the club than any of us. But Morry never told tales out of school. He knew when to keep schtum, and he won the trust of everybody at the club.'

Leeds' biggest fan back then lived just up the road from me. His name was Herbert Warner and he was a lot closer to Leeds manager Don Revie than Keston was to Bill Nicholson. A jeweller and market-stall holder, Herbert was a confidant of 'The Don' and would often be called upon to entertain the players. He would walk into the changing room and crack a few Jewish jokes and, in hotels the night before a big match, he relaxed players by organising bingo and carpet bowls sessions. In 1972 he was even allowed to display the centenary FA Cup at his Barnsley market stall after Leeds had beaten Arsenal to win the trophy.

'I travelled with the players down to Wembley,' Warner recalls:

And we had a few laughs. I sat in the main stand near the Royal Box, which was a great view. After all the civic celebrations, Don let me bring the trophy home to show friends and family who were coming round to the house. It was a spur-of-the-moment thing, but I decided to take it to the market. People could not believe it. They said 'Is that the FA Cup?' I didn't do any trade because people were more interested in having their pictures taken with the Cup. I didn't think of the risks. I played golf with his wife Elsie and followed the team all over Europe. It meant that I neglected my business in Barnsley, but I never missed a match anywhere. I'd sit there until just before they were due to go out and afterwards would have a drink with them in the players' lounge.

Warner died in the early 1990s, a few years after Leeds manager Howard Wilkinson asked him to stop travelling on the team bus. Keston, who is now in his eighties, finally fell out with the club during the Sugar era. Several other clubs have had their Jewish superfans, but the era when a devoted supporter could become part of the furniture is long gone. Ronnie Teeman, a lawyer who represented players like John Giles, Peter Lorimer and Joe Jordan, viewed the 1960s and '70s as a Golden Age when football was a common denominator for Jews and Gentiles: 'You see, what could a Jew talk to his non-Jewish workmate about? Religion? No. That was taboo. But he did have something in common, and that was sport. It allowed him to communicate and converse.'

Morris Keston's chutzpah in 'converting' to Christianity, albeit for the duration of the Egyptian tour, showed just how far some Jewish fans were now prepared to go to follow their 'new religion'. Football was becoming the secular faith of the Jews, in some cases providing an alternative to a *shul*-based Jewish identity. Communal leaders watched this phenomenon with growing horror, linking the rise in match attendance to a rise in apostasy. In a *Jewish Chronicle* Community News item, a Mr A. Cohen 'deplored the excuses given for non-attendance at our synagogue's Hebrew classes. These ranged from having to attend ballet dancing classes to having to get in early at the Arsenal Football Stadium.' In his novel *Blood Libels*, Clive Sinclair has a rabbi denouncing 'shabbat-desecrators' from the pulpit. 'The man who does not keep the sabbath holy,' declares the rabbi,

is no Jew, just as a woman that beats her child is no mother. Nothing is determined by biology – as we above all peoples should know – but by the heart. If your heart is not in it, neither are you. Many of you, I know, will be running to football matches this afternoon, making a mockery of your presence here. To them I say leave now. You are no Jews. Your religion is football!

The second and third generations retained their ethnic cohesion but, as the historian Todd Endelmann has noted, a growing number 'associated traditional ritual, worship and belief with the poverty and Old World habits of their parents and grandparents'. This was certainly true of my own parents, who had grown up in the backstreets of inner-city Leeds and were desperate to make a break with the past. They and their friends were proud to be Jewish, but as youngsters they had rebelled against the religion's stifling laws and customs; if they weren't working on Saturday, they would spend their leisure time at the cinema, the shops or the match.

In Manchester, the home of two of England's biggest teams, an alternative *shabbat* ritual, dating back to the 1920s, continued to be followed by City fans in the Golden Age. A group of season-ticket holders would meet at the Grosvenor Hotel in the city centre. There, as Sydney Lea recalled, they would 'have a couple of drinks and a few games of billiards' before hailing a taxi to the ground. Lea remembered cutting short his honeymoon in the 1920s to make sure he made it to the club's first ever game at Maine Road.

Sydney made the occasional 'concession' to the spirit of the rest day – 'I used to smoke when I was watching football, but when my old man came with me I didn't because I didn't want to hurt his feelings, it being the sabbath and all' – but on the whole felt no guilt about his religious laxity. Martin Bobker, who worked in a waterproof garment factory, described his 'typical weekend as un-Jewish'. Starting with a Friday-night trip to the greyhound track at nearby Salford, followed by billiards and then cards at a friend's house, his sabbath continued with more billiards at lunchtime and then a visit to the City ground. For Joe Garman, another young Mancunian Jew from an immigrant family, watching football had become part of the special day. Religion, he said, was never allowed to get in the way of his love for football, his lack of orthodoxy 'suiting my own whims'.

The Manchester community's affections were equally divided between City and United. The Jewish TV dramatist Jack Rosenthal frequently introduced football themes into his work. I remember, as a boy, being enthralled by his sitcom *The Dustbinmen*, whose central character, Winston Platt, was a Colin Bell nut. In one memorable episode, Winston, unable to get into Maine Road, gave a running commentary of the match to his gang while sitting on a wall outside; from the crowd noises he was able to identify players, free-kicks, corners and, of course, goals. Rosenthal was actually a devoted Red, but had gone to both Maine Road and Old Trafford since the 1930s. In his later years, according to Colin Shindler, the two old friends would 'moan on a daily basis about the awfulness of modern football and particularly modern footballers', rhapsodising nostalgically about the great days of Matt Busby and Joe Mercer. 'Jack and I sat around the dinner table,' wrote Shindler, 'discussing why Alex Ferguson reminded Jack of angry drunken Scottish dockers he used to meet in the pubs of Salford in the 1950s and 1960s and why Kevin Keegan reminded us of self-centred teenagers. Football was a constant topic of conversation between us.' For Shindler, the Blues were 'a broad church, an open synagogue. Nobody cared what you did on Saturday morning if you were at Maine Road on Saturday afternoon.' This is how it was for me, too, standing in the noisy, intimidating Elland Road Kop, rubbing shoulders with working-class Loiners from the 'rougher' part of the city, part of the great melting pot of post-industrial, multicultural Leeds.

In the 1950s, Manchester City's Jewish fan base had become so large and influential it was able to threaten the end of Bert Trautmann's career. Around 25,000 people demonstrated outside Maine Road when the club signed the German goalkeeper – a former prisoner of war – but the row was defused when Rabbi Altmann appealed for calm in the *Manchester Evening Chronicle*. An individual German, reasoned the rabbi, could not be held responsible for the crimes of the Nazis. 'If this footballer is a decent fellow,' he argued. 'I would say there is no harm in it.'

In *Manchester United Ruined My Life*, Shindler gave the impression City was the 'Yiddisher club' but, as Mason Glass recalled, many Jews supported United – if somewhat furtively:

I used to sometimes lie to my *bubba*. She thought I was going to a *shiva* [a mourning house] on a Saturday afternoon. One particular *shabbas* I went to see United against Bolton Wanderers and returned to the household at 7 p.m., and all my aunties and uncles were there as usual. And one of my uncles said, 'Was it a good game?' and my *bubba* looked at me in astoundment. And she wasn't very happy that I was going to football matches on a Saturday afternoon. That wasn't the first time I was caught out – and it wasn't the last.

These Mancunians, along with Morry, were typical of an increasingly secularised second generation who viewed the traditional Saturday rituals as outmoded. Brought up in the Jewish East End, Keston had won a scholarship to Hackney Downs. Like Leslie Goldberg at Lovell Road, he had received a secular education, although the grammar school's catchment area included a large

Jewish population and it closed on High Holy Days. 'The families were financially poor,' its historian, Geoffrey Alderman, noted. 'But their economic and social aspiration knew no bounds.' Nor did the passion many of them displayed for football. Ivan Cohen had his first ever fight at 'Grocers', as the school was known, over a throw-in. 'It was with an Arsenal fan and it was very bloody,' he said. 'Once, for a Spurs–Arsenal match at The Lane, we all tried to bunk off early, but our deputy head, Mr Briarley, had anticipated the situation and was standing at the station, waiting to stop us.'

Not all the Jewish boys liked football: Keston's classmate Harold Pinter was, like Jacobson, keener on table tennis. But for aspirational Jews, both Spurs and Arsenal stood for success, glamour and escape. 'It was about a migrant community integrating and being accepted,' said Cohen. And, for many of these boys, the first step towards this acceptance and integration came in the stands at Tottenham Hotspur.

From the Swastika to the Star of David

In the 1930s, according to a *Manchester Guardian* report, Jews made up a third of the average crowd at White Hart Lane – equal to about 11,000 supporters regularly attending. At a 1934 north London derby the *Daily Express*'s Trevor Wignall discovered he 'was nearly entirely surrounded by them . . . the majority of my neighbours were partisans of the Spurs. They were vociferous to a degree but they were good losers in that they agreed that their team was outplayed.' Arsenal might have been the émigrés' club, attracting the more affluent, suburban Jews, especially during the Chapman era, but Tottenham had always been the main attraction to football-mad Jews in the capital. Algernon Lesser had discovered, as far back as 1911, that 'the results of the games in the football leagues [on Saturday] after-noon are most keenly discussed and loud is the wailing and great the distress among the supporters of "the Spurs" if Tottenham Hotspur have had to lower their colours'.

Founded in 1882 by members of the Hotspur Cricket Club, who wanted an activity to keep the team fit and together throughout the winter, Spurs' earliest religious links were actually with Christian groups. Their first secretary was a churchwarden at the Church of England's All Hallows Parish on Tottenham High Road, and their first president was leader of the local YMCA. Sixteen years later they switched from the River Lea marshes, the old stomping ground of famous amateur teams like the Old Etonians and the Wanderers, to a purpose-built stadium in Northumberland Park. In 1899, they moved down the road to The Lane. Given that the majority of London's eastern European immigrants lived in the Spitalfields-Whitechapel-Stepney area at the time – by the first decade of the twentieth century believed to be the largest Jewish community in Europe – and were much closer, geographically, to West Ham, it seems odd that Tottenham were, even then, known as the Jewish Club.

In 1921, a *Jewish Chronicle* reader explained his allegiance to 'God's Chosen Football Club' by referring to his 'epiphany' at that year's FA Cup triumph. This only confirmed some West Ham fans' depiction of the club as a magnet for glory-hunters. The Hammers were an unfashionable team with a localised profile. From their earliest days as Thames Ironworks FC, strongly linked to the workers at the Thames shipyard, West Ham were a close-knit 'family' run by a small and protected group of chairmen, directors and managers. When Arnold Hills, the owner of the shipyard and brainchild behind the football club, gave the team access to his privately owned

Memorial Ground he expressed the hope that local dock workers would form the majority of the support. Very few, if any, Jews worked on the docks. Jeremy Dein's father Lou, a waiter at Blooms, was the exception that proved the rule. Whereas the rest of the Deins, including future Arsenal vice-chairman David, moved to north London and supported the Gunners, Lou became a West Ham fanatic. 'When I was six, we used to take four buses from Gants Hill to Upton Park,' Jeremy remembers. 'We would be right at the front of the queue for tickets. We'd get the best seats. The turnstiles would open at 1.30 p.m. My father used to arrive with a big bag of salt beef sandwiches, some of them for us, some of them for the turnstile guy. That ensured we got row A seats.'

Glory-hunting might have played a part, but there is another, even simpler, reason why so many East End Jews became passionately devoted to Tottenham: ease of access. Driving or using combustion-engine-powered vehicles on the Sabbath was strictly forbidden, but catching the tram or the train was not. White Hart Lane was located on the High Road that linked north London to the heart of the City. The public transport network – the system of electric trams that spanned large swathes of the capital and the Stoke Newington and Edmonton Railway, which opened in the 1870s, went from Liverpool Street, near Spitalfields, to Tottenham and Edmonton – made access to the stadium from the east and centre of London relatively easy. As a *Jewish Chronicle* correspondent noted: 'In those days, before floodlights were invented, almost all games took place on Saturday afternoons from about two o'clock. It was possible to be in synagogue until the end of *musaf*, to nip home for a quick plate of *lokshen* soup, and then board a tram from Aldgate to White Hart Lane.' No other ground in London was as easy to get to from the East End. For secular Jews who were happy to travel by train, the Stoke Newington and Edmonton Railway from Liverpool

Street, near Spitalfields, allowed them to observe their new *shabbat* ritual of cheering on the Spurs.

Morry Keston remembers:

I had two friends at school who were mad about football: David Fisher and David Abrahams. They were cousins and argued constantly about which team was best, or whether George Ludford of Spurs or Ted Drake of Arsenal was the better player. On the opening day of the season in 1943, Arsenal were away at Chelsea, Spurs at home to Palace. It was easier to get the train from my home to White Hart Lane Station than travel across London to Chelsea, so we went to the Spurs game. That was the beginning of my Spurs obsession. I went to every home game during my youth and, apart from an eighteen-month period doing National Service, I've watched all but two of Tottenham's home matches since 1952. I missed one of those because I tripped on the pavement and badly injured my shoulder. The other I missed because of a triple heart bypass operation. I begged the surgeon to let me go, telling him 'I don't want to lose my home record!' He said: 'If I let you go we'll lose you.'

Keston has been called many things over the years – Hanger-on, Superfan, Fan of Fans, Mr Spurs – but his favourite description came from Greaves, who once dubbed him 'our twelfth man'. Yet despite, or more likely because of, this, he was always kept at arm's length by the board. '[He] has hung on so successfully over the years, despite endless discouragement from the club,' wrote Davies in *The Glory Game*, 'that he is now about the closest to the players of all the outside fans.'

According to Keston, 'In the sixties and seventies the Tottenham board was a closed shop. The chairman, Sidney Wale, took an instant dislike to me. I think he saw me as some sort of threat to his position, but I can't understand why. I was only ever interested in supporting the team and enjoying my friendships with the players. Somebody once gave me five shares of Tottenham. They were worth only £3,000 in those days. I sent a letter to register – but they refused to register me. People used to say to me: "They don't like you because you're Jewish." They didn't want any outsiders.'

After a Greaves-inspired Tottenham beat Chelsea to win the 1967 FA Cup, Keston reinforced both his self-appointed title of 'Spurs' Biggest Fan' and his pariah status with the board by holding an alternative victory party. Instead of going to the club's official Cup final banquet at the Savoy, nearly all the players, along with a fair smattering of Chelsea stars, celebrated at Morry's Hilton bash. Two weeks later, on a plane coming back from Zurich after watching a European game, he found himself sitting next to Wale. 'Did he say anything to me? No, he did not. "Hello, Mr Wale" – no answer. This, because twelve days before I had made that party. Pat Jennings told me that my party had gone down like a lead balloon with him.'

As the sports writer Mihir Bose has pointed out, before Irving Scholar's emergence in the 1980s there was 'unofficial apartheid' between Jewish supporters and Gentile directors. Keston's ostracism came to symbolise the community's estrangement from the board. From raising the swastika at White Hart Lane in the 1935 England–Germany international to fifty years on – when the club's Jewish chairman and Jewish manager were equally upset to see Israeli blue-and-white flags fluttering on the terraces – and through to the present day, the idea of a large Jewish fan-base has unsettled the club's owners. It was not until 1973 that a 'Happy Yom Kippur' message finally appeared in their matchday programme – a gesture

Arsenal had been making, and benefiting from, for years. North London might be home to the majority of the capital's 200,000 Jews, but even in the last thirty years, when the likes of Scholar, Alan Sugar and Daniel Levy have been in charge, the link has been constantly downplayed. Irving Scholar and David Pleat were both strong supporters of Israel but, throughout their careers, they chose – like Goldberg, Spiegel and Dulin – to play down their Jewishness. Scholar refused to be interviewed for this book, insisting that religion had nothing to do with football. Pleat was reluctant at first, still worried about the prospect of an anti-Semitic backlash. In 2002 Levy turned down Israel's request to play their Euro 2004 qualifiers at White Hart Lane; the chairman felt no obligation to proffer an explanation.

Arsenal, on the other hand, have always accepted, and very often embraced, the connection. In 1965 they moved forward a League match against Northampton Town, and delayed their original kick off time by over an hour, to avoid a clash with Yom Kippur. The relationship blossomed during the Chapman era; when the legendary manager died, in 1934, his *Jewish Chronicle* obituary called him a 'great friend of the Jewish people' and praised him for charitable efforts towards a number of causes, including the Norwood Jewish Orphanage and Bethnal Green Aid Society. In a letter to the paper his successor, George Allison, wrote:

> I am happy to think we have a large number of Jews who derive healthy entertainment and get enjoyment from the demonstrations of sportsmanship which they see at the Arsenal ground. For many years it has been our great pleasure to contribute to Jewish charities and to help those deserving causes which Jewish organisations have 'fathered' and I am conscious of the fact that we are only able to do this to the fullest degree

because of the support which we receive from the Jewish community.

By 1951, when Hapoel Tel Aviv toured Britain, the club's fan-base had grown considerably. Of the Israeli side's three matches – against Manchester United, Glasgow Rangers and Arsenal – it was the one at Highbury that created the most excitement. In his programme notes, Arsenal manager Tom Whittaker highlighted the 'good relations between the Jewish and non-Jewish supporters of the club'.

And yet it is Spurs who remain, in the eyes of the English public as well as their own fans, 'God's Chosen Football Club', so much so that their fans declare themselves to be foot-soldiers of the 'Yid Army'; many have little idea of the Y-word's etymology: in the 1930s, Mosley's British Union of Fascists marched through the East End shouting 'Down with the Yids', a term of opprobrium equivalent to words like 'Nigger' and 'Paki'. Glanville has argued that the taunt was originally a disparaging reference, by fans of other London clubs, to Jewish hangers-on like Keston. This might have been so, but the anti-Semitic epithet was popularised by the 1960s sitcom *Till Death Us Do Part*. Sitting in his living room with a West Ham scarf draped around his neck, the show's bigoted anti-hero, Alf Garnett, would frequently rant against 'those Spurs Yids'. Garnett's antipathy fed off a longstanding rivalry between the two clubs, inflamed by some East Enders' resentment of the Jews who had 'deserted' Whitechapel for White Hart Lane. Ironically, the actor who portrayed Garnett – Warren Mitchell – was himself a Jewish Spurs fan. In one episode, Alf claimed that the Blitz was Hitler's attempt to bomb the ground: 'Third set of floodlights past Southend!' Although his son-in-law pointed out that floodlights didn't appear until after the war, the connection was reinforced in the national psyche.

Critics have pointed out that the 'Yid Army' chant gives racist fans the licence to respond with offensive songs like 'Spurs are on their way to Auschwitz' and 'He's only a poor little Yiddo'. For many years, every time Chelsea played Tottenham 'Yiddo! Yiddo!' would be chanted in a guttural, threatening echo with added Nazi arm movements. 'Once, at Stamford Bridge, someone started bellowing "Fuck the Yids, fuck the Jews," at me and my brother,' the writer and comedian David Baddiel, a well-known Blues fan, revealed. 'This happens a lot at Chelsea, whether Tottenham are playing or not. If similar language were being used in en masse singing and chanting about Afro-Caribbeans or Indians, it would be a cause for national outrage.' Spurs fans like Ivan Cohen, however, argue that supporters have 'reappropriated the Yiddo slur as a badge of honour'.

From the Rebbe to the Revie

I, personally, experienced little anti-Semitism as a Leeds United fan in the 1970s. There was one incident, recounted in my book *Promised Land: A Northern Love Story*, in which I was interrogated by three fellow Koppites. They were attempting to sniff out interlopers – the fashion being, in the mid-1970s, for away fans to 'take' the home end – and, very quickly, detected my outsiderness. I had, back then, a north Leeds accent, and this unholy triumvirate were tough, hard-core, south-of-the-river Loiners – 'proper Leeds' – quite possibly members of the Service Crew hooligan gang. When this moment, and my subsequent beating up, was recreated in a stage adaptation of the book, some members of the audience questioned its authenticity. But it certainly took place, as did the 'Yids' taunts when supporters from rival Yorkshire clubs visited Elland Road. Occasionally, when United played the likes of Huddersfield Town or Bradford City in minor cup competitions, I would hear 'Does your rabbi know you're here?' chants – which actually made me feel quite proud.

My rabbi certainly knew I was at Elland Road. Occasionally, at a midweek game, we would bump into each other in the car park. As my schoolfriend Anthony Gilbert, who eventually became a cantor at one of the Leeds synagogues, said: 'Our generation went to *shul*, came home, had a nice meal, and then – it didn't matter if it was winter or summer – *shabbas* stopped at three o'clock because they went to the match at Elland Road. It was that special day in the week. Maybe the fact that they went to Elland Road was part of the *shabbas* as well, as far as they were concerned.' In 1974, when Britain went to the polls, uncle Louis complained in the *Jewish Gazette* about 'Leeds Jewry losing its sense of perspective [by thinking] that Downing Street is of less importance than Elland Road, that Don Revie needs more consolation than Harold Wilson – or is it Heath?'

Louis was the community's unofficial historian: 'I am proud and happy that I am a Jew,' he once wrote, 'and even prouder and happier that I am an English Jew from Leeds.' I have lived in exile down south for many years now but every time I come back to the capital of God's own country I think about this sentence. All three things – my Leedsness, my Jewishness and my Englishness – have interacted to form my identity. And all three came together in the form of Revie's great Leeds side. My city has been the home of Manny Cussins, Michael Marks, Montague Burton, Arnold Ziff – who founded Europe's first shopping mall – and councillor Karl Cohen, the 'demolition man' who knocked down the slums. They were all civic visionaries who helped transform the city's fortunes. They all played their part in helping to rebuild the city in the Golden Age – to the extent that it was unrecognisable from the dirty old town of the late nineteenth century. For me, supporting the mighty Whites has always been two things: a marker of my Leeds Jewish identity and a way of overcoming Jewish parochialism. When I first stood on the Kop, I was aware of belonging to a minority culture, but that didn't seem to matter. On the contrary, as a teenager, being Jewish and a football fan amounted to the same thing. Either way, Saturday remained the most important day of the week. In the morning, walking to *shul* with my friends, any mention of God was likely to be a reference to Billy Bremner.

5

The Showmen:
When Harry Took Orient to the Ball

CLAVANE'S CIGARETTES

H. ZUSSMAN (LEYTON ORIENT)

'We had lost somewhere, and I'll never forget Harry, tears
in his eyes, as he sat us all down. It looked to him like
we were sinking into the Third Division. We all thought
he was Orient, we all owed him something. "You will send
me to the grave," he said, "you're breaking my heart."'

Terry McDonald

Harry Zussman: The Fairy Godfather

In April 1962, with one game to go until the end of the season, Orient chairman Harry Zussman rang up Swansea boss Trevor Morris. The Os were neck and neck in the Second Division promotion race with Sunderland, and Harry promised Morris a new hat if his team got a result against the Wearsiders. Morris suggested a new suit, and Zussman immediately agreed. Orient striker Malcolm Graham's brace saw off Bury, Swansea held Sunderland to a 1–1 draw, and the East Londoners were promoted to the First Division for the first, and only, time in their history. As Harry rang up his tailor to order Morris the most expensive suit on offer, his fellow director Leslie Grade asked Graham to choose anything he wanted. Graham, his head still spinning with emotion, requested a glass of champagne. 'I should have said "Can I have the rented clubhouse we're living in to own ourselves?"' he later reflected. 'Leslie was so elated by our success and the fact that we were going up into the First Division that I think he might even have agreed to it.'

*

Before the Golden Age, Leyton Orient were known as London's Cinderella Club. For many years, bucket collections would be held at their stadium to pay for the players' wages. In the early 1960s, guided by their cherubic, cigar-smoking East End fairy godfather and his two cigar-smoking West End impresario friends, Leslie Grade and Bernard Delfont, they were known as the Showbiz Club. Even posh, and-soon-to-be-swinging, Chelsea momentarily deferred to this triumvirate of rags-to-riches Jewish entrepreneurs. A few months into the Os' first ever season in the top flight, with the wheels about to fall off, Zussman summoned manager Johnny Carey to an emergency board meeting. Grade asked Carey what it would cost to keep them up. 'Mr Grade, save your money,' the former Manchester United and Ireland captain replied: 'You've had your fun. This is a dream.'

The dynasty lived the dream long before that dreaded phrase entered the football, and popular culture, lexicon. Grade and Delfont, the flamboyant and canny brothers, who between them ran theatres, theatrical agencies, film studios, record companies and a television station – ruled British showbusiness between the 1940s and 1970s. 'My father, Leslie, loved the Orient,' said his son Michael. 'He said to my uncle: "Bernie you should come, it'd do you the world of good, get away from the business, you'll love it. A complete distraction from all the actors." So Bernie goes along. The idea is they'll put Bernie on the board, he'll put a few bob in. Bernie goes to his first match, and at half-time they came round with the figures. He thought he was back in the theatre. "What are the takings?" he says. "Oh my God." Orient were always hand to mouth. They always seemed to be on the brink of dying.' And yet, because of Zussman's devotion to this messy, muddy, bedraggled bunch of nobodies from the backstreets of East London, they were not just kept alive but taken on a once-in-a-lifetime journey to fantasyland. From the moment he took over, in 1949, until his premature death from a heart attack thirty-two years later, the short, plump shoe manufac-turer, almost always bespectacled under a homburg hat, gave his life to the Os.

Despite a considerable relocation away from East London, Orient have always had a special place in the Jewish community's heart. By 1937, when the club themselves moved from Clapton to Leyton – Clapton Orient had fielded a Jewish goalkeeper, Monty Berman, during the early part of the decade – barely a third of London Jews still lived in the East End, and numbers were steadily falling. The majority of working- and lower-middle-class Jewish families tended to take two routes out of the East End. Those who gravitated east-wards preferred Orient to West Ham, the latter being perceived to be unwelcoming. The other axis, predominantly middle-class, was in Golders Green, Edgware, Hendon and Finchley. In these north-west suburbs, the socially-mobile and anglicised 'migrants' tended to opt for either Spurs or Arsenal, although a significant number retained an affection for the good old Os. 'Most Jews went to Tottenham, or maybe Arsenal, because of the success and always being First Division,' said Mark Lazarus, whose playing career began at Brisbane Road. 'But their first love was Orient really.'

Lazarus' mother Martha and his sister Rosie were mainstays of 'Kosher Corner', a section of Brisbane Road that was, until recently, forever *heimishe*. Bernard Josephs remembers the West Stand's un-official Jewish section 'issuing friendly Yiddish curses to the players, unless of course they were playing a blinder'. Bernard Sonenfield, a superfan to rival Keston at Spurs and Warner at Leeds, was known as 'Ooosee' on account of his habit of shouting 'Ooos' at regular inter-vals during a game. He eventually graduated from the unofficial Jewish section to the vice-president's lounge, joining three other East Enders-made-good: Arnold Pinkus, who was nearly as wide as he was tall, Alf Nathan and Derek Weinrabe. At half-time, Jewish jokes would be told as salt beef sandwiches and chopped herring were served. 'I shlapped all over the country to watch one of the most mediocre teams in England,' said James Masters. 'From Carlisle to Plymouth, from Torquay to Hartlepool, and how could I ever forget the exotic locations of Grimsby, Wrexham and Macclesfield? I'd wear the same pants for each game, keep ridiculous superstitions and even break up with a girlfriend if her presence coincided with a losing run.'

Frank Cass, the son of a north London cabinetmaker who became a successful book publisher – like Hecht's, his list was eclectic, including everything from the writings of Soviet-Jewish refuseniks to the *Goon Show* scripts – introduced 'an army of people' to the delights of Brisbane Road. 'The Jew likes hopeless causes,' he wrote. 'Supporting Orient means supporting the helpless and the hopeless. It's like saying "Next year in Jerusalem", the plea and prayer for better times ahead. Paying to see Orient is the nearest some Jews come to giving to charity.' Zussman, a snappy dresser who could always be spotted in the directors' box smoking his expensive, ten-inch cigars, gave so much to the cause he died penniless.

Brian Winston, who took over from Harry as chairman, recalls:

I'd say to him 'Harry, is everything sorted, have you got a will? Have you taken care of the grave?' 'No problem,' he said, 'it's all there.' He expected me to do it all. When he died, I did. But we found letters in his bedroom from the *shul*. We'd said every year: 'Harry do you realise you haven't got burial cover?' So we went off and we managed to buy a double block for him. And I buried him. You have never seen in your life the attendance of football dignitaries in Willesden Cemetery. There were 200 people from football. They all came. Harry was a fabulous fella. But he was too generous. You'd go to lunch with Harry and before you could get the bill he'd already left his credit card. Harry died without any money to his name. He'd had a Rolls Royce right through the war. He and his wife lived in the Cumberland Hotel. So there was a few bob there, some-where. But it all went. It was down to the way he lived. He was too generous, and his business was dying. And what did he know about fashion shoes when he got into his seventies? He put all his money into the Orient.

At the beginning of the 1960s, powerful social and political forces – economic mobility, occupational diversification and growing toleration – were weakening the established bastions of Anglo-Saxon Protestantism. The gates of elite sporting institutions, from prestigious golf clubs to the Football Association itself, remained closed, and at big football teams, wealthy, well-connected shoulder-rubbers like Keston were excluded from the corridors of power, but the doors were opening up at the lower level. At unfashionable clubs, local businessmen like Zussman and Winston at Orient, Manny Cussins at Leeds, Jack Dunnett at Notts County and Bill Rubin at Southend were coming through. 'The whole concept of a football chairman changed,' said journalist Dennis Signy. 'These new Jewish chairmen were full of bonhomie, the exact opposite to the old-style chairmen. But they weren't in it for the money.' The People's Game seemed to embody the old saying: 'The best way to make a small fortune is to start out with a big one.' It certainly wasn't like the property market, where dealers like Jack Cotton, Charles Clore, Harry Hyams and Harold Samuel were propelled into the ranks of the nouveau riche; of the 108 people who made over £1 million each in property deals between 1945 and 1965, seventy were Jewish. 'The chairmen are wealthy businessmen who have invariably sunk large amounts of capital into their clubs with little hope of any return for the investment,' explained a 1975 *Jewish Chronicle* article on 'Soccer's Men at the Top'. 'They do it, quite simply for the most part, just for the love of the game.'

'My father, god rest his soul, was a football fiend,' Michael Grade said. 'He loved football. He would go anywhere to watch football. As a kid, he bunked in at Arsenal, Spurs, anywhere, over the wall. He had no affiliation. He would go where he could get in. He says to me one day, he says: "I think I'm going to go into Leyton Orient. I like Harry Zussman. He's a nice man." He and Harry were very close. They adored each other. Thick as thieves. And they had a fantastic run. They got into the top division, which was unbeliev-able for a club like that.'

From the East End to the West End

In *An Empire of Their Own*, the American writer Neal Gabler described how once-impoverished eastern European movie moguls wove a new reality from their American dreams. Brisbane Road was hardly Hollywood but, for a brief, scarcely believable, moment in the Golden Age, Zussman, Grade and Delfont reinvented it as a dream factory; a glitzy, glamorous theatre of sport. West End celebri-ties were not only invited to games, they were often made to sing for their supper. Before a big FA Cup tie with title-chasing Burnley, Arthur Askey entertained the crowd with his trademark long whip, urging them to pack together tightly to create more room on the terraces. Bernard Delfont, born Boris Winogradsky in Russia, was known to the British public as the portly, dapper chap who always greeted the Queen as she stepped out of her car onto the steps of the London Palladium for the Royal Variety Performance. Orient players would often be treated to the best seats at top West End shows. 'People would cut a vein in their arm to get tickets to the Royal Variety,' said team captain Sid Bishop. 'We went to it about four or five times. In the dressing room before one game I turned to Les Grade and jokingly said: "Do we have to go to that bloody show again this year?" He said: "Bernard, Bernard, listen to this saucy bugger." It was all taken in good spirit.' Such performance-related perks were par for the course. 'We would go up to the West End and try on all sorts of nice suits and coats,' said Graham. 'If we wanted anything, it was simply added to Les Grade's account that he had with the shop. It was great. We didn't have to pay for a thing.' After Graham's two goals against Bury secured promotion in 1962, Signy recalled: 'No one could believe it. This was the big time. It was football with a smile. There was this new showbiz side. Harry and Leslie were pioneers. It was showtime at the Orient.'

For Leslie and Bernard, showbusiness was not just about fame and fortune, it was a passport to social acceptance. For Harry, football was the same: a means to an end.

'What was there for Jews back then?' asked Michael Grade. 'Jewish outsiders got involved in football clubs because suddenly it was open to them. The professions were closed so where, they thought, can we make a difference? Showbiz and football were both opening up.' In *The Glory Game*, Keston told Davies: 'Chelsea's a bit different. They get the show business crowd.' At the height of the Golden Age, director Sir Richard 'Dickie' Attenborough would invite hip Hollywood stars like Clint Eastwood and Steve McQueen to lunch before games. Twentysomething Jewish entrepreneur Greg Tesser, who was in with the Kings Road crowd, watched as a 'bunch of eclectic Yiddisher celebrities' – including hair stylist Vidal Sassoon, goggle-eyed comedian Marty Feldman and United States Secretary of State Henry Kissinger – mingled with David Hemmings, Terry O'Neill, David Bailey, Michael Caine and John Cleese at the Bridge. 'Marty lived above me in Wellesley Court in Maida Vale,' wrote Tesser, 'and I introduced him to Osgood. I do not know which of them was more star-struck. Feldman at the time was one of the most sought-after comic performers in the country, but even so I remember him saying wistfully to me: "I wish I had Osgood's talent."'

Orient couldn't quite compete with such an A-list, or such West End largesse, especially after both Leslie and Bernard left the board. But the sports promoter Barry Hearn, Winston's successor as chairman, recalled a strange encounter with Old Hollywood on the dilapidated terraces. Hearn, who is not Jewish, was born in

Dagenham, where there was 'a considerable amount of anti-Semitic feeling in the 1960s – by then some Jewish people were becoming successful, and there was a lot of envy.' He didn't think about such things until, one day, a pensioner standing next to him behind the goal asked what he was doing after the match. 'Going to see *Moses* with Mum and Dad,' he replied. 'Oh,' said the old man, 'my daughter in Hollywood was costume designer for that.' That evening, when he saw the credits at the cinema he realised the man's daughter was the legendary designer Edith Head. Head, like so many other Jewish migrants, had escaped her ghetto past to make it big in the movies. Along with moguls like Carl Laemmle, Adolph Zukor, Sam Albert, Jack Warner and Louis B. Mayer, she was part of a pioneering wave of immigrant filmmakers. In a parallel life across the Atlantic, eastern and central European refugees were building their reputations in posh West End theatres – and run-down football stadiums.

Not all were welcomed with open arms. John Bloom, who made a fortune selling washing machines and cheap holidays to the masses, liked to portray himself as a friend of the housewife, pal of the working man, scourge of the City and enemy of the establishment. All of which cut no ice with QPR fans during his doomed hostile takeover bid. 'He was a playboy, he'd just got caught up in a call-girl scandal,' said Michael Grade, then a journalist covering the story for the *Mirror*. 'At a meeting at Loftus Road he arrived with a really expensive camel-hair coat, six City lawyers from one of the top firms and all his advisers. And they sat there in a hub. And a fan pointed at Bloom and said: "I want to tell Mr Bloom that he can't buy this football club like he buys his women." Great cheering. But Orient fans and players loved my dad and Harry.' Once, on a train to Derby, defender Malcolm Lucas complimented Les on his reversible cardigan, which was lemon-coloured on one side, light blue on the other. Les told Lucas if the team won he could have it; they did, and the player kept it, 'for important dos.' On another trip, on the way back from Scunthorpe, Phil White was given Grade's smart new Crombie overcoat as a reward for striking the winning goal.

Brian Winston remembers that Leslie was very close to Harry:

They were so similar in character. Leslie was an incredible bloke. He used to say things to Harry like 'I'll get you Liberace, I'll get you Sinatra.' I remember one game against Fulham, we came in at half-time 6–0 down. We finished 7–1. Leslie came across to me in the Fulham boardroom and put his arms around me. He said, 'Whatever they say, we drew the second half.' You'd enter a room and Harry was one of those guys who said: 'Come in, you're welcome, there's love and happiness in this room.' Brian Clough would never go into a boardroom, anywhere in football, including his own at Forest. But at the Orient, Cloughie would knock on the door and say: 'Mr Chairman, can I join you?' There was always a lot of drink flowing, although Harry had to give it up after becoming an alcoholic.

Michael Grade says: 'Harry was larger than life. He was very good in defeat. The boardroom was always full of laughs. Always a million laughs. There was lots of booze. Open house. It was regarded as the friendliest boardroom in football. No question about that. The club had a heart, and that came from Harry. He was remarkable. Harry was a short, fat man. Larger than life, heart of gold. It was a hand-to-mouth existence, though. He'd go into the dressing room if they lost and say: "You're killing me!"'

It was just as likely, though, that his appearance after a match heralded a lavish night ahead. Zussman often came into the Orient dressing-room handing out £20 notes for beer. 'Which was quite a lot of money in those days,' goalkeeper Frank George remembered.

'Win, draw or lose, Harry always came out afterwards with some money – a few quid to go and enjoy ourselves with.' At the end of the 1960–61 season, even though they had almost dropped into the old Third Division, Zussman gave all the players, along with their young wives and children, a free holiday in the Channel Islands. Most of them had never flown before.

Sid Bishop recalls:

We had a collection for Harry while we were there. He and Leslie Grade had turned up to pay us a visit while we were out there enjoying ourselves for a week or ten days. Stan [Charlton] must have got word they were coming, because he organised a collection for the chairman, as a thank you for treating us to the holiday. We bought him a sealskin cigar case. Harry, who reminded me a bit of Max Miller, thought it was a wonderful gift. The next thing we knew, he announced: 'If you get promotion next year, you and your wives and families can all go to Majorca for a holiday.' He really thought it could really happen – and it bloody well did. Everyone – not just at Orient but in football – loved Harry.

The Lord–Cussins Spat

Everyone, that is, apart from Bob Lord, the epitome of the outspoken northern businessman. The Khrushchev of Burnley, as Arthur Hopcraft memorably labelled him, was actually a visionary chairman and, in many ways, cut from the same cloth as Zussman. In 1960, the Lancashire team became the smallest town ever to win the League: an astonishing achievement. But Lord made a number of enemies during his twenty-six years in football – and three of the biggest happened to be Jewish. In the 1950s, as he and his team were beginning their extraordinary ascent, he frequently clashed with *Daily Express* sports editor Henry Rose, who he believed displayed a marked preference for the more glamorous northern clubs like Manchester United and didn't give teams like Burnley their due. In the 1960s, Zussman became his bête noire and spent most of that decade banned from the Turf Moor directors' box. 'He hated Harry and he hated me,' said Winston. 'I've never had any anti-Semitism directed against me, except by Bob Lord.' And in the 1970s Lord had a huge falling-out with Leeds United chairman Manny Cussins.

Rose, like Zussman, was a showman, a larger-than-life Jew who embraced, rather than hid, his ethnic difference, part of the new breed of American-influenced sports journalists who had broken through in the mid 1930s. A distant cousin to *The Front Page*'s Walter Burns, he was a precursor of the self-important, personality-driven, red-top populism that prevailed after his tragic death in 1958. He was born in Cardiff, the son of Russian Jewish immigrants who came to Britain from Odessa around 1895. In the First World War, as a seventeen-year-old fighting with the London Rifles, he was saved from drowning in a Flanders shell-hole after his fellow soldiers defied enemy fire to form a search party. This brush with death, he revealed in his frank autobiography *Before I Forget*, motivated him to 'make the most of my life'. By 1938, when he won widespread praise for criticising the England team's notorious Nazi salute in Germany, he had become a celebrity, his photograph appearing on promotional posters all over the country. On one occasion, he received a letter from a young fan in an envelope decorated with a rose and addressed to 'Henry, Manchester'.

'They were not happy about it,' wrote Rose of the English players, whom, he claimed, had been blackguarded by the FA into giving Heil Hitler salutes:

And they are not happy about it now. Hapgood, the captain, looks along the line. There is a shuffle and, orders being orders, hands are raised. They are lowered again as one anthem finishes (I detect relief) and raised again with some diffidence. There was a good deal of talk about it among the players before the game, and there has been a good deal since. There was no unanimity about the decision of the committee in charge that the salute should be given . . . A member of the team told me: 'I know that when my father sees a picture of me giving the salute, he won't be pleased.'

'Good for you, Henry!' exclaimed his *Express* colleague G. W. Sinfield, congratulating Rose for his courageous stance in Berlin. However, in *Before I Forget*, the self-styled 'ace' sportswriter finally came clean about what really happened:

The inside story of that salute is worth a laugh. Actually it all began with a brainwave from Lionel Manning of the *Daily Sketch*, one of Fleet Street's most able newspapermen, and worked up by us both. Apart from the actual matches, hard news is scarce on these tours. With the idea of working up a stunt, Manning put into the heads of the Football Association chiefs the question whether a Nazi salute should be given by the players in Berlin or not. They had not given the suggestion a thought. We put it into their minds and sold them the idea. Immediately, they became ponderous. They had secret meetings and had to work up some sort of expression of opinion. We were kept supplied with good newspaper stories for days, reporting the dithering from day to day until the actual decision was made. Thus are big newspaper stories born.

Glanville called Rose 'the outstanding journalist of his day, every-thing was flamboyance and everything was showtime,' but was irri-tated, if also amused, by egotistical stunts such as arranging his own paging in hotels. Often, when he attended a match for the *Express*, a flunkey would stand outside the ground carrying a placard which read: 'Henry Rose Is Here'. Glanville recounts:

When he came to a hotel he'd tip the concierge to say, 'Telephone call for Mr Henry Rose,' and then he'd come striding in, in all his majesty and glory into the foyer, to take this call, which probably didn't exist. It mattered to him. To me it's unim-portant. What matters is what you write: if people like it, great. He said he had practically every ticket collector and station-master bribed within a huge radius of Manchester. They would say things like: 'Ticket collector from Cheadle Station here Mr Rose. George Roughton of Manchester United has just passed through the barrier.' He was an old breed of journalist, always on stunts. They had this wonderful love-hate relationship with him at Anfield. He went into the press box, and the whole of the Kop booed him. But he lapped it up. He said if they hadn't been stopped they'd have given him a gangster's funeral.

Rose was given a hero's funeral six days after his death in the 1958 Munich air disaster. If the Manchester United team were devastated by the horrific crash, the band of northern journalists that followed the Busby Babes to Belgrade were all but wiped out. Rose's send-off was no more than he might have expected. Vast crowds assem-bled along the six-mile funeral route, many arriving at the Jewish cemetery in taxis that had no meters running. The *Express* gave him a great send-off, too. 'The moment that silenced the heart of his kingdom,' ran the headline over his last ever double-page spread, a moving report of 'the biggest funeral procession ever seen in Manchester'.

Lord was actually on Rose's side on one issue. Both men agreed that TV coverage was a threat to the game's survival. When the BBC highlights programme *Match of the Day* began in 1964, Lord turned their cameras away from Turf Moor and maintained a ban for five years. In 1974, at a Variety Club function, he declared: 'We have to stand up against a move to get soccer on the cheap by the Jews who run television.' By this time, the idea that the Football League – 'we' – was still *Judenfrei* was slightly out of date. At least six of the league's ninety clubs had Jews as their chairmen, with a further twenty directors covering a dozen or so outfits. But the myth of absence prevailed. Manny Cussins also felt it was time to make a stand – but against the bigoted butcher's anti-Semitism. The Leeds chairman, who as a thirteen-year-old had sold chairs and tables from a handcart for his immigrant father, threatened to walk out of the Elland Road boardroom if Lord came to Burnley's match there. Lord retaliated by ordering his own board to boycott the game. It was a neat trick, turning the offended into the offender, and, astonishingly, he managed to get away with it.

Cussins was not the first Jewish chairman of Leeds; wallpaper magnate Albert Morris had briefly been in the chair in the late 1960s. He had made his fortune in the furniture retail business, building up a chain of stores, which he sold for £1 million, before founding John Peters, which controlled over a hundred retail outlets by 1975. When he travelled with the Leeds team on away trips, he would slip away early on the morning of the match to sell furniture in one of the fifty-three stores. Just as Orient had a group of vice-presidents to raise funds, so Leeds United, who when Cussins became director were an obscure, second-rate outfit, set up the 100 Club to forge stronger ties with local businessmen. It was one of the earliest examples of corporate sponsorship; Cussins, Morris, Arnold Ziff, Howard Levison, Bobby Caplin, Martin Goldman, Gabby Harris and many other wealthy Jews – and non-Jews – all paid £100 to watch games from a club room in the new West Stand. Whenever any of them were interviewed, they expressed their eagerness to 'give something back' to the city that gave their families refuge.

In the community I grew up in, these rags-to-riches businessmen were big *machas*. They had left the inner-city ghetto in their droves and played a key role in Leeds' economic, political and cultural resurgence. Ziff, whose father had fled the Russian pogroms at the turn of the century, kick-started the retail revolution when he opened the Merrion Centre. There was, however, a price to pay for integration. 'The language has changed,' lamented the traditionalist *Jewish Chronicle*. 'Yiddish is rarely heard and hardly ever spoken at public meetings. Its sons speak with pride of Leeds' prowess on the football field.' The city's Jews had dominated the clothing industry, producing household names like Marks and Spencer, Burton, Barratts, John Collier and March the Tailor. Many of them became intimately acquainted with Revie's inner sanctum, providing suits, kits and even – as in the case of Ziff's Stylo company – football boots. Everywhere I looked, there was an 'uncle' – all my parents' male friends were 'uncles' – involved in some capacity with the Mighty Whites. One used to give Jack Charlton his bag of 'left-overs' – cut-offs and seconds – to sell to his team-mates. Another managed a factory run by Cussins and was best mates with Bill Fotherby, a future chairman of the club. Gabby Harris became soul mates with Allan Clarke, and, as the former centre-forward once told me, secretly donated thousands of pounds to the club's annual Christmas parties to pay for the children's presents. The fathers of my Selig Brodetsky schoolfriends all seemed to have roles in the big Revie family – as doctors, lawyers and testimonial organisers.

I witnessed, at close hand, the resentment this bred in some sections of the Leeds crowd. Towards the mid 1970s, there was a tangible atmosphere of menace at Elland Road as a 'them-and-us' mindset developed between the working-class, south-of-the-river fans who stood on the Kop and the north-of-the-river season-ticket holders in the West Stand. The latter, at times, would be depicted by the former as 'rich Jews' who were part-time supporters and not 'proper Leeds' or 'Leeds through and through'. I began to hear anti-Semitic chants and, when we played Spurs, the obligatory concentration camp hissing noises would occasionally be directed towards the West Stand. When Revie moved into Cussins' big house on the hill, a newspaper report gave his new mansion the 'how the other half live' treatment. It had central heating, a sun lounge, two bathrooms, a four-car garage block, spacious drawing and dining rooms, a playroom and a kitchen and an adjoining annex with separate living accommodation. And, concluded the article, it was in Alwoodley, where 'all the Jews now live'. This was not entirely true; many of us still resided at the bottom of the hill in the lower-middle-class district of Moortown. But, in three generations, the community had gone from being working-class tailors to middle-class professionals. Ziff was well known for his philanthropy. But no matter how many Steinways he donated to the Leeds international piano competition, or how much money he raised for Leeds parish church, he was never quite accepted as 'one of us'. Like his fellow businessmen, he became obsessed with the football club; so much so that, in the week following his death, his sons Michael and Edward sat *shiva* – a week-long Jewish mourning ritual for close relatives – during half-time at Elland Road. On the whole, his rise was viewed as symbolic of an upward mobility that had benefited the city – but there were audible, Lord-esque mutterings about a 'race' that appeared to be exercising undue influence on the local economy.

This narrative was not peculiar to west Yorkshire, but part of a national trend. In 1961, the year both Delfont and Cussins became football directors, a survey revealed that 44 per cent of British Jews belonged to the upper two social ranks – professional and inter- mediate – while only 10 per cent belonged to the partly skilled and unskilled sections of the workforce. 'Half-Gentile, half-Jew; a last, lost tribe of self-made Yorkshiremen and Israelites,' was how David Peace described the 1970s Leeds board in *The Damned United*. 'In search of the promised land; of public recognition, of acceptance and gratitude.' Not everyone portrayed the tribe's journey so sympa- thetically. In the period bookended by the unscrupulous activities of slum landlord Peter Rachman, as revealed during the 1963 Profumo affair, and the Guinness scandal of the 1980s – in which businessmen and brokers manipulated the stock market to inflate the price of Guinness shares and assist a £2.7 billion takeover bid of the Distillers group – grasping, Faginesque stereotypes resurfaced in the national conversation. During the Lord–Cussins spat a number of columnists expressed sympathy with the Burnley chairman's point of view. The Jews, some argued, were becoming far too powerful in television: what about the Grades and Sidney Bernstein? The game's traditionalists insisted it would be a tragedy if the Football League sold out to a race that was disproportionately represented in the entertainment business. When Jews had been poor, they had been accused of taking the jobs of working-class Englishmen; as they successfully integrated and became better off, distaste was expressed for their drive, 'ruthlessness' and commercial acumen. At times, this resentment expressed itself in crude forms: swastikas daubed on gravestones, anti-Semitic chanting against Spurs fans and, on several occasions, synagogues being bombed or burned to the ground.

Mostly, however, it was channelled through a genteel form of bigotry, a cultural insistence on homogeneity, an intolerance of difference. Even in the Golden Age, it seemed, anti-Semitism remained a pervasive irritant.

6

The Fighters:
When Marky Tried to Lap Wembley

CLAVANE'S CIGARETTES

M. LAZARUS (CRYSTAL PALACE)

'For me the hardest player [of my era] may surprise you – Mark Lazarus the former QPR winger ... He didn't look for trouble but when it came his way, look out, Lazarus could stand up like one of the old-fashioned bare-knuckle fairground fighters.'

Rodney Marsh, *Priceless,* 2001

Mark Lazarus: The Tough Jew

In March 1967, for the first and only time in his life, Ike Lazarus went to see his son, Marky, play a game of football. The match, which took place in front of 97,951 spectators at Wembley, was the League Cup final between Marky's team, Third Division Queens Park Rangers, and First Division West Bromwich Albion. As everyone down Petticoat Lane kept telling Ike, it was like David against Goliath. And, as Ike kept replying: 'Well, you know what happened in that one.' As expected, Albion got off to a flying start, taking a two-goal lead. But Roger Morgan pulled a goal back for the underdogs after the break and then Rodney Marsh equalised with a wonder goal. In the closing minutes, the ball ran loose to Marky who clipped in the winner. It was the most important goal in QPR's history. Marky ran towards the team's fans and began to set off on his trademark lap of honour. But his team-mate Les Allen ran over to him and pulled him back. 'You can't do that here,' said Allen. 'You bloody mad? You can't lap the whole of bloody Wembley.' Lazarus stopped, shrugged, smiled, waved to where he thought his dad was sitting and went back to the centre circle.

*

At the Selig Brodetsky, possibly as a reaction against the endless dissection of the Torah, although most probably a petulant response to Abie's orange peel ban, my friends and I decided to compile a list of the greatest *schtarkers* of all time. My number one Jewish strongman was Samson, whose doomed heroism particularly appealed to me. In second place I selected the biblical warrior Judah Maccabeus, whose followers, the Maccabees, were constantly lauded in our festivals; a rebel army that took control of Judaea, they founded the Hasmonean dynasty, which ruled from 164 to 63 BCE, reasserted the religion, expanded the boundaries of the Land of Israel and reduced the influence of Hellenism. And third was Mark Lazarus, the pugnacious QPR winger, famous for his winning strike at Wembley. My dad liked Lazarus because he reminded him of the tough Jews he'd grown up with on his council estate. He used to drive me into his old neighbourhood, telling stories about the bad things he and his gangs got up to back in the day. He revered the Yiddisher boxers who defended the estate from invading gangs – more often than not Irish. On these frequent tours of his childhood, I would feel a kind of envy, a nostalgia for an ugly-beautiful past. His generation had fought their way out of poverty, but their struggles remained part of the secret, vanishing world he still inhabited in his imagination: a lost, glamorous underworld of resilient, Runyonesque immigrant hustlers. When I read *Tough Jews*, a brilliant book about Jewish-American gangsters, I came across the following sentence: '[They left] the world of their heads to thrive in a physical world, a world of sense, of smell, of grit, of strength, of courage, of pain.' Unlike my father I came from a mollycoddled generation, the first not to directly suffer religious bigotry or institutional discrimination – and thus the first not to develop the skills necessary to protect us against potentially evil outside forces. We no longer felt threatened. There was no need to fight our way out. We were to be doctors not streetfighters; accountants not *schtarkers*.

When QPR won the League Cup in 1967, news of Lazarus' Jewishness spread rapidly through the classrooms of our tiny north Leeds school. True, we Brodetskians had already discovered that Les Goldberg once played for the Mighty Whites, but it was so long ago that he was still sporting the ancient, and less-than-mighty, blue-and-yellow strip. Lazarus was a here-and-now Jew, a powerful symbol of athletic excellence. He was Judah Maccabeus made flesh, independent, free and strong; determined to reach his goal, to attain it undaunted by obstacles, however great, to kick away all obstructions. A black eye for a black eye, a broken tooth for a broken tooth, he floated like a butterfly and stung like a bee. He was Muhammad Ali, Mark Spitz and Norman Bites-Yer-Legs Hunter all rolled into one. When I watched him on *Match of the Day*, he appeared to be a charismatic fusion of chutzpah, brutality and flamboyance. Like Zussman, the Grades and Rose, he had integrated openly, unashamedly, stylishly, into English football. Despite my obsession with Revie's awesome team, Lazarus was – and remains – one of my favourite ever footballers. Jews have a favourite sportsman the way Catholics have a patron saint: a mythic figure who has shown us the way. In English football, of course, there haven't been too many Jewish players to choose from, but that has only enhanced their mythic status. At Selig Brodetsky, my head was filled with biblical warriors, men who were rugged, bold and fearless. The problem for my headmaster, and other community elders, was that late twentieth-century *schtarkers* didn't wear *yarmulkahs*. They were secular, often assimilated, and usually married to Gentiles.

Lazarus was once accused by a rabbi of 'letting my people down . . . and I said, "Oh yeah? I tell you what, you don't get no better Jew than me. I won't have anything said against Jews that is detrimental." But that rabbi would. He'd stand there and he'd take it.' Lazarus didn't have a barmitzvah and he married out. 'I'm an atheist,' he told me. 'But I suppose my Jewishness came out in the way I used to stand up for myself in the dressing room. I had an overactive Jewish lip. I acquired quite a reputation.' Lazarus' only regret is that it may have been his overactive lip that prevented him from becoming England's first Jewish footballer. His East End childhood had toughened him up, preparing him for the on- and off-pitch battles to come. In the early days, he found boxing to be a far more welcoming sport. After signing for Fulham and Chelsea as a schoolboy, he quit for a while to concentrate on the fight game. 'But when I started playing again, I got spotted and signed professional forms for Orient, which meant that I wasn't allowed to carry on boxing. Where I came from, we were all fighters. We had to be. We had to stand up for ourselves, just like my dad's generation did against Mosley and his Blackshirts.' Alec Stock, Orient's manager, took Lazarus with him to QPR before First Division Wolves signed him for a then club record fee of £27,500 in 1961. But he clashed with his new boss, Stan Cullis, and was sold back to the west Londoners.

Lazarus says that Cullis was 'a sergeant major type who was never happy, even when we won. Nothing was good enough for him and we had a personality clash. I always stood up for myself and other people. With his background and attitude it was never going to work. Being a Jew I couldn't accept bollockings for no apparent reason. He bollocked you when you were winning 3–0 at home. He had influence at the FA, another reason I think I didn't play for England. He was like another manager I couldn't stand: George Petchey, a coach at Palace. I used to offer him outside three times a week. I'd say: "I've had enough of you, me and you outside." George wouldn't have that. He wouldn't take me on. When I played against him I used to slaughter him every time.'

On one occasion, after helping one of his many clubs, Crystal Palace, to one of his many promotions, he ran up to the directors' box and stripped off his shirt and socks in front of the startled board members. On another, in the middle of an FA Cup game against Poole Town, he took his striptease act a stage further, flying down the wing in his jockstrap; he had run over to the touchline to replace his torn shorts, but, as he threw them to the bench, a team-mate had passed the ball to him. Several of his 'stunts', as Henry Rose might have called them – like the John Barnes' banana-skin-back-heel a couple of decades later – were about making a point. Unlike Orient's half-time showbiz turns and Chelsea's celebrity parades, his flamboyance was as much about crowd-taunting as crowd-pleasing. 'I think it was his way of saying: "Look, I'm a Jew. Look what I've just done,"' said Barry Hearn. 'I think he was saying: "Put that in your pipe and smoke it."'

Before Allen stepped in at Wembley, Lazarus had been about to perform his trademark goal celebration. This involved running past his own fans, shaking as many of them by the hand as possible, and then lapping the entire ground. It used to delay the restart by several minutes. Hearn remembers him, in one of his spells at Brisbane Road, 'running around the whole of the stadium when he scored a goal, milking it like mad, with a big smile on his face and his arms aloft'. But often, at away grounds, the celebration would act as a retort to the vile bigotry he had to put up with as Britain's first high-profile Jewish footballer. At the end of 1962, the *Jewish Chronicle* launched an investigation into what the paper called a 'vicious campaign' against him. It detailed a series of ugly incidents, including a bottle being thrown at him at Brighton. During one match at Sunderland home fans called him a 'Jew bastard', said he should be sent to the ovens and informed him he was lucky to be alive. Those who visited the Den in 1971 will never forget the vile, anti-Semitic abuse he received. At Shrewsbury, Lazarus responded to racist heckling by flicking the ball up and juggling it from one knee to the other – then turning to his abusers and waving at them. The referee booked him for inciting the crowd. Perhaps it should have been for chutzpah. At the Loftus Road training ground, he once knocked out a racist team-mate during a five-a-side session. Most of the anti-Semitic comments, though, tended to come from opponents.

Managers would tell their full-backs to insult me and get me riled. My mum always said to me that if anyone called me a 'Jew bastard' I should go up and smack him on the chin. We had to fight back. I used to get a lot of abuse on the pitch from players. Enough to make me want to turn round and give them a right-hander. The left-back at Gillingham said something to me once, and I got him on the sly. A lot of the crowd saw it. Fortunately for me, the ref didn't, so I didn't get sent off. I also once gave a big centre-half at Scunthorpe a right-hander. Again, no sending off. I never got sent off for any of them.

In his autobiography, Rodney Marsh, himself a renowned crowd-pleaser, described Lazarus as the hardest player he had ever come across: 'Mark came from a very tough boxing family and had no problem having a row with anyone.' Lazarus' maternal grandfather was Harry Solomons, the British bare-knuckle champion, and two of his twelve brothers, Harry and Lew – both known as Lazar – became well-known boxers. Harry was a respected welterweight who fought for a British championship when he was only sixteen, but it was his younger brother who sprang to fame in the 1950s, fighting for the British title at welterweight and middleweight. Famously, Lew knocked out gangster Charlie Kray in three rounds. 'You had to fight,' he said, 'you had to look after yourself with the cobblestones.' Money was scarce, and, as his father struggled to put food on the table, Mark watched his brothers compete. 'They were hungry,' he said. 'Literally. We all were back then.' Barry Silkman, whose mother Ginny was a relative and went to games with Keston, his dad's business partner, used to watch Ike [Lazarus' father] walking down the streets of Whitechapel, challenging every anti-Semite he came across to a fight. 'He was a tough guy was Ike, you didn't want to cross him,' said

Silkman, 'but big-hearted. Same with Marky: lovely fella, didn't go looking for trouble, but if someone called him a Jew they'd be horizontal.'

Silkman, the last British-born Jewish footballer to play professionally in the top divisions before Joe Jacobson in 2007, would go on to display a similarly pugnacious attitude to life. A clever, skilful player on the pitch – one of football's wandering Jews, Silky wore the colours of Hereford, Crystal Palace, Plymouth, Luton, Manchester City, Maccabi Tel Aviv, Brentford, QPR, Fulham, Orient, Southend and Crewe – he got into a fair few scrapes off it. Now an agent, he had fall-outs at nearly all of these clubs, including one with David Pleat whilst on loan at Notts County. 'I came in one morning and told Pleaty his place was a pisshole,' he said, 'and that his staff were fucking shit. And that I was going.'

The most violent bust-up of all came at Fulham, when Bill Dodgin took over from Bobby Robson as coach. As Silkman recalls it: 'At QPR my youth team manager had been Dodgin. I went to Fulham, got on great, then Dodgin took over. I was sitting in the changing room and in he walks, the new manager. Everybody stands up. The chief scout introduces me and says I'll be signing on as a full professional next week, and Dodgin says, "Yeah I know him, I'll talk to you about him later." I never signed. Some time later, I was playing cricket at Craven Cottage. Under a steel staircase, I took the bat out of George Cohen's hands and put it right down on his [Dodgin's] head. I nearly killed him. It nearly ended my career. I never kicked the ball anywhere for a year.'

Marky's father Ike was the classic East End patriarch: the toughest of men with the quietest of voices. Even after Marky shot to fame in 1967, whenever he visited Petticoat Lane, market sellers would refer to the QPR star as 'Ike's son'. As a kid, Lazarus senior had joined the Judean Social and Athletic Club, founded in 1902 by

brothers Dave and Barney Stitcher to encourage Jewish participation in sport. In his early thirties he put his streetfighting skills
to good use, becoming part of an unofficial security force that
protected Jewish neighbourhoods against Mosleyite raids.
Following an article in a BUF newspaper claiming 'the alien race'
had infected football with unsportsmanlike habits, such as jeering
at referees and verbally abusing opponents, a group of Blackshirts
attacked players taking part in a match near Cable Street between
the Jewish People's Council and Edgware. A few weeks later, on
4 October 1936, thousands of anti-fascists trying to stop a BUF
march clashed with police in the Battle of Cable Street. Jews had
always faced hostility in the East End, especially during the anti-
alien backlash at the turn of the twentieth century, but in the
1930s there was a new, and far more terrifying, context: the rapid
rise of fascism in Continental Europe. Ike was among the demon-
strators who chanted the Spanish Civil War slogan '*No Pasaran*' –
'They Shall Not Pass' – as police tried to clear a path for the
Mosleyites. They did not pass, the march was called off, and Mosley
was humiliated. 'My dad was a quiet man,' said Lazarus, 'but he
could really handle himself. And if anyone came to him and said
they'd been beaten up by a couple of Blackshirts, my old man
would be on to it.'

Bobby Fisher, who was looked after by his uncle Mark during
his early days as an Orient player, was brought up on such tales of
derring-do:

I had spent a bit of time with Mark as a kid. My adopted
parents split up, so I went to live with my gran and granddad,
Ike and Martha. It was like an extended family in Chadwell
Heath, with Mark living around the corner. Ike was a fantastic
character. We'd go to Petticoat Lane, and everybody knew Ike.

You couldn't go past a stall without someone saying: 'Ike, how you doing?' I remember him saying: 'We showed Mosley where to go. He weren't too mouthy when we sorted him out.' Ike was one of the blokes on the top of the building throwing bricks at the fascists. He was shouting at them: 'You're not going to get away with it.'

Mark Lazarus is the same age as my dad and belongs to a generation that came of age in the shadow of the Holocaust. 'As they were faced with the image of dead, degraded Jews being bulldozed into mass graves,' wrote Rich Cohen in *Tough Jews*, 'here was another image, closer to home.' Marky, like my dad, grew up in an era when you had to fight to survive, to belong, to be accepted. Fighting was in the family's blood.

'We were watching Mark play at Orient once,' Fisher continued, 'and this guy near us stood up and said: "You Jew bastard, why don't you fuck off back to where you came from?" and Mark's uncle Joe said: "Tell you what, mate, say it one more time and you'll never say it again." Uncle Joe was small, he didn't look too intimidating. Five minutes later, Mark's got the ball again and someone's whacked him and he's gone down injured. This geezer says: "You Jewish bastard," and Joe got up and gave him a whack. He did him, knocked him out. And he stood over him and said "Told you you wouldn't say that again, didn't I?"'

The women were hard nuts too. Delia Zussman, daughter of Harry, would take on all comers. 'I remember when they started on Bobby Fisher at Blackpool,' said Brian Winston. 'Bobby [who was mixed-race as well as Jewish] was getting the monkey chants, there was a lot of racist abuse. You sat close to the pitch at Blackpool, and people threw bananas. One bloke standing in front of the directors' box, she had a right go at him: "Shut your mouth, that's my husband". And he didn't say a word after that.' Fisher's mum, Mark's sister Rose, once assaulted a referee after a game because he had booked her Bobby. As Bobby says:

> My mum came to every home game. At quiet times during a game I could hear her when I was on the pitch: 'C'mon Bobby,' that sort of thing. It wasn't funny at the time, although everybody else thought it was funny. If I got injured she'd be the first to get up and shout at the player who fouled me: 'You dirty bastard, how can you kick my son?' We're Jewish East Enders, you see, we protect our own. After one match, in which I'd been booked, someone came running in going: 'Fish, Fish, you gotta get out to the front door!' 'Why?' 'Your mum's attacking the referee' 'What?' I went out there in my gear to see my mum at the main gates with the ref behind two linesmen and Mum with an umbrella trying to hit him, and there's the doorman trying to keep her off. She looks at me and says: 'This bastard booked you. You didn't foul him,' and I go: 'Mum, come on.'

'Rosie was a character,' said Winston. 'As Orient chairman, I had more problems with Rosie than I did with Bobby. Rosie was so protective of Bobby. Like any mum of any child. At times he would say: "Mum, please. I'll deal with this." At times, she was an embarrassment to him. She had a mouth like the Blackwall Tunnel. "Why did you drop my son, why isn't my son playing?" But she was a loveable character. She and my wife would talk all day about the East End and the old days and all the great yiddisher characters. All gone now.'

Barry Silkman has similar stories to tell about his own mother, Ginny – a cousin of Mark's – who was 'a bit *meshuga*, lunatic is probably the word. But she was the strongest Jew, physically and mentally, of the lot of them . . . We had a stall at Petticoat Lane. One day, Mum's selling two dresses for £6 or one for £3 10 shillings. This man wants one dress for £3. She says no, and they argue, and he says: "All you Jews should have been gassed in Germany." My mum went bang. She hit him. He's literally hit the floor, gone. His woman comes over, and Mum's headbutted her, smashed this woman's nose to pieces, put her nose round the side of her face. That's how my mum was. But there were some tough guys back then.'

From Wingate to Maccabi

In 1947, foreign secretary Ernest Bevin told his American counterpart that 'anti-Jewish feeling in England now was greater than it had been in a hundred years'. At the beginning of the year, Mosley's Blackshirts, released from internment and even more determined to drive the Jews from the East End, were organising fifteen outdoor meetings a week in London, selling papers outside tube stations, daubing walls with graffiti and attacking synagogues. As cinemas showed the full horror of Auschwitz and Dachau, the streets were taken over by uniformed mobs who insisted Hitler was right. 'Their speeches and their literature depicted us, the Jews, as coarse, ugly caricatures with long beards and dirty fingernails, dressed in black gabardines,' recalled the hair-stylist Vidal Sassoon, who before picking up a pair of scissors was a member of the 43 Group, a crudely armed paramilitary force set up by battle-hardened war veterans. 'And they hurled the same abuse that I remembered from the 1930s. I was too young to do anything about it then but I had never forgotten the fear. When you've got a thousand throats all screaming "Yids, yids, we've got to get rid of the yids", it's pretty terrifying. They'd wear uniforms, insignia, the whole thing. I don't remember when we decided to fight back, but the pictures we were seeing from Auschwitz, Buchenwald and Dachau gave the slogan "Never again!" real meaning.'

Ike Zazarus was one of the thousand-odd street-fighters in the 43 Group. Well organised and ruthless, their members assaulted fascist speakers and broke up BUF meetings. Their tactics reignited the pre-war divide between passive assimilators and confrontational anti-fascists; as with the 1935 England v. Germany international and the Battle of Cable Street, the Board of Deputies, despite its new complexion, urged the community to reject the group's direct action. The *Jewish Chronicle* advocated a third way, citing the example of Wingate FC, the first exclusively Jewish team to compete in a Saturday league. Founded in 1946, by Major Harry Sadow, Frank Davis, George Hyams and Asher Rebak – all recently demobilised – the club were named after the British Army General Major Orde C. Wingate, who worked with the Jewish Defence Forces between 1936 and 1945. Rejected in turn by the Athenian, Delphinian and Spartan leagues, they eventually played and lost their first match in August 1948 in the London League. The founding fathers, shocked by the post-war resurgence of Mosley's fascists, wanted to improve relations with the Gentile population. 'Mosley was marching again in Ridley Road, and the stereotyped image of the Jew was making a comeback,' explained Davis. 'We decided to fight it by setting up our own football club, and I think we did a very good job in proving that being a Jew didn't mean you were a little fat gown manufacturer. All right, so a Jew wasn't a coalminer, but he could be a sportsman who moved around with a great deal of grace.'

According to Bobby Fisher:

On the pitch I was tough. You had to have a very thick skin, being called a Jew bastard. At Orient I was very close to the guys in the stand, they were only a couple of metres away, in your face. It was with a venom, not just trying to put you off your game, but real hate. Looking back, it made me a lot stronger. I'm mixed race so I got it twice over. I'm not religious, but it made me feel proud to be Jewish. When I coached at Wingate, I saw a lot of good Jewish amateur footballers come through the ranks. They always stood up for themselves, hated being criticised. But they were maybe a bit too stubborn. At times, in fact, I found them impossible to manage. They found it difficult to be criticised without giving something back.

As the only exclusively Jewish team competing in a senior amateur sporting competition in the whole country, Wingate became the standard-bearers for their community. They made no effort to hide their religious background and played in a navy blue and white strip with a large Star of David emblazoned prominently on both their shirts and shorts. With players mostly drawn from ex-Jewish Sunday league teams, they became one of the most successful amateur sides in the London area. During their first seven seasons in the Middlesex League, they never finished lower than seventh, and several players were selected for the Middlesex FA County representative teams. In the 1951–2 season they won promotion to the London League, then they captured the prestigious amateur London League Trophy in 1958 and were accepted into the Athenian League in 1964. They nurtured players like Ivor Harrison, an inside-forward who signed for Queens Park Rangers in 1949, and Bernard Black, who signed on for Millwall in 1953. Jack Silver, who played at inside-forward in the early 1950s became one of the capital's outstanding amateur footballers. He played for the London FA representative side before managing the team in the late 1950s. In 1961, eight of their players, alongside their manager and assistant, were selected to represent Great Britain in the Maccabiah Games, an international Jewish athletic tournament. They pulled off a huge shock by beating Israel in the final.

Like Wingate, the British Maccabi Association was set up to counter the stereotype that the Jewish people were physical cowards. Before the Second World War, there had been little interest in establishing a British arm of this previously marginal Zionist movement; emphasising physical recreation as part of a new mindset grounded in military skills, the World Maccabi Union had initially received scant support when it set up its first branches in the 1930s. It was perceived as too aggressive and ideological, too rooted in a secular nationalism that had never really caught on in Britain. But in the 1950s, in the wake of the Holocaust and the creation of Israel, its membership grew to 6,000, easily dwarfing the numbers involved in the youth club movement and the Jewish Lads' Brigade. By the 1960s, as a new generation of young Jews began to immerse themselves in the national game, and Zionism gained a strong foothold, it was seen as the ideal way of channelling football mania away from the full-blown, and damaging, integration so enthusiastically embraced by the pre-war leadership. Anglicisation, it was felt, had gone too far, and even appeared to be threatening the community's demographic wellbeing. Following a rise in intermarriage and a fall in the birth rate, Anglo-Jewry was beginning to shrink. Something had to be done.

Wingate were about Becoming English, about proving, as the novelist and avid fan Clive Sinclair wrote, 'that Jews could be athletes as well as bankers'. Not just athletes, but good sports, too. In their first two seasons, the club's adherence to sportsmanship and Corinthian fair play produced no sendings-off and no penalties.

Jack 'Kid' Berg, a *schtarker* who fought with the Star of David on his shorts and was a muscular rebuttal of theories of Jewish physical inferiority.

Louis Bookman was the first Jew to play in England's First Division, but depictions of him were invariably informed by crude stereotypes.

The boys of the pioneering Norwood Orphanage team line up for inspection in the very first years of the twentieth century.

Teams from Brady Street (above) and the Jewish Free School (below) pose proudly with hard-won trophies.

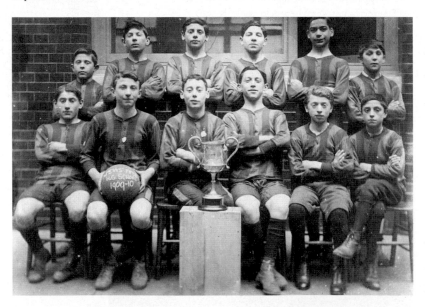

Leslie Goldberg, star of Lovell Road School, celebrates his call-up to the England Schoolboys side. A glittering career appeared to beckon.

Micky Dulin's brief career with Tottenham Hotspur in the late fifties was curtailed by serious injury.

The Swastika flies above White Hart Lane during the 1935 friendly between England and Germany. A propaganda coup for the Nazis, this episode was an exemplar of the alienation between the Tottenham board and their many Jewish fans.

Mark Lazarus (standing, fourth from left) celebrates scoring the most important goal in QPR's history to win the 1967 League Cup final.

The three impresario brothers Lew Grade, Bernard Delfont and Leslie Grade. Leslie would bring some unprecedented showbiz sparkle to Leyton Orient.

David Pleat, posing with two Nottingham Forest teammates in 1963, shortly after being hailed in the press as 'the New Tom Finney'.

Manny Cussins, chairman during Leeds Utd's golden era, welcomes new manager Brian Clough to Elland Road, unaware of the extraordinary drama that would follow the appointment.

The ebullient journalist Henry Rose, whose career was characterized by a number of flamboyant stunts.

Barry Silkman, product of an archetypal Jewish East End upbringing, poses at Leyton Orient's Brisbane Road with two young Jewish fans.

Irving Scholar, Spurs chairman until 1991, was one of the prime movers in creating the Premier League, but was ousted from his position before he could take the club into an exciting new era.

Edward Freedman, described by Manchester United's Martin Edwards as 'the best signing I've made' revolutionised the merchandising and marketing operations at both Old Trafford and White Hart Lane.

Infamous for 'that miss', Ronnie Rosenthal was also one of the first foreign imports into English football at a time when the domestic game remained an insular and somewhat drab spectacle.

Dean Furman of Oldham, one of three Jewish players at Boundary Park. The club also has three Jewish directors.

Lord David Triesman, the first independent chairman of the FA, and a passionate advocate of reform, with Sepp Blatter, Nicolas Sarkozy and Gordon Brown at the Emirates stadium in 2008.

Whereas Maccabi were about Staying Jewish. Their teams played in both Gentile Saturday and Sunday league competitions, but their main purpose was to stem the tide of drift and defection, to restore pride in Jewish achievement, to be part of a national and international network that, at its peak, had 150,000 members in over thirty different countries worldwide. The renowned journalist Reg Drury, a Gentile cockney, occasionally guested for a Maccabi team in Hackney and, according to Glanville, displayed the 'wit and speed of response that went with the territory'. Drury was shocked, however, to find himself on the receiving end of some 'anti-goy' abuse – even though he wasn't entirely sure in what way he'd been abused. 'You weren't *gornisch* today,' a spectator shouted at him at the end of one particularly unpleasant match. Glanville had to explain that the word was a corruption of the Yiddish phrase for 'nothing'.

After the war, Maccabi clubs sprang up all over the country – in Sunderland, Manchester, Leeds and Brighton. In London, organisations were founded in Tottenham, Edgware and Holborn, with an immigrant branch, the Bar-Kochba, formed in West Hampstead. The Maccabi Union Cup became an integral part of the annual Jewish calendar, as did a representative match, often watched by thousands of spectators, between players from its northern and southern leagues. In 1950, the southern section expanded to two divisions, taking in new clubs from areas such as Hendon, Leyton and Edmonton. Maccabi and Jewish Sunday league teams competed in the Jewish Chronicle Cup, established in 1957, with the finals of the competition held every April or May at Wingate's ground in Hendon. It often attracted large numbers of spectators and Jewish celebrities such as Alma Cogan and Frankie Vaughan; the singer was himself a renowned centre-forward.

A *Jewish Chronicle* article, published in the early 1970s, congratulated communal leaders for restoring what the paper called 'the spirit of Judaism' in its youth clubs and sport organisations. 'Before the war, through playing sport, and watching others play sport,' it concluded, 'our youth were becoming less Jewish. This is no longer the case.' This was only half-true. Although more insular in their playing habits, as evidenced by the rise of Maccabi and Jewish-only football leagues, they were far more outgoing in their spectating habits.

I have never played for a Jewish-only team. I went to the Judean Club as a boy and took part in football and table tennis competitions. I went to Jewish cubs and scouts. But, at my mixed secondary school, my burning ambition was to get into the Roundhay first team, not play in the Jewish league. At Roundhay boys' grammar, all we ever talked about – Jews and non-Jews – was Leeds United. When my fellow co-religionists and I gathered in the gym for morning Jewish prayers, away from the main C of E assembly, or went to *shul* on Saturday there was only ever one topic of conversation. Forty years later, nothing has changed. One of my ex-schoolfriends has written countless books about Leeds United, another is a sports agent, I am a sports journalist. I can't speak for them, but my trips to Elland Road still feel like illicit journeys into a forbidden world of sense, smell, grit, strength, courage and pain.

Writing about the Manchester community across the Pennines, David Conn observed:

Given the hemmed-in closeness of where we lived, the weight of rules, the omnipresent feeling of being outsiders, a minority, with persecution in the past and the threat of it still drummed into us, it is difficult to overstate how important football was to the Jewish men of Manchester. The game is passionately loved by millions, everywhere, and for the same reasons, the blessed release, and so it was for us. Playing it, hungrily, at every opportunity, and watching it, supporting your club . . . Jewish men felt a sense of belonging, to the wider community, when they rubbed shoulders in the vast crowds at the football. The game was in the air we breathed.

From Under-the-counter to Over-the-top

If for some young Jews, football offered a strong sense of belonging, for others the sport was also a conduit to a slightly seamier strand in British society. Jewish support for Tottenham Hotspur had grown rapidly in the immediate post-war period, and the area north of the railway line, roughly between White Hart Lane and the North Middlesex Hospital, became known as 'Little Russia' following the migration of White Russian refugees from the 1917 Revolution. It was an intimidating neighbourhood, the police only venturing there in pairs, and it spawned a subculture of fearless, colourful characters who appeared to have stepped straight out of a Damon Runyan short story. Need a new watch? A diamond ring? Ticket for the Spurs? Then One-Armed Lou, Johnny the Stick and Fat Stan were your men.

Johnny 'the Stick' Goldstein, one of the first ticket touts, was a familiar figure outside White Hart Lane in the 1950s and '60s. As hacks huddled together in the big grey car park, waiting for titbits of gossip, they would spot Johnny hanging around Danny Blanchflower, the Spurs captain. Glanville remembered him having a long, loud and Pinteresque argument with a posh journalist about Jews and art. 'Rembrandt was a Jew,' Goldstein insisted. 'No he wasn't,' replied the journalist. A few months later, the tout hobbled up to Glanville's colleague and stared at him for a few seconds. 'He was,' he shouted, before hobbling off. One of Dulin's strongest memories of his time at Tottenham was Goldstein and One-Armed Lou selling tickets at well over the official prices. 'Johnny gave players 10 shillings above the ticket cost,' he said. 'If it was £2 he'd give you £2 and 10 shillings. He made a living out of it. He'd sell them on for £2 more. If Frank Sinatra came over and you wanted tickets, you'd see Johnny. But you had to give him tickets for games.' Goldstein, who was buried in the Tottenham shirt given to him by Greaves, his idol, was once invited to attend an FA investigation into black market FA Cup final tickets. 'Willingly,' he told the governing body, 'provided I am able to name the FA and League officials who have bought tickets from me for Sinatra concerts.' The invitation was suddenly dropped.

Lou, recalled Glanville, was 'a tough egg with a very fierce temper and physical menace'. He had made 'big killings' as a ringside gambler; perching in a neutral corner, he'd work out how referees were marking their cards by the movement of their pencils – and adjusted his odds as he calculated the points for each boxer. Renowned for being a gangster with chutzpah, he insisted on being paid out under a sign bearing the legend 'Betting Prohibited'. On one occasion, when ordered to 'keep moving' by the police, he jumped up and down on the spot – and was taken into temporary custody for insolence. The story he told about how he lost his arm was, according to Dulin, utter fiction: 'He said his ship got torpedoed in the war. He was in a boat for sixteen days, desperate for food, saw a fish and tried to grab it. A shark bit his arm off. But I heard he actually lost his arm in a car accident as a kid. His claim to fame was that he killed somebody. He hit them with a billiard cue. Got away with it because he had one arm, said they'd attacked him.'

Brian Glanville claims:

Lou was a very violent man. He once had a terrific altercation with the Spurs player Bobby Smith at a party. He broke a bottle and said 'Come on.' He was a gangster, really, and yet very thick with the Spurs team. He allegedly saved the grandchild of Pat Murphy, the managing editor at my newspaper, the *Sunday Times*, by scooping him up from an accident and whizzing him off to hospital. Once, on a train going northwards to some Spurs match or other, I saw Johnny in an altercation with a large, plump, young fan. 'If I ever need anything from you, Johnny . . .' said the fan, his lip curled on the edge of some contemptuous phrase. Johnny looked up wearily from his seat. 'Your tongue will get you hung, son,' he said. The fan subsided.

Stan Flashman, pompously, called himself an 'entertainment broker', boasting he could provide a ticket for anything – a Wimbledon final, Last Night at the Proms or even a Royal garden party, he was rumoured to have sold invitations to Princess Anne's wedding. Fat Stan would feed journalists stories in return for payment in 'Nelsons' – Nelson Eddys: readies. The son of an East London Jewish tailor, he initially made a living selling pots and pans and sheets and ties in Houndsditch. While working in a warehouse he saw a fan selling tickets outside White Hart Lane. 'So I bought a couple and sold them to a punter and made a tenner,' he said. 'I quickly realised that if you go up to someone offering to sell there are only two things he can say – yes or no. So I hung around buying and selling for a couple of hours; made £40. That was more than a week's wages for me in those days.' His richest harvest came from cup finals. Many players and managers used to give him under-the-counter tickets in return for notes in the hand. On the eve of the 1971 Arsenal–Liverpool FA Cup final, as Flashman was showing journalist Norman

Giller a wad of tickets from his Highbury contacts, there was the sound of a police siren outside his flat. 'We looked out of the window to see two police cars pulling up and four officers getting out,' said Giller. 'They were clearly intent on an arrest. "They can't touch me without evidence," said Stan as he started to flush the tickets down his toilet. There was a commotion outside Stan's front door, and then the police went off holding on to a neighbour they had come to nab on a hit-and-run charge. I left a cursing and cussing Stan with his arm down the loo seeing what he could retrieve.' Fat Stan would prowl the streets of London in dark glasses, dealing in cash. He was once handcuffed and gagged by rivals, who relieved him of wads of Cup final tickets and £1,000. But he revelled in his reputation, graduating to a mansion in Totteridge with his wife Helen, who had been working as a nightclub hostess when they met. Outside the house sat a Mercedes-Benz, registration 777 SF.

In the 1990s he went 'legit', one of a growing number of Jewish entrepreneurs buying into football clubs. At Barnet, however, his methods tended to deviate somewhat from the norm. 'One minute he was the most generous person in the world,' said his long-suffering manager Barry Fry, 'the next a monster.' On one occasion, when Fry complained about interference in team selection, Flashman declared: 'You won't be alive to pick the team – you'll be in the cement under the M25, you cunt.' Like Zussman, he would give his players cash-in-hand bonuses – if they won – but supporters were abused, television crews assaulted and photographers attacked. Once, during a contract dispute, he threatened to break his centre-forward's legs with a baseball bat. The player scored a hat-trick against Watford the following game. 'It was just my way of motivating him,' he told Fry.

7

The Thinkers:
When Pleaty Got the *Platz*

CLAVANE'S CIGARETTES

D. PLEAT (TOTTENHAM HOTSPUR)

'When I first started in football something always used
to crop up, like a moronic centre-half in a dressing room
saying, "He's a Jew you know."'

David Pleat

David Pleat: The Invisible Jew

In May 1983, Raddy Antic's last-minute goal against Manchester City secured another season in the top flight for Luton Town. When the final whistle was blown, Luton manager David Pleat, in beige suit and loafers, hop-skipped-and-jumped his way across the Maine Road pitch in one of the most bizarre footballing celebrations of all time. Some spectators expected the men in white coats to be following in hot pursuit with a straitjacket. One of them, Pleat's sister, actually feared for his life. 'There was a horse on the pitch to stop fans running on,' she said, 'and I was thinking: "That horse is going to run him over." I was sitting there thinking: "You stupid man." But it was pure, unconfined joy.'

*

David Pleat has spent most of his life keeping calm, keeping his head while all around him lost theirs. His playing career roughly coincided with that of Lazarus', but his way of dealing with anti-Semitic slights was to ignore them rather than to knock the anti-Semite's block off. And yet his moment of fame – of chutzpah – puts all those Lazarus laps of honour, keepy-uppy exhibitions and touchline stripteases in the shade. Indeed, his demented charge across a football pitch on a misty Manchester afternoon in May 1983 set the tone for a new kind of managerial euphoria; after it a steady succession of English gaffers could be seen manically emoting on the touchline. Of course, like the QPR winger's aborted attempt to lap Wembley, and indeed Zussman's tears after Orient's shock promotion, it stood for something more. In Yiddish, *platz – platzen* in German means 'to burst' – has two applications: either you can burst, or split, laughing (as I did whilst watching Pleaty's jig of joy, over and over, on YouTube) or you can burst, in an emotional sense, come apart at the seams. In the East End, where Pleat's Lithuanian ancestors settled after fleeing the Tsarist pogroms, the word is pronounced 'plotz'; which, strangely enough, was the family surname before they anglicised it to Pleat. 'I was just in a daze,' he said. 'I didn't know where I was. We'd scored in the last minute. I knew we'd done it. It was the pinnacle of an achievement. It was the emotion of it, the culmination of a build-up. It had taken us four years to get to this one season in the top flight. If we'd gone out at that time we'd have never got back. In one minute it could have all gone backwards.'

The Hatters' adoption of a stylish passing game showed that, no matter how impoverished a club they were in resources, they could still play – and think – themselves into the Big Time; that an imaginative approach to coaching, alongside the canny recruitment of talented unknowns – like Brian Stein from Edgware Town, Mal Donaghy from Larne and Kirk Stephens from Nuneaton – could, against all the odds, sustain a small, unfashionable team in one of the world's best leagues for eight years. 'We would win 5–4, 4–3, 3–2,' said Paul Elliott, another of Pleat's great discoveries. 'It was all attack, attack, attack.' Although Bookman had made his mark at the club back in the 1920s, it was Pleat's success which established an unlikely Jewish footballing presence in south Bedfordshire; to such an extent that the *Jewish Chronicle* once claimed, possibly tongue in cheek, that they were 'probably the most Jewish club of the lot, boasting a Jewish chairman [David Kohler], Jewish manager [Pleat] and that most exotic of species, a Jewish player [Barry Silkman].'

Pleat's father Joe, like Ike Lazarus, was a secularised, second-generation immigrant, a 'temperamental' rather than 'religious' Jew. He stood up for his beliefs, spoke out against bigotry, fought against Mosley's Blackshirts at Cable Street. He was once thrown out of a Nottingham hospital for punching two patients who'd called him a 'Yid'.

By contrast during a distinguished fifty-year career, as a player, pundit, tactical analyst – but mostly manager – it's Pleat's cerebral nature that has stood out. He has approached the game, perhaps informed by the anti-Semitism experienced by his parents, in a low-key, intellectual rather than chest-beating, emotional way. He made his debut, as a seventeen-year-old for his boyhood team Nottingham Forest, in the same year the *Jewish Chronicle* documented a 'campaign of abuse' against Lazarus. In many ways, Pleat's career was the apotheosis of the anglicisers' approach to integration: self-effacement, the dread of being conspicuous, the fear of social ostracism, a touch of paranoia. Like Lazarus, he represented the second and third generation's drift away from the faith through ignorance, indifference or intermarriage. Like the fans, the showmen and the fighters of the Golden Age, he rejected segregation and ghettoisation, both imposed and self-imposed.

Ever since the eastern European invasion, Jews have been keen to fall into line as loyal British subjects of the Mosaic persuasion. Despite the excesses of Mosley's Blackshirts in the 1930s, and the rioting that followed the brutal murders of two sergeants in 1947, an anti-Semitic ideology has never taken hold of the British national imagination. In the post-war years and after, discrimination persisted in the higher echelons of society – but there was a growing sense of emancipation, an atmosphere of inclusivity, an incorporation into the mainstream of society. And yet, as he has admitted, Pleat never felt as if he was 'one of us' – and his ethnic profile was so low he was rarely identified as a Jew. So much so that several of the key figures interviewed for this book were surprised by this 'revelation'. 'I have not wanted to draw any attention to my outsiderness,' he said. 'I'm assimilated. I've integrated without a fuss. Mind you, I can remember Paul Elliott once saying to me "You understand what we black players are going through. You're an outsider, like me."'

During an era when many squads were almost entirely white, he often fielded an almost entirely black team at Luton, showcasing such trailblazers as Elliott, Stein, Mitchell Thomas, Ricky Hill and Emeka Nwajiobi. At the funeral of Stein's father Isaiah in 2011, Elliott was shocked to see his old gaffer so upset – an example of the second type of *platzing*. Pleat's parents had been cremated in the same cemetery and, listening to the eulogy for the anti-apartheid activist, who had been adopted by a South African Jewish family before escaping to England, had brought back long-suppressed memories. 'It wasn't the same, I know,' said Pleat, 'But my mum and dad had to go through so much. They never spoke about it. My father suffered anti-Semitism at work. My mother couldn't speak a word of English when she came to England. She worked her socks off, but she suffered also at her work.'

'I'd never seen him so emotional,' said Paul Elliott.

Well, just once before – at Maine Road in May 1983. I'll never forget that game. It was only my seventh for the club and I was only eighteen. He took us all aside, one by one. He said to me: 'Listen Paul, you've done fabulously so far for this club. You have a massive future in the game. Even if we go down we will come back greater. You will go on to great things.' I said 'Boss, we'll stay up.' Back in the early 1980s, both football and society were ugly. There was a moronic minority that had a strong presence in stadiums. We had eight black players in the side at one time. He told us to let our talent do the talking, otherwise we'd let the bigots win. At the end of the City game, when he ran across the pitch, I didn't think it was the same man. I thought: 'Jesus Christ, is that the boss?' He was so unco-ordinated. He was out of his comfort zone. His subconscious mind had clearly come to the fore. Normally he was very calculated in everything he said and did. He never panicked, was always calm, analysed everything very carefully. But those two moments – at the funeral and the City game – I saw this different David.

Brought up on a council estate in Nottingham, Pleat has always felt different. There was only one other Jewish family in the neighbourhood, and, although his parents weren't religious, they never forgot their roots. His maternal grandfather, Israel Noah Fishman, came over from Poland in 1910, followed a year later by his wife, who died soon after Pleat's mother Eva was born. A match was then made with an Austrian lady, who proceeded to give birth to two daughters. Eva changed her name to Fish and learned to speak English with a broad Yiddish-Cockney accent. Whenever David came back from a football match after a defeat, she would greet him with the words: 'So, where was the goalkeeper?' She had five records, all 78s, which featured Cossack and Russian-Jewish folk songs, and used to light the candles on Friday night to usher in *shabbat*. Her husband Joseph, on the other hand, was the very model of an assimilated Jew; inheriting the acting bug from his father, who had been a chorus singer in a Lithuanian Yiddish theatre; he quickly learned, and would often recite to his children, Shakespeare's great soliloquies.

In the beginning, Joe Plotz was as much of a football nut as his cousin Ralph Finn. Like many 'aliens' growing up in Whitechapel, he'd been anglicised at the Oxford and St George's Jewish Lads' Club, founded by the social reformer Basil Henriques. Henriques wanted the club to 'provide a refuge from the appallingly overcrowded homes and hideous, monotonous slum streets' and 'give physical recreation to half-starved, poverty-stricken, underdeveloped boys and girls'. Joe enthusiastically embraced the anglicisers' motto of 'a healthy mind in a healthy body', taking part in myriad football and boxing matches. After being rejected by Orient, however, he decided to become an actor – until Eva refused to tour the country with his theatre troupe. So, like everyone else of his generation, he settled for tailoring. Joe often took Susan to the music hall in Nottingham, and kept a magic box of greasepaint by his bedside. 'Once he played a blind man in an amateur production,' Susan recalled, 'and he was going around, for a while, acting blind. He became someone else. That idea, that you can be somebody else rather than yourself, started me off wanting to write drama.'

Susan went to Oxford University and became a successful TV dramatist, writing seventy-four episodes of *Coronation Street* before moving on to *Juliet Bravo* and *Brookside*. David became 'someone else' when he joined Forest. The family had moved to Nottingham during the war to escape the Blitz, and Pleat became smitten as a nine-year-old at a 1954 Forest versus Leeds game. Four years later Pleat recalls another wonderful match, between Forest and West Brom: 'I remember that match as clearly as my barmitzvah, which was three days earlier. My parents did not discourage me and actually supported me fully, but maybe in their heart of hearts they would have preferred me to pursue a "proper profession".'

At the age of fifteen, the press hailed him as 'the New Tom Finney' after he scored a wonder goal in England Schoolboys' 5–3 defeat of Scotland at Wembley. Thereafter Pleat's career conformed to the Becoming English narrative: head down, keep schtum, don't rock the boat. Even in the Golden Age, when many doors were opening, he preferred to mute his Jewishness. 'When I was a kid we were made to feel as if we were foreigners in the country we were born in,' said Vidal Sassoon. 'Before you conquered the fascists you had to conquer the fear.' Pleat's biggest fear, which he never really conquered, was that anti-Semitism would hold him back, possibly ruin his career.

His failure to embrace his ethnicity unreservedly was a far more typical Golden Age response than Lazarus' flamboyant antics. Both players only made an impact after the maximum wage was abolished. 'Curiously,' Glanville noted in 1961, 'the New Deal itself coincides with the emergence of two Jewish footballers in First Division football, after a long period in which there wasn't a Jew in the whole of the Football League . . . All this leads me to wonder whether we shall now see an influx of Jewish players into football [and] the Jewish professional might see in football management a career for his future.' There was, however, no influx – and Pleat was to become the only British Jew ever to manage a top club.

I've always been aware that I am, for whatever reason, different. When I was young I was concerned about it. I was different, why was I different? Why do I have to be different? From time to time it hit me. But there were so few people like me in the game and from time to time an anti-Semitic comment would hit me. I know there is something different about me – and they know it, some of them. I remember some of my contemporaries at Lilleshall all doing this is-he-or-isn't-he thing. They're going: 'I'm sure Pleaty's a four-by-two' [rhyming slang for a Jew]. I'm not that type who says: 'Fuck off you cunt.' So you sit there and everyone's looking at you. 'C'mon, Pleaty, it's your round, you tight?' When I hear the occasional comment it stays with me for a day or two, then I forget about it. Then I have a conversation and it reminds me. I am very sensitive, I feel hurt.

After playing in the 1961 Maccabiah games in Israel, Pleat had been horrified to read all about his involvement in his local paper, the

Nottingham Evening Post. 'All of a sudden it's "What's this about the Maccabiah?" The other players, who'd had ignorance bred into them by their parents, didn't understand, made a joke of it.'

He only really stopped feeling different when he became Tottenham manager in 1986 – and in subsequent stints at White Hart Lane as director of football. Just like his dad at St George's, he finally felt he belonged. Not that he made a great deal of his Jewishness; on the contrary, he objected to all the Israeli flag-waving and 'Yid army' chanting. But with two Jewish businessmen running the club, Scholar and Paul Bobroff, and a support base that included a large number of co-religionists, he felt as comfortable as he ever had in his career with his dual identity.

During his first – and only – full season as Spurs manager (he harbours dark thoughts about his infamous 1987 sacking: despite a successful first season at White Hart Lane, he was forced out after disclosures about his private life. But he chose, on that as on many other occasions, to suffer in silence), the team finished third in the League, lost to Coventry in the FA Cup final and reached the semi-finals of the League Cup. His great tactical innovation was to play with one striker – Clive Allen, who scored forty-nine goals in all competitions – to accommodate the talents of Glenn Hoddle, Chris Waddle and Ossie Ardiles in a flexible 4-5-1 formation. Ardiles, one of the first foreign players to 'invade' England in the late 1970s, was a key figure in his great side, the talisman in a sublime midfield. Along with fellow coaches Howard Wilkinson, Jim Smith and Ron Atkinson – all, like Pleat, managers who had started out at non-League sides – he was part of an emerging group of bright, young, Lilleshall-trained coaches. Of them all, perhaps, he was the one most open to Continental thinking. One national newspaper voted his highly praised Tottenham team, operating a system inspired by the French sides who stormed the 1984 European Championship and

1986 World Cup, 'the most entertaining team in the country'. Writing in the *Independent* eight years later, Glenn Moore waxed lyrical about 'some of the best attacking football of the last two decades'. Citing his influences as Alec Stock, one of the first English managers to go to Italy, Harry Haslam, Brian Clough and Peter Taylor, Pleat summed up his philosophy in two words: thought and imagination: 'I've always said that the coaching in this country lacks imagination. It's straight-line football. I was thrilled when I did an FA coaching course at Lilleshall. That got me thinking. I like imaginative football. I could lose a game and still be semi-content like a lunatic, a *meshugana*. If we did clever things which we'd done on the coaching field, if we replicated what we did in training it was great; if we replicated what we did in the week and won – I was in another world. Fantastic.' Pleat's teams, according to Scholar, 'always tried to play football the way it should be played – on the ground. The game is called football, not airball or skyball. His teams played "the Tottenham way"'.

From Cohen to Lorimer: Is He or Isn't He?

The abuse that greeted Pleat, and the Tottenham board, on his return to Kenilworth Road in 1987 shocked many neutral observers. Scholar, normally as reticent as Pleat when it came to public proclamations of ethnicity, was so angry he confronted Luton chairman David Evans in the directors' lounge after the game. Despite giving his blessing to Pleat's departure from the club, Evans had spent the previous months attacking his ex-manager's 'betrayal' in the press, stirring up a huge amount of hostile feeling in Luton fans.

Luton fans had chanted against Pleat on their first visit to White Hart Lane after his departure, but in the return fixture they greeted him, and Spurs, with a wall of incredibly intimidating abuse. Irving Scholar remembers it as 'one of the nastiest atmospheres I had ever witnessed at a football ground . . . As David Pleat took his place in the dug-out, some stupid fellow held up a white placard with the word "JUDAS" emblazoned in black ink, directly above it . . . about two minutes from the end a stockily built lad of around twenty marched past the front of the directors' box. He was looking straight ahead of him, chanting what I can only describe as a highly provocative, racist, anti-Semitic song, which I had first heard some years previously at Maine Road. It went: "The Jews are on their way to Auschwitz. Hitler's going to gas them again."' Faced with such a blatantly anti-Semitic barrage, the irate Scholar marched straight to the directors' lounge after the game and challenged Evans, before announcing to his colleagues that he was no longer prepared to stay where he was obviously not wanted. He left, followed immediately by the rest of the Spurs board.

The intolerance that provoked most Jewish players in football, like Pleat and Dave Metchick – who played for Fulham, Orient, Peterborough, QPR and Brentford – to go 'under cover', led to several, farcical, is-he-or-isn't-he? cases of mistaken identity. When George Cohen helped England to World Cup glory, in 1966, the defender was lauded by the Jewish, national and international press. The *Jewish Chronicle* had even traced his ancestry back to Abraham Cohen, a nineteenth-century bare-knuckle fighter. Finally, after all these years, a Cohen had done the nation proud. On an England tour of America two years earlier, the Fulham defender had been the subject of a celebratory piece in the *New York Times*. After reading the article, headlined 'Why a Cohen Is Playing Football for a Living', which highlighted the rarity of 'a nice Jewish boy' playing such an 'alien' game, he rang up the editor to explain that he was not actually 'of the faith'. 'I have a Jewish great-grandfather,' he said, 'but that's it, really. Neither my father nor my mother was a Jew. I have always been Church of England.'

The is-he-or-isn't-he? question was given a surreal twist in the late 1970s when Peter Lorimer, a star of Don Revie's all-conquering Leeds team, received a telephone call from a man representing Hapoel Haifa. 'The offer was to both play and assist with the coaching,' wrote his agent Ronnie Teeman. But before he could take the position up, Lorimer needed somehow to circumvent the Israeli Football Association's rules, which only permitted a club to play Israeli citizens. If Lorimer wanted to play, then he would have to quickly become one. The quickest route would have been to invoke the 'law of return,' enacted when the state was established in 1948, which guaranteed that a Jew from anywhere in the world could return to the land of his forefathers and be entitled to citizenship. Though not born of a Jewish mother, Lorimer would have been eligible as a convert to the faith. The Hapoel Haifa representative suggested that Lorimer visit a rabbi in Leeds to be rushed through the process and obtain the necessary certification. Even when Teeman pointed out that the conversion process usually involved at least two years of study, and included the daunting prospect of a ritual circumcision, the Hapoel Haifa representative remained undaunted and suggested the quick fix of visiting a 'progressive' rabbi in New York who would be happy to wave Lorimer through. Teeman, understandably, was somewhat cynical. 'As to whether his conversion and all it – quite literally – entailed was in vain, I do not know as I never asked him about it or saw him in a synagogue.'

Lorimer travelled to New York and received the paperwork, but the Israeli FA declared the conversion certificate invalid – so he ended up coaching the team instead. 'I didn't convert,' he said. 'A newspaper picked up on it, and it was seen as a bit of a joke over here, but over there it was a serious matter. But it wasn't allowed.

If I had been Jewish I would have been allowed to play. But something good came of it, in that it helped to change the climate. A year later they lifted the ban. And it broke down a few barriers the other way, too, in that it paved the way for players like Avi Cohen, Ronnie Rosenthal and other foreign players to come to England.'

Part 3

The New Age

Being English

'I have spent the best years of my life becoming a true
Englishman. And now the whole country is turning alien.'

George Mikes, *How to Be a Brit*, 1986

In the New Age, the Jews finally became English. The die had been
cast many years earlier when 'sporting contact with Gentiles', as the
Jewish Chronicle put it, 'had been pursued too vigorously.' Despite
the backlash of the late 1960s and early '70s, the early anglicisers'
dream of converting a Yiddish-speaking community of eastern
Europeans into an established and confident community of
Englishmen would be realised in the last decade of the twentieth
century. During this final phase of integration, two things happened
in English football – mirroring, and to some extent galvanising,
developments in society as a whole – which speeded up the anglicisation of its forgotten tribe. Firstly, as anticipated by Pleat's Luton,
the West Brom side that fielded three black regulars and several
other teams of that era, an anti-foreign, post-imperial, generally
backward-looking game has been transformed into an inclusive,
multicultural, global sport. At the same time, the influx of television revenue, rampant commercialisation and the arrival of a new
breed of mega-rich foreign owners has transformed it into a high-
profile, obscenely lucrative branch of the international entertainment industry.

During this revolutionary era, as Jews entered the middle-class professions, the middle-class professions entered football. The international entertainment industry feeds off middle-men – a role historically played by ethnic minorities. Sociologist Edna Bonacich coined the phrase 'middle-man minority' to describe the familiar immigrant paradigm: lacking financial capital of their own, such communities devote themselves to the acquisition of knowledge, which converts into affluence when they become the bankers, lawyers, accountants and doctors of migrant folklore. In the New Age, all of these fields have been touched by this final phase of a 100-year Anglo-Jewish odyssey, though of course middle-men have been around ever since medieval European governments restricted money-lending to Jews on the grounds that they were morally inappropriate for Christians. In the Dark Ages, and then Renaissance Europe, Jews weren't allowed to own property or enter the professions. This established something of a pattern, with non-Jewish rulers enjoying all the benefits of usury while condemning the 'money-grubbing parasites' who financed their endeavours.

Although as David Goldberg, the emeritus rabbi of the Liberal Jewish Synagogue in London, has observed: 'It has been easier and safer to be a Jew than black or Muslim,' and while my generation has felt more secure than previous ones, we remain lumbered with our parents' and grandparents' nomadic baggage – in particular, their constant fear of a return to penury or even social ostracism. Such insecurity has sunk deep into the recesses of the Anglo-Jewish psyche.

In writing this book, I was told on numerous occasions that, although I was setting out to celebrate an obvious, if hidden, success story, I would only succeed in reinforcing the age-old stereotype of the grasping businessman. This stereotype, of course, predates the New Age. 'The Jew [in England] is portrayed as Fagin,' Alan Sugar told the *Jewish Chronicle*, 'and you won't shake that out of people's heads. It's an underlying thing – that the Jews are a little bit sharp, a little bit quick, not to be trusted, possibly. If you ask a group of non-Jews in a pub what it is that they don't like about Jews, this is what they'll come out with . . . that they hoard money.'

And so, even after the 1992 revolution, when the presence of Sugar and his like in the game's upper echelons became a given, it has been a struggle to be totally accepted, to belong, to become 'one of us'. It could be argued that, from one point of view, the struggle to complete this epic quest – which began with the Jewish Naturalisation Act of 1753, gained momentum with political emancipation in 1858 and was set back several decades by the 'alien' invasion of the late nineteenth century – has actually driven some of the key changes in English football over the last thirty years. I finished this book in May 2012, just after an English team owned by a first-generation Russian Jew had been crowned European champions – and the manager of the England national team had been anointed by a fourth-generation Russian Jew. In a final push to prove themselves as loyal, patriotic insiders, a previously marginalised tribe of foreigner outsiders have finally 'arrived'. As *Times* columnist David Aaronovitch wrote:

> My immigrant grandparents were illiterate and my grandmother was one of those recalcitrant women, much maligned these days, who never mastered English. Perhaps part of her always remained gossiping over the washing in some village on the shifting Polish–Russian frontier. Their children, however, were not Russian or Polish. They were British. Today you will walk many a country mile before you encounter anybody more British than the Chief Rabbi Lord Sacks. The very expectation on the part of others that it would be otherwise – this Britishness of the newcomer – may itself help to intensify it.

8

The Israelis:
When a Cohen Flew to the Moon

'The whole situation was unreal. Every moment was like being in a dream.'

Avi Cohen

Avi Cohen: The Great New Hope

At the end of 1978, at a fogbound Heathrow airport, whilst waiting for his flight back home to Israel after watching a Liverpool match, a Reds fan spotted the club's chairman Peter Robinson. Walking over to introduce himself, he said: 'I know a really good player back in Israel you should sign.' Pini Zahavi's chutzpah paid off, and, seven months later, Avi Cohen flew in from Tel Aviv.

*

For Willy Meisl, the 1953 Hungary debacle exposed a myopic, safety-first approach that, 'like the Maginot Line' – as he put it – had failed to repel 'foreign invaders'. Twenty-five years later, when the first stream of foreign imports began to trickle in, the English game was still an introverted fortress. The New Age began in 1978 – the year Viv Anderson became the first black footballer to play for England – when the Football League, under pressure from the European Community, lifted its ban on overseas recruits, preparing the way for the parting of the Red Sea in 1992, the year football changed for ever. Following the World Cup in Argentina, Spurs manager Keith Burkinshaw, liberated by the abolition of the two-year residency rule, snapped up victorious Argentinians Ossie Ardiles and Ricky Villa. When, on a sudden whim, Zahavi touted Cohen to Robinson at the end of the year, he would never have dreamed that the Israeli would be part of a trickle that would eventually lead to a flood. Today, only a third of top flight stars are English.

Of course, in 1978, football remained, notoriously, an arena for the expression of racist and xenophobic attitudes. But the gradual increase in the number of black and mixed-race players, many of them second- or third-generation descendants of post-war immigration from the Caribbean, followed by the influx of overseas stars, created an environment in which outsiders could more easily become insiders. And as Jewish middle men like Zahavi – agents, networkers, marketing and merchandising gurus – came to the fore, and home-grown Jewish players became a dying breed, a new group of outsiders arrived – Israeli Jews – who raised fresh questions about the dual nature of Anglo-Jewish identity.

In 1990, Norman Tebbit infamously claimed that 'a large propor-tion of Britain's Asian population fail to pass the cricket test. Which side do they cheer for? It's an interesting test. Are you still harking back to where you came from or where you are?' Strictly speaking, my patriotism should be tested every time the England football team play Lithuania; or, perhaps, given Vilnius was part of the Tsarist empire when my great-grandparents fled to England, Russia. A few years ago, when England played Israel, several people asked me which team I would be supporting. This idea of split loyalty would have amused my Israeli friend, Ronnie Goldman, whom I visited in the mid-1970s, a year after my barmitzvah. We had met at a Jewish summer school in Taunton and bonded over football in general and Leeds United in particular. When he invited me to spend the following summer at his Tel Aviv home, my parents were delighted. They felt that my obsession with football, which they had blamed for my drift away from the faith, might now bring me back to the fold.

It was during this visit, however, that I came to realise just how 'truly English' I was. The Goldmans were a warm, loving family, and I was made to feel very welcome. But I amused them, and Ronnie's friends, with my clichéd Englishman abroad routine, sitting on the beach every day on a deckchair, a blanket draped over me, devouring the *Daily Telegraph* from cover to cover. At least, Ronnie's mother joked, in starting with the sport and working my way towards the news pages I was keeping to the Hebrew tradition of reading from back to front. Israel is a beautiful country but, from that moment on, I realised how deeply attached I was to the emotional landscape of England: freedom, ease, dependability, fairness, composure, reserve – and above all sportsmanship.

Much to my surprise, despite ending up a secular, assimilated English Jew who supports the creation of a Palestinian state, there is still a part of me that remains overly anxious about attitudes towards Israel. So when Cohen joined Liverpool in 1979, I couldn't help worrying, in the classic diaspora-Jewish manner, whether his arrival might revive anti-Semitism at football grounds. What if he flopped? Wouldn't this confirm the *Airplane* gag? Worse, what if he was a big hit? Wouldn't his success highlight, by comparison, the paucity of homegrown Jewish footballing talent? And wouldn't he be a target, like the Tottenham 'Yids', for anti-Semitic abuse? Cohen lasted only twenty months at Anfield, but when he died in a motorcycle accident in 2010, aged just fifty-four, I found myself moved to tears by the tributes and obituaries, particularly the ones emanating from Liverpool. Despite making only twenty-four appearances for Bob Paisley's great team, the red half of Merseyside went into mourning on hearing of his death. 'He quickly integrated himself into the football club when he joined us,' said Kenny Dalglish, 'and spent a lot of time learning English, which really made him popular. He certainly left his mark.'

Being Israel's first footballer to play abroad, he became, for a while, the Great New Hope, the man who would finally, as the original 1936 Maccabi Code had predicted, 'prove Jews to be physically and morally courageous' on the playing field. Since its foundation sixty-four years ago, sport has been one of the ways the Jewish state has attempted to sell itself, particularly its brawn, to the world. Avi's friend, Shaul Adar, had grown up watching Cohen in an era when, he said, 'every Israeli male was excited about Thursday nights because, between eight and nine on TV, we could watch *Game of the Week* featuring a top English match played the previous Saturday'. Everyone had a favourite First Division team, and half of the country's football pools involved predicting the results of English matches. In the late 1970s, Adar and his friends enjoyed 'a full-blown love affair' with a game that had been exported to Palestine during the British Mandate. It had not always been thus. For his parents' generation, who had been involved in a bloody struggle for independence, it had been more of a love-hate relationship.

Kaduregel – the Hebrew word for soccer – had taken root during the thirty years of British rule, from the end of the First World War to 1948, often acting as a litmus test for Jewish–British relations. In 1935, when German Jewish athletes defied Hitler's ban on attending the Maccabiah Games in Tel Aviv, the protest was as much against the British, who had barred refugees from entering Palestine, as the Nazis. FIFA admitted the Palestine federation only after it was agreed a national team would include Arabs and Christians as well as Jews – but on a tour of Egypt the letters LD were sneakily added to the team's shirts, indicating the Hebrew words for 'Land of Israel'. In World Cup qualifiers for the 1934 and 1938 tournaments, not one Arab player was included.

When independence came, in 1948, and the surrounding Arab countries declared war, the country's first prime minister, David Ben Gurion, sent a football team on a propaganda mission to America. Some of the eighteen players, who had been selected from the best clubs in Tel Aviv, Haifa and Petah Tikva, had joined the British Army to fight the Nazis. They included Hungarian-born centre-back Israel Weiss, a member of the 'Jewish Division' set up by Winston Churchill in 1944, and the team's captain, a *schtarker* called Shmulik Ben-Dror, who had risen to the rank of officer. 'He was a very, very hard man,' recalled the journalist Asher Goldberg.

'He was seriously injured [during the war] and spent a long time in hospital in Italy. His body was full of shrapnel. They were taking pieces of shrapnel out of him for the rest of his life.'

But some of the others chosen to fly the new flag of Israel had actually fought to overthrow the British. One of them, Eliezer Spiegel, joined the Irgun, a militant Zionist underground armed movement which assassinated British officials. In 1946, they blew up the King David Hotel in Jerusalem, the nerve centre of British rule. This resulted in twenty-eight British (on top of sixty-three non-British) deaths and, along with the kidnapping and hanging of two army sergeants a year later, provoked anti-Jewish rioting in British cities. A year before the King David bombing, Spiegel had been arrested and sent to an Eritrean camp for three years. 'We used to play football there, against a team of the British,' he said. 'I used to play very well. So, one of the soldiers, a captain, said he would arrange for me to go to England and play there. It would have been a dream come true to play in England – but I told him I wouldn't go. They wanted us to be far away. I wanted to return to Israel first.' And yet, even for Spiegel, 'making it in the West' remained the ultimate goal: the ultimate Jewish fantasy.

A year after the foundation of Israel, he finally got his big chance, turning out for Maccabi Tel Aviv at Molineux. The *schtarker* blew it: 'I touched the ball ten times. The ten times we kicked off. A newspaper had printed which hotel we were staying in. I was waiting outside, after we lost 10–0 to Wolves, and I saw this man in full military uniform coming towards me. I thought: "That's it, the British have found me. I'm to be arrested." It was the captain from Eritrea, now a colonel and retired. He'd read in the paper I was here. He said he was sorry for Africa, and happy I got to England eventually. He was bored now. He said he drank cups of coffee all day.'

A year later, in 1950, Hull City's visit to Israel drew the ire of Zionist newspapers. 'We have not forgotten as yet the "friendship" of the Britons,' one reminded its readers. 'The blood which was spilled like water because of, and through, them has not dried up as yet . . . it is too soon to have relations with "Albion the Traitor". She has to prove first that she changed her mind and atoned for all her sins. Therefore let the Hebrews not play against the Britons on the bloody soil.'

The mood began to soften in 1951, when Hapoel Tel Aviv toured Albion the Traitor, taking on teams in big cities with Jewish populations, like Manchester and Glasgow. The greatest interest, due to the greatest concentration of 'British Hebrews', was in north London. Tickets sold out quickly for the Arsenal clash and, on the evening of the game, the first floodlit match ever played at Highbury, over 45,000 saw the Gunners cruise to a 6–1 win. Both the match programme and the specially arranged BBC radio commentary were provided in English and Hebrew. The programme noted that:

> . . . many foreign clubs have visited Highbury over the years but none have attracted so much widespread interest in London as Hapoel Tel Aviv. It is a well-known thing about touring sides in England that the English football fan does not take kindly to such matches. This cannot be said about the visit of Hapoel Tel Aviv and we can say without doubt that this match has created more active interest than any foreign visiting club in modern times.

Three years later, 13,000 fans braved torrential rain to see Arsenal beat Maccabi Tel Aviv, and when Hapoel returned to Britain in 1957, more poor weather kept the attendance down to only 8,754; the *Jewish Chronicle* reported that the 'majority' of those who saw Arsenal's 10–1 victory were 'of Jewish ethnicity'.

Not to be outdone, Bill Nicholson arranged for two Israeli coaches to study Tottenham's methods throughout the 1961 close season. When his great double-winning team visited Israel in 1962, over 40,000 fans packed into the Basa Stadium to see them beat a representative national side 2–1. Two years later, Nicholson invited Yossi Mirmovitch, the Israel manager, and his assistant, David Schweitzer, to White Hart Lane on a three-month coaching programme. The Israeli FA hoped these visits would legitimise the new nation-state in the eyes of an often hostile outside world; with a bit of luck, one of Mirmovitch's team would be picked up by Spurs or another top team. This almost happened when Mordechai Spiegler impressed Ron Greenwood during his trials at Upton Park. But the scorer of Israel's only goal in World Cup history, a wonder strike against Sweden in 1970, was refused permission to join West Ham, the FA invoking their two-year residency rule.

It was to be another nine years before the long-awaited breakthrough happened. And it was Liverpool fan Zahavi, a journalist at the time but soon to become a super-agent, who announced the news.

As Shaul Adar recounts: 'After Pini broke the news Avi had signed for Liverpool, for months there was an Avi Cohen festival. I was a kid and I remember it as something amazing. Pini had all the scoops, of course. Every day the TV followed Avi around, everywhere he went. He became the most talked-about player in the country. He was playing for Liverpool, who we all saw once a week on Thursday night – and once a year in the European Cup Final. It was like a fourteen-year-old maths pupil doing a Ph.D. Being at Anfield was beyond the imagination of most Israelis. We had no clubs in any tournaments. At the end of the 1970s Israeli football was nowhere. We felt isolated. And there were virtually no foreign players in England. During Cohen's two years Israelis became even more obsessed with English football.'

Cohen had not, it must be said, been an instant hit. Back in the late 1970s, the domestic game lacked cosmopolitan flair, foreign coaches and a global reach that would attract millionaire, let alone, billionaire owners. The old-school attitude at Liverpool, the League Champions and, arguably, the most powerful team in Europe, was to play, train and enjoy their Wednesday afternoon bonding sessions down the pub. 'They didn't really know how to deal with a non-Brit,' Cohen would later reflect. 'The whole experience was new to both of us.' Before his first training session, he noticed that his peg in the changing room was next to Dalglish's. Mustering up the courage to speak to the great man, he mumbled: 'Me, you, same.' This prompted only a blank, intimidating stare. After an awkward impasse, he elaborated, again in Tarzan-speak: 'You, me, same.' King Kenny had absolutely no idea what Avi was on about. Cohen tried again: 'Me, you, same. Both of us learn English.' The joke broke the ice, but the Israeli still felt completely out of his depth: 'From the first minute of my first game to the last minute of my last, two years later, I was shell-shocked.' Back home, he had been fêted for his smooth passing and distribution of the ball, for his ability to read the game, anticipate play and tackle strongly. His debut at Elland Road went so badly he spent the next six months languishing in the reserves. 'For Avi,' said Adar, 'being there at that time was like someone today from Hackney Marshes being invited to have a trial at Barcelona.' When asked to sum up his two years at Anfield, Cohen went even further. 'It was,' he said, 'like a man stepping on the moon.'

He kept asking Zahavi why one of the world's best teams had signed him. 'I didn't think I deserved to play for Liverpool,' he said. 'Even when I played I thought they were much better than me. No-body said to me: "Avi you're better than them." I was alone. Nobody helped me. I suddenly found myself at the top of world football. It was incomprehensible to me. The gap was huge. I thought I was in a place I didn't belong.' In his second appearance for the club, at home to Aston Villa at the end of the season, he sliced an attempted clearance over Ray Clemence's head into his own goal. But five minutes into the second half, his low, angled, right-foot strike – one of the goals that secured a second consecutive title for the Reds – sent the Kop into paroxysms of glee. When he heard them singing 'There's only one Avi Cohen' he felt a shiver down his spine. 'For me,' he said, 'I think this was the moment Israeli football finally arrived.'

From Avi to Avram

Cohen's signing inspired one of Bob Paisley's rare forays into intentional humour. When a *Jewish Chronicle* reporter rang up the Liverpool manager to enquire whether Cohen was orthodox, Paisley replied: 'Orthodox what? Orthodox midfielder? Orthodox defender?' If Avi was an orthodox Jew, the journalist explained, he couldn't play on a Saturday. 'But I've got half a dozen like that already,' joked Bob. In fact, Cohen was so unorthodox he actually turned out for Liverpool on Yom Kippur – to the great horror of his country's press. Some Israeli writers even invoked the concept of divine retribution to explain the goal he gifted Southampton with his badly misjudged back pass that day. It was, perhaps, a sign of the community's increasing secularisation that the incident failed to similarly scandalise Anglo-Jewry. Anglicisation had, as the anti-integrationists warned, been accompanied by a decline in religious observance. The baffled Swindon Town historian Dick Mattick had noted, back in the 1920s, that 'Harry [Morris] would never play on the Jewish Day of Atonement.' But Pleat had never given it a second thought throughout his playing career and was surprised to be reprimanded by Brian Winston when the Orient chairman presented him with the Second Division championship trophy in 1982. Winston, not in the greatest of moods after the Os' relegation to the Third Division, reminded the Luton manager of a phone call between the two earlier in the season.

> I'd rang him and said: 'David, what are you going to do for our Luton–Orient game?' He said: 'What do you mean?' I said: 'You can't go to our match. It's on Yom Kippur' He said: 'Well, I'll be honest. I've got to. I'm the manager and I've got to be there.' I said: 'What are you going to do when you walk out on to the pitch, look up to heaven?' He said: 'Are you going?' 'No,' I said, 'I can't because of my family.' David said: 'It's different for me, the team need me at the game.' 'Well,' I said, 'I'm just phoning to tell you I won't be there.' So he went, and I didn't. And the bastard won 1–0.

Thirty years later, the wheel came full circle when a small section of the English media criticised West Ham manager Avram Grant for missing a crucial match to observe the Jewish Holy Day. Citing a similar incident in 2007, when Grant had fasted for Yom Kippur the day before his first game in charge of Chelsea, ESPN reporter Kevin Palmer wrote: 'News that he [Grant] is set to miss next weekend's game at Stoke as he prepares to observe the Jewish festival . . . confirms his commitment to his religion runs deep and he has always placed that devotion above sporting ambitions.' This unsympathetic tone, however, was untypical of the game's wider reaction, especially when Grant disclosed he was paying tribute to the relatives who had starved to death in Russia. To Jewish footballers like Oldham's Dean Furman, his stance was a source of great pride.

It was uplifting for him to stand up and say it doesn't matter how big football is, this is my life, I want to live it like I want to live it. And I think everyone should have that choice. And I think that we, as Jews, should have that choice. It's good that you see people at that higher level doing things like that. It shows to everyone it's a big thing to be Jewish. In football, as in life, you've got to be your own person. Most people respected that. From my experience there is a lot of tolerance now of Jews in football. And that's partly down to Israelis like Avi, Ronny Rosenthal, Eyal Berkovic and Yossi Benayoun. They broke the mould.

Cohen's stay on Merseyside might have been brief, but it paved the way for Rosenthal, who in 1990 became the first non-Brit to be signed by an English club for more than £1 million. Rocket Ronny was far more of a success during his three-and-a-half-year stint at Anfield. He scored two memorable hat-tricks – the first on his full debut, the other a perfect one against Charlton – and his seven goals in the 1989–90 season's final eight matches helped Liverpool lift their last title. Rosenthal's habit of coming on to nick a goal in the later stages of a game earned him the sobriquet of 'supersub'. He moved to Spurs, where he scored eleven goals in 100 appearances, and then finished his career at Watford. But Rosenthal remains best remembered for what has come to be known as 'That Miss'. In a 1992 game at Aston Villa he ghosted past a defender, rounded the goalkeeper and then prepared to roll the ball into an empty net. Sliding his foot under the ball, he then watched in dismay as it crashed against the bar. It was a blunder which came to define his career – and, for a while, Israeli football – becoming embedded in football folklore. 'The ball bobbled a little, and I caught it with the wrong part of my foot,' he explained. 'Nine times out of ten, ninety-nine times out of 100, when you are trying to pass the ball into an open goal it is easy and it goes in. But ridiculous things happen, the ball bounces differently, and it changes direction. But if you asked me if I'd want to do it again I'd say "yes". It put me on the map.'

This last sentence was a conscious echo of Israeli basketball star Tal Brody's famous statement after Maccabi Tel Aviv had reached the sport's European Cup final in 1977. Brody's 'We are on the map' declaration had become the country's sporting mantra – and, somewhat inevitably, it would be the headline that greeted the next Great Jewish Hope's arrival in England.

The problem was that Eyal Berkovic, known as 'The Magician' – *Ha-Kosem* in Hebrew – was a far less loveable character than either Cohen or Rosenthal. He played for five British clubs and was branded a big-mouth at nearly all of them. He made his mark at Southampton, scoring twice in a famous 6–3 victory over Manchester United in 1996. But his petulance alienated Celtic fans and landed him in trouble with high-profile figures like Kevin Keegan, his manager at Manchester City. At West Ham he enjoyed a brief period of popularity after scoring the decisive goal against Spurs on his debut, but in a notorious training-ground bust-up with John Hartson he was kicked in the face by his team-mate. The Welshman was roundly condemned in the media, but there was little sympathy for his victim. 'You especially feel the hostility in the press,' said Berkovic. 'Even when Hartson did that the press blamed me. If my head had been a ball it would have been in the top corner of the net. He was my best friend at the club but that morning he came in drunk. What a disgusting guy.'

Yossi Benayoun had a more benign temperament. A humble, but equally talented, unlocker of defences, he was born into a Moroccan family, his Sephardic background typical of many Israeli footballers.

On arrival in the country, like many immigrants from Arab countries, his parents were shunted into a remote, charmless 'development town', overshadowed by a nuclear reactor. With its high unemployment rate and pervasive atmosphere of hopelessness, they struggled to raise their family. However, at the age of eleven, Yossi was spotted by a football scout and, two years later, was being hailed as the poster boy of a new Israeli golden age. As a kid – a slight, fragile figure – he would hitch-hike with his father to the training grounds of Hapoel Be'er Sheva, the only senior team in the oppressively hot Negev Desert. Virtually every day, for five years, they would wait hours at a time for a car to stop and pick them up. He vowed that whatever he did with his life he would always strive to be exceptional and would never give up. Highway 54 was his road to paradise.

'It's a normal life in Dimona, like anybody. My family still live there, in the desert. It's a different life from England but it's my home. It's one of the smallest and poorest cities in Israel. It was hard because we had no money, nothing, but I never wanted for anything, and we never felt we had anything missing. The love we had as a family was enough for everything and always at the middle of the family was me. What little we had they gave to me so that I could play football because they could see I had this talent. I was a football player from ever since I remember. My dream was to play in the Israeli premier division. I went to Ajax at fifteen and it ripped my family.'

Homesickness drove each member of his family back to Israel until finally only Yossi and his father, Dudu, were left. The Israeli press said he was too soft.

It was very hard, difficult. My girlfriend, Mirat [now his wife] was also just fifteen. It was just too hard for everyone. It was just not the right time. A year later, I was called in and offered a four-year contract as a first-team player. But the day after I had to say: 'Sorry, I want to go back to the Negev.' It was hard, especially for a family who had nothing. The money was important, but there are lots of things which are more important. You have to be happy; if you are not then money doesn't matter. A lot of people gave my family cash, well-wishers, but when I went back I returned it. There was a lot of criticism. The press in Israel, the journalists, are very hard. When I went back they wrote horrible things, saying I would never be a player, I would never be able to make it in Europe and didn't have the character. They just didn't understand. Everyone in Israel loved and supported me. They liked the stories that I had nothing, my family had nothing, and I came out and had great success.

His career seemed to be over before he had even turned sixteen. Benayoun kept longing for his mother's north African cooking and for his childhood sweetheart. His predicament received disproportionate coverage back home. All of Israel seemed to be counting on him to become its first big international star. Within five months he returned to Israel crestfallen, going back to Be'er Sheva to rebuild his career. He played brilliantly in the 1997–8 season, scoring fifteen goals, but failed to save his team from relegation.

We had to win our last game of the season to stay up. In the last minute we won a penalty, and I had to take it. The other players were aged twenty-nine to thirty-two. I was called 'The Kid' – I was only seventeen. It was a very experienced team, but none of the other ten players wanted to take it. No one. And I missed. The goalkeeper saved it. But I chipped the rebound into the net. Yet it wasn't enough. In the other match, the other team scored in the last minute too, and we went down.

A photograph of him weeping after the game, still looking like a little boy, lingers in the memory of many Israeli football fans. For an entire nation his tears, and the courage he demonstrated, became an enduring image. They took The Kid back and loved him again. He went to a bigger team, Maccabi Haifa, who were champions twice in four seasons and did well in Europe, twice beating the French giants Paris Saint-Germain. These games, and a spell at the Spanish club Racing Santander, attracted the attention of several English clubs, and he joined West Ham in 2005. His debut, against Blackburn, was a startling experience.

> Look at me. I don't have one muscle in my whole body, for
> the first twenty minutes I couldn't breathe. I wanted the gaffer
> to take me off but I was too ashamed to say it. The pace of
> the game was different to anything I'd ever experienced. Even
> the training took some adjusting to, but Teddy Sheringham
> told me to take it easy, to build myself slowly and I would get
> used to the English pace, and he was right. When Yaniv Katan
> [his fellow Israeli international] arrived here the first thing he
> said to me was, 'Yossi, can you believe we're in the same team
> as Teddy Sheringham?'

West Ham was Grant's last club in England. Despite grumblings about going AWOL at Yom Kippur, the vast majority of his English critics, and there were many, ignored his ethnicity. His nationality, however, was another matter. Israel was still a novice in footballing terms, and his lack of a formal UEFA managerial qualification attracted strong criticism when Roman Abramovich appointed him

Chelsea manager in 2007. There were hints of a conspiracy, one columnist even suggesting the existence of a 'Jewish Russian mafia'. Finishing second in the Premiership, and reaching the 2008 Champions League final – something the fans' deposed idol José Mourinho had failed to achieve – did little to win over the sceptics. A year later, the lugubrious coach was brought in to save a struggling Portsmouth side, but, after going into administration and being deducted nine points as punishment, Pompey dropped out of the Premier League. The following season, Grant also presided over West Ham's relegation from the top flight. 'He was a monumental disaster and a calamity as our manager,' declared David Dein's nephew Jeremy Dein, a devoted follower of the club. 'But, despite the fact that his season there was a total disaster, I never heard a word of anti-Semitism at Upton Park. Not one word.'

Like Pleat's parents, Grant's mother had discouraged his interest in football, once cutting up a new ball so he would turn his attention to his studies. 'My late wife had a fiery temperament, and she gave Avram a hard time,' his father Meir explained. 'He was bright and did well at school. But, as he got older, he was not prepared to invest in his studies and only wanted to play football. Aliza wanted him to become a doctor or lawyer. I would tell her, you cannot change him.' This was a familiar story: first- or second-generation immigrants, desperate for their offspring to have professional careers, determined to stop them entering the insecure, short-lived, world of football. But, in Grant's story, there was the added poignancy of the immigrants in question, who were deported from Poland to Siberia during the Second World War, losing most of their family in the Holocaust. He had been a teenager when he found out that his paternal grandparents and five of Meir's siblings had died in this way – and that his father had buried them with his own hands. 'I was with friends one evening, speaking about football,' said Grant, 'when suddenly I heard screams from the bedroom which froze my blood. I ran there and saw my father, Meir, screaming out in the most terrible anguish in his sleep. Through those shocking screams I learned from my mother about the Holocaust and the nightmares that haunted my father and continued to haunt him for sixty-five years night after night. All my life I have lived under the shadow of the Holocaust.'

Meir Granat has indelible memories of that time:

After the Nazis arrived they moved us south to near Warsaw. We stayed there for six months and moved around some more, but in 1941 we realised things were looking bleak in Poland and decided to take our chances in Russia. We were exiled to the far north. Guards dropped us off in a forest and said, 'Build a home or die.' When it is so cold, the body needs to eat more. It was -40 in winter, and what little food we could glean was rock hard. In such circumstances, people who are not young stand no chance. We were so far north that in the summer there was no darkness, and in the winter, no light. When I buried my father, I cut off my *peyot* [sidecurls] and removed my *kippah*. I had lost my religious faith before his death. To survive, you must look forward in hope, never back.

9

The Revolutionaries:
When Dein Bought Some Worthless Shares

CLAVANE'S CIGARETTES

D. DEIN *(ARSENAL)*

'Once we'd seen the FA, and we realised that the door
was a little bit ajar and we could kick it open, we moved
quickly . . . running our own clubs we needed to be pretty
tough. We were relatively young and we came from a
business background and we were hungry.'

David Dein

David Dein: The Mad Optimist

In 1983, on his way to the sugar market, a young trader bought some shares from an old man. When he arrived home, his mother became furious and threw them out of the window and sent him to bed without supper. Nine years later, he woke up to find the shares had grown into a gigantic beanstalk.

*

When David Dein bought those unissued Arsenal shares from Peter Hill-Wood, for £290,250, the club's chairman could not, for the life of him, understand why anyone, particularly a nouveau riche sugar trader like Dein, would want to invest in a football club. The one lesson he had learned from his family's long association with the game was that nobody made any money from it. 'I think he's crazy,' said Hill-Wood. 'To all intents and purposes it is dead money.' In their five decades of running the 'establishment club', the Hill-Woods, a classically patrician, Old Etonian dynasty, had restricted the number of outsiders allowed into their inner sanctum. Brian Glanville once asked Peter's father Denis, during an interview in the latter's old stockbrokers' office in the City, what had happened to the Enclosure Club in Highbury's West Stand. The writer had thought it 'an agreeable enough institution'. Hill-Wood explained it had been closed down. 'It's the Jews,' he said. 'They take over.'

Glanville recounts:

Little could [Denis] realise that under his son Peter's regime, 'They', in the shape of David Dein, would emerge from north London obscurity eventually to be the propulsive force of the club . . . Thus did I call Dein the Lopakhin of our football, meaning the serf's son who, in Chekhov's great play *The Cherry*

Orchard, takes over the estate from the aristocrats his father once served and chops down their beloved cherry orchard. Dein, however, chopped down nothing; rather did he build it up.

Whether he foresaw the game's future transformation by television's billions is a debatable point, but Dein would eventually become one of the first ever directors to make vast amounts of money from selling his shares. When the first Hill-Wood, Samuel, became chairman in the late 1920s, Dein's grandfather, Abraham, who had fled from the Ukraine, owned a small tobacconist shop in the West End. David's father Isadore, who supported Leyton Orient, worked at the shop on Saturdays, so his two football-mad uncles, Izzy and Lou, took him to games with his brother Arnold. Izzy became David's football mentor; well-connected at Highbury, he would allow his young nephew to keep the compliment slips that came with their tickets. Before moving out of the East End to Forest Gate, the Deins had opened a small shop in East Ham, which is how Lou, a Yiddish-speaking waiter at Blooms, caught the West Ham bug. The rest of the family preferred Highbury to Upton Park, despite the anti-Semitism they occasionally experienced. 'Sometimes I'd go with my father and uncle to Arsenal away games,' Dein's nephew Alan recalled, 'and we'd hear some people call out: "Jews among us."'

Dein, like Pleat, has spent his whole life ignoring such slights. On one occasion, when faced with some borderline anti-Semitic banter in a Premier League boardroom, he chose to suffer in silence whilst his fellow director Danny Fiszman walked out. Fiszman, a multi-millionaire diamond dealer, was the son of Belgian Jewish parents who had fled the Nazis during the Second World War. Born in Willesden at the end of the conflict and initiated into Highbury's Clock End, he bought his first tranche of shares from Dein in 1991 – which, by then, were certainly no longer regarded by Hill-Wood as dead money. Dein's refusal to join Fiszman in taking such a strong gesture is typical of a man who has always preferred to play down any reference to his ethnicity. When he became vice-chairman, he hated journalists pointing out the huge gulf in class and upbringing between him and the public-school merchant banker who ran the club.

One of the ways he 'rebuilt the orchard' was by putting Highbury on a more commercial, customer-friendly footing, pilfering ideas about modernisation from the United States. He introduced mascots and big screens, described by a horrified Hill-Wood as 'dreadful things which make a terrible racket', and turned the ground into an all-seater stadium. Each morning, he told his friend Alex Fynn in the late 1980s, at the beginning of the George Graham era, he would look into his shaving mirror and see 'Get a winning team' etched on his forehead. The appointment of Graham as manager certainly brought great success, but it was the 1996 capture of an unknown French coach, Arsène Wenger – the result of Dein's wide and extensive network of contacts – which completed the meta-morphosis of English football's establishment club into a cosmo-politan, outward-looking, European superpower, ushering in a decade of glory unparalleled since the 1930s. The astonishingly successful reinvention of Arsenal, would not, Wenger told *L'Equipe* magazine, have been possible without the Dein revolution.

In ten years, Dein revolutionised not only Arsenal, but the whole of English football. Apart from Josef Venglos at Aston Villa, an English club had never taken the risk of appointing a foreign coach. 'It is pretentious to say it but my arrival was a strong sign,' says Wenger. 'Dein is a mad optimist. He is open-minded to new ideas. Before bringing me in, he was one of the people behind the birth of the Premiership in 1992.'

That inauguration changed football for ever. The other 'midwives' were Tottenham's Irving Scholar, Liverpool's Noel White, Everton's Sir Philip Carter and Manchester United's Martin Edwards. According to Paul Bobroff, who in 1982 – a year before Dein's 'crazy' investment – had taken over Spurs with Scholar, the Scholar–Dein axis 'drove the revolution . . . they were the main ones at the time. There wasn't much sympathy from football to our point of view. That's why Irving and David at the time could never get elected to any of the committees. They didn't want people like us. They saw us, maybe, as a threat.' It was Dein who successfully lobbied the FA to support the new breakaway league, having been deputed by the 'Big Five' – as Spurs, Arsenal, Manchester United, Liverpool and Everton were then collectively known – to approach the governing body. 'A number have claimed they were the movers and shakers behind the Premier League,' said Keith Harris, the former football League Chairman, 'but it was Irving and David who were the main ones. And it's no coincidence that they are Jewish.'

It was also no coincidence that they challenged their clubs' conservative, ageist and reactionary administrations just as Margaret Thatcher was opening up her government's doors to establishment outsiders. Five of her Cabinet were Jewish. As one of them, her chief problem-solver Lord Young, noted, 'in the 1980s we became an entrepreneurial society, and part of that was the turning of sport, especially football, into business. Irving and David went into football the way others went into property or retail.' In the 1970s, when Young had been the head of a London property specialising in building industrial estates, he occasionally went to watch QPR with Scholar. A decade later, when the latter tried to break the BBC/ITV hold over televised football, Young invited him to a meeting at the Department of Trade and Industry. '[Young] made it clear,' wrote Scholar, 'that his solution would be to try and promote some form of competition by finding a cable or satellite company that was prepared to bid. He asked me whether I knew Michael Green of Carlton Communications. I had known him since the age of seven, when we used to sit next to each other in Sunday morning Hebrew classes.'

As someone who became a left-wing activist in the 1980s, and who is proud of his tribe's longstanding involvement in the British Labour movement, I found it galling, for a while, to watch Thatcherism's appropriation of Jewish entrepreneurialism. But Harold Macmillan's snide observation that Thatcher's first cabinet contained 'more Old Estonians than Old Etonians' produced a slight mellowing on my part. Secretly, I felt proud that the children and grandchildren of the immigrant generation were getting up the establishment's noses. Still, it was hard to accept that Jewish allegiances were changing. Twenty-six of the twenty-eight Jewish MPs in the 1945 parliament had represented the Labour Party, and the political alignment of Anglo-Jewry remained distinctly left of centre until the late 1960s. But rapid upward mobility had clearly produced a shift in political preferences, and by 1990, when Thatcher left office, the social geography of the community had completely changed. The Iron Lady had at least challenged the ingrained anti-Semitism of the wealthy land barons who dominated her party. Macmillan, a Tory grandee who was prime minister in the late 1950s and early '60s, often made jokes about Jews and Jewish politicians, derisively calling the Liberal MP Leslie Hore-Belisha 'Horeb Elisha', a jabbing reference to Mount Horeb, where the Ten Commandments were handed down to Moses. Macmillan was one of the Tory parliamentarians who forced Hore-Belisha out of the government in the early 1940s for allegedly conspiring to force Britain into a war on behalf of the Jews on the mainland.

Thatcher, by contrast, had no time for racial bigotry or for those who countenanced it. She was unusually free of even 'the faintest trace of anti-Semitism in her make-up', as Nigel Lawson, her chancellor of the exchequer, wrote in 1992. Alan Clark, a senior Tory politician, wrote in his diaries that some of the old guard, himself included, thought Lawson could not possibly, 'as a Jew', be offered the position of foreign secretary. Lawson's 'Jewish parentage was disqualification enough,' a *Sunday Telegraph* editorial agreed in 1988. When I asked Lord Young about this, he laughed it off – 'typical Alan' – and recalled how Thatcher used to refer to the Jews of Finchley, her constituency, as 'her people'.

Scholar, Bobroff and Dein, like Young, Lawson and Leon Brittan, were the new Thatcherite whizz kids on the block, precursors of the dynamic breed – led by Alan Sugar, David Gold, Danny Fiszman and Daniel Levy – who reaped the benefits of the following decade's football boom.

Scholar, a property developer who made his millions at European Ferries, was, like Dein, a boyishly enthusiastic fan with a trainspotter's knowledge of his club's history. On becoming Spurs chairman in 1982 he instituted football quizzes on the team bus – which he frequently won. As he wrote in his 1992 memoir *Behind Closed Doors*, 'our disenchantment arose from the fact that for a long time, the Spurs board had a reputation for meanness'. As someone who had been hooked on Tottenham ever since his uncle Gerry had taken him to see Arthur Rowe's famous push-and-run-side in 1952, and was besotted with the great Double-winning team of 1961, he craved a return to the expansive brilliance of the 'glory-glory' era. He was fired as much by his love for 'the old East Stand camaraderie and atmosphere' he remembered from his first game – a 2–1 victory over Cardiff – as his desperation to oust the stuffy old guard, the Richardson and Wales families who had run White Hart Lane for decades, 'a rather dull lot, out of touch with the supporters and jealously guarding their inheritance'. A frustrated Scholar felt that: 'With my property expertise I could be of some use to the board. But clearly they did not feel the need for any outside expertise . . . They had not really competed with the other major clubs in the transfer market since Bill Nicholson resigned as manager in 1974. The directors were a very old-fashioned group, and many people took the view that they would rather the team played behind closed doors.' As Bobroff remembers:

> Tottenham had a reputation for not being that keen at board level on Jewish people. Irving had approached the board to try and get involved, and every approach was rebuffed. I can recall one of my uncles, who was friendly with a director at Tottenham. They had done some business together. I don't recall my uncle ever being invited, even on the odd occasion, to the boardroom or the director's box. We faced huge and bitter opposition at the time. So we had to break the door down.

They had both, independently, come to the same conclusion after attending a dispiriting meeting organised by Arthur Richardson, a board member for almost twenty years, in which the seventy-five-year-old chairman unveiled plans for a highly expensive new stand. Having won the FA Cup in 1981, Spurs faced a financial nightmare after the rebuilding of White Hart Lane almost left them penniless. 'That meeting was so appallingly done,' said Bobroff, whose property company Markheath Securities had an executive box at Spurs. 'They had so little proper information. You could see this had all the makings of a full-scale disaster. I went away from it quite concerned that my football club was in the hands of people who didn't have a clue what they were doing. They were in well over their heads.' Worried about the club's massive debt, Scholar had asked a number of awkward questions. These went down badly with Richardson, as did a series of letters offering to help – all of which were ignored.

At the annual general meeting Richardson tried to stop Scholar airing his views. 'He knew I was not a shareholder,' wrote Scholar, 'and felt I was not entitled to ask questions.' After the meeting, the Tottenham manager Keith Burkinshaw told him the financial problems precluded him from signing new players. Scholar acquired a full list of shareholders and wrote to them all, inducing them to sell with a hard cash offer. The main obstacle to overcome was a rule which 'made the Spurs board the cosy closed shop it was [giving] the directors the right, without having to give any reason whatso-ever, not to recognise the registration of shares to anyone they did not approve of'. Scholar's solicitor put him in touch with Jonathan Metliss, a Jewish lawyer and 'a keen football supporter who under-stood my excitement and enthusiasm', who discovered that the board could not stop him buying shares. Scholar's great coup was in persuading Sidney Wale to sell the vast majority of his holding to him. After spending around £600,000 on acquiring proxy voting rights, he then received a call from Bobroff, who told him he'd bought 13 per cent of the company's shares. As a result of Bobroff's purchase, the pair now controlled 50 per cent of the company's shares and were in an unassailable position. 'The board were still saying it didn't matter,' said Bobroff, 'because they were not regis-tering the transfers. The doors were only broken down when I got our solicitors to bring over a big pile of proxies and share-transfer deeds. We only had a discussion after that. That was when the younger Richardson [Geoffrey] said to his father, who was dead against us: "It's over."' At an extraordinary general meeting, Bobroff proposed that the Richardsons and Ken Kennard be removed from the board of directors. The following morning they resigned, and the game was up. 'Everything had happened so quickly, that I found it difficult to take it all in,' wrote Scholar, who was only thirty-two at the time. 'Tottenham had always been my greatest passion: from the days of standing on the terraces as a young boy, to the time I got my first season ticket in the East Stand in Block D, Row D, Seat 117. I can remember the excitement of eventually acquiring a seat in the old West Stand, which in those days was virtually impossible. Now I was the major shareholder.'

Bobroff knew he had arrived when, driving into the ground on his first morning, he received a respectful salute from the gateman. The rest of the day was an eye-opener: the new directors discovered money stuffed into drawers, an unwelcoming attitude by switchboard operators, poor media relations and a lack of tills in the club shop. After selling £5 million of shares, which wiped out the debt in one stroke, they floated Spurs on the Stock Exchange. This was an unprecedented move by a football club, but these were the giddy 1980s, and anything seemed possible; the financial markets were buoyant and there was new money in the City. English football, Scholar recalls, had been: 'a young man's game ruled by old men, a sort of sporting version of China, where you must be at least eighty to be chairman. This was almost the norm at Spurs before I arrived, and after a generation of the Richardsons and the Wales – "Mr Richardson and Mr Wales to you, young man" – the idea of a chairman who was not that much older than the players and a good deal younger than the coaching staff came as a shock'. Scholar had grown up believing that Tottenham were the great aristocrats of north London but was upset to have seen them descend to something more akin to one of the less salubrious locations described in Charles Dickens' *Hard Times*. Mirroring the team's declining fortunes, the White Hart Lane offices were tatty and unprepossessing and in desperate need of a lick of paint. All this would change.

The new Spurs owners were ahead of their time. They diversified into leisurewear, computer systems and merchandising and constructed a row of executive boxes intended to 'elevate the match-day experience'. In trying to make the game more marketable and commercial, they were treated with great suspicion by the butchers, bakers and candlestick-makers who ran the Football League. They upset several of the game's top officials when, not long after taking over, they closed down the Ladies Room at White Hart Lane. 'Women weren't allowed in the football boardrooms,' said Bobroff. 'It was men only. Jewish wives don't appreciate that sort of thing. I remember at Aston Villa, the men were in a room and the women were behind a glass screen at the other end. It was prehistoric, some of it. Those guys, they regarded the boardroom as a good old booze-up where men could be men and talk to each other as men. But you can't have Jewish wives stuck in a room behind a glass screen.'

A breakaway division had first been mooted in 1985, when representatives of the Big Five invited several other clubs to join them in an autonomous Super League that would negotiate its own lucrative television and sponsorship deal. Three years later the quintet attended a secret dinner hosted by ITV mogul Greg Dyke. As Dein looked on, Scholar asked Dyke: 'If we were ever to change things to create a new league, would you buy the television rights?' Dyke had anticipated this question, but wondered, as he would later put it, 'whether they had the nerve to do it'. A brief examination of both men's meteoric ascents would have revealed that neither Scholar nor Dein were lacking in chutzpah.

Surprisingly, up until the 1980s, the pair had never bumped into each other on the north London circuit. They had both played in the same Jewish football league. A pacey right-half, Dein would meet Fynn, one of his Golders Green team-mates, outside the local tube station before every game and dream about starring for Arsenal. He was also a member of the local Maccabi side. He still has a diary, which is in pristine condition, detailing all the matches he ever played in – and all the ones he watched. One entry begins: 'Arsenal lost, what a disgrace, 1–1 half-time.' In another, he has written: 'School starts again. Arsenal 2, Blackpool 3.' He once showed Edwards, the Manchester United chief executive, a section about the 'greatest game I've ever seen . . . Arsenal were 3–0 down to Manchester United at half-time . . . ended up 4–5, all the team played well except for Kelsey.'

Both jet-setting businessmen, Scholar and Dein's horizons were far broader than the blazered old guard's. They both liked to visit football stadiums on their frequent trips abroad. They had both been to America, seen the future – and it worked; in the mid-to-late 1980s, as the terrible disasters at Bradford, Heysel and Hillsborough took their toll, they both advocated a fresh approach to the game based on the US model. While spending his summers at his wife's family home in Florida, Dein had been struck by the way the NFL was marketed: the razzmatazz, food, franchising, merchandising and pre-match entertainment all made the American football game a fun, family-friendly day out. It was this that led to the innovations at Highbury that had so horrified the former establishment. And they were also both impressed with the rebranding of Major League Baseball as 'The Show' – an apt description of today's all-singing, all-dancing, wall-to-wall-Sky-TV Premier League.

But it was Scholar who took the first big leap, recruiting Dein's old team-mate Fynn, now a director at Saatchi and Saatchi, to run an innovative marketing campaign. Fynn's brainwave was a television advert in which the Spurs team, cult comedian Peter

Cook and an ordinary fan – 'Mrs Ridlington' – urged supporters to 'come and join the 35,000'. Just over 35,000 fans turned up at White Hart Lane for the next home game against Coventry – the highest attendance of the season. 'Irving was the one of the first guys to see the value of television and merchandising,' said Fynn. 'He went too far too fast at times. He applied his business acumen in a way that other chairmen had not. 'They smell the liniment and their brains go,' he once told me. But he was also a huge Spurs fan. When Tottenham introduced their clubcall, the joke went around that they were the club at the top of the national list because, wherever he was in the world, Irving would call the line.

Scholar's signings on the pitch – Chris Waddle, Paul Gascoigne and Gary Lineker – reflected a swashbuckling approach intended to restore the glory, glory days of Nicholson's 1961 double team. Scholar had pulled out all the stops to sign Gascoigne in 1988, stealing him from under Alex Ferguson's nose. In his 1999 autobiography, Ferguson claimed Gascoigne was wooed into signing for Tottenham after the club had bought a house for his impoverished family. Marketing guru Edward Freedman, another inspired appointment, watched as Scholar desperately tried to bring the Newcastle player to the club: 'Everyone knew Gascoigne was the player. But we didn't really have any money at Tottenham. Irving Scholar fought like mental to get him. Finally, at the board meeting, they said: "Yes, go for him," and he said to me afterwards: "They said I could go and buy him. They think I'm going to go into a supermarket and buy a tin of beans." Liverpool, Man United wanted him. But Irving was like a dog with a bone. He got Gascoigne to come by cajoling, by persuasion, by not giving up.'

Scholar's off-the-pitch signings – commercially astute businessmen like Fynn and Freedman – were equally imaginative. Six years after

Freedman's arrival, Spurs were turning over more in merchandise than any other club, including Manchester United. Freedman, who introduced a rapid retail expansion, cutting back on licensing and cranking up the manufacture of Tottenham's own goods, remembers:

> Irving was slightly mad, but he was one of the visionaries of football. He was way ahead of anyone else. He walked into Tottenham and he thought: 'This is ridiculous.' The shop was run by an ex-footballer who'd broken his leg. He was a nice guy, but there was no commercial, marketing or PR nous. The football world was a very closed world. Their main thing was that they play football on Saturday. I had expertise in an area they didn't have expertise in. Irving was very interested in what I was doing. I virtually became his right-hand man.

Freedman, the grandson of a Lithuanian immigrant, had grown up in Stamford Hill. His father, who had been on Orient's books, employed Lew Lazar, Mark Lazarus' brother, and he followed the boxer around the country with his friend Edmund Freudman, who was eventually signed by Chelsea, but left after refusing to play on a Saturday. Freedman's games master, the Nazi refugee Yogi Mayer, was a big influence on him, but after playing for the QPR youth team he decided to pursue a career in the fashion industry. He built up a chain of men's clothes shops and ran InterCity plc's retail operation before being headhunted by Scholar.

> I got on well with Irving. We were both big Spurs fans and liked similar stuff: salt beef sandwiches, Jewish jokes, football . . . But he liked my merchandising ideas most of all. We took merchandising to another planet. We got the players going out

onto the pitch in sweatshirts which we then sold in the shop and put in the programme, starting a mail-order operation. We were flying. People didn't understand what was going on. Spurs were so far ahead it was embarrassing. I found it funny, though, how David [Dein] used to pick Irving's brain. I'd be in the office with Irving, and David would phone him up and ask him his opinion on something. I said: 'Irving, get real.' 'What do you mean?' he said. 'All that man ever does is phone you and get information from you, and all you do is get zero from him.' The next day he rang up David and said he'd had enough of it. But you're talking about revolutionaries when you're talking about Irving and David. They were both thinking on a level people like me could relate to. They were both visionaries.

In May 1992, after deciding the revolution would be televised, all twenty-two First Division clubs resigned from the Football League to take advantage of a £262 million Sky rights deal. Irving, however, was nowhere to be seen. While Dein had been busy picking his brains and reinventing himself as one of the game's most influential movers and shakers, Scholar had fallen out with Bobroff after running up crippling debts to finance a new stand. With Barcelona threatening to repossess Lineker, Tottenham's star striker, Scholar turned to Robert Maxwell, who then reneged on a £1.1 million loan. City banks had to ask the accountant and corporate troubleshooter David Buchler to rescue the club, and, after going through five different backers, manager Terry Venables finally found one who would do the deal: Alan Sugar.

'That Irving Scholar made mistakes one cannot doubt,' wrote his biographer, Mihir Bose, 'but his greatest fault has been to love Tottenham and football to excess. His crime was to be too enthusiastic for change in a world which sees all change as the devil's work and all ideas for reform as a disguised grab for money . . . He was always pushing against the tide, and the tide in football always runs against change.'

According to Buchler, Sugar brought financial serenity to Tottenham. 'There was no calm in 1991,' he said. 'There were the receivers, then Paul Gascoigne had to be sold. But it all, eventually, calmed down, thanks to Alan. He didn't have the football vision that Irving Scholar had, and I don't think he'd claim to have that. But financially he put the club on a decent footing.'

And so it was Sugar, not Scholar, who represented Tottenham at the historic Royal Lancaster Hotel meeting in May 1992 – and cast the vote that completed the required two-thirds majority for a new, breakaway Premiership. In a phone call his autobiography would later suggest went 'down in the annals of football history', Sugar, whose company was the main supplier of satellite dishes to Sky, advised the Murdoch-owned channel to 'blow them [ITV] out of the water' by trumping their rival's bid. Sugar had not only kicked Scholar off the board, he had also banned him from the club. And yet without his visionary predecessor there would have been no Premiership in the first place – and he wouldn't have made a cool £47 million when eventually selling up to Daniel Levy at ENIC.

From Silver to Gold

Leslie Silver decided to bail out of football just as the Golds and the Sugars were getting into their stride. When Leeds won the last ever First Division title in 1992, the club's chairman was hailed as a local fan who, in the tradition of Zussman and Cussins, had run the club he loved out of a sense of civic duty. This was only partly true. Silver was actually born and brought up in Walthamstow. His grandparents had emigrated to London from Poland in 1899, and he had supported Arsenal as a youngster. The son of a craftsman in a clothing factory, he used to stand on the terraces at Highbury, watching his heroes Alex James and Cliff Bastin. At the age of seventeen, he joined the RAF, flying dangerous missions in Halifax bombers. After the war, like so many demobbed soldiers, he was awarded a gratuity – which he used as a starter fund for the Silver Paint and Lacquer Company.

I left school at fourteen, which we did in those days. I worked in the clothing factory, where my father also worked. When the bombs started falling at the back end of 1940, one of the first raids that we had knocked this factory out in the East End of London. We moved up to Leeds, on the assumption that the war would finish in six months; then we'd be back in the East End. But we never went back. I wanted to get involved in the war. You chaps don't understand it. Your generation – thank goodness – hasn't suffered the experiences that our families suffered. I hated fascism and I wanted to do my part. In the RAF, we had to fly 250 hours of operational missions. When I returned on leave, my father never showed any emotion. When I told him I'd completed my 250 hours of missions, he closed his eyes, leaned his head against the wall and said: 'Thank God for that.' When I went home on leave during the war, an uncle said: 'What are you going to do when you get demobbed?' I said, 'Well, I can tell you one thing. I'm not going back into the East End clothes trade.'

I interviewed Silver just after Manchester City had won the 2012 championship, and the contrast between his title-winning squad, which had cost just £8 million to assemble, and mega-rich City, whose Arab owners had spent £930 million, could not have been more glaring. During the 2011–12 season, City's wayward Argentinian star Carlos Tevez had been on £250,000 a week; twenty years earlier, Jon Newsome, the Yorkshire-born defender whose goal against Sheffield United helped Leeds win the League, had taken home a mere £400.

Like Zussman, Silver was a moderately wealthy businessman who emotionally, as well as financially, invested in his club, selling his paint company and risking his house. He had built up a business empire with factories in Yorkshire, London and Newcastle and renamed the company Kalon Ltd. In 1985 he acquired Leyland Paints, which grew to become one of the largest paint manufacturers in Europe. When Cussins invited him on to the Leeds board in the early 1980s, football wasn't viewed as a money-making enterprise or an investment opportunity. Howard Wilkinson's side had won promotion to the top flight and only two years later become League champions, thanks to the increasingly old-fashioned virtues of graft, organisation and determination. Silver was, himself, the very model of an old-school chairman, not a million miles away from the Hill-Woods' version. He viewed the role as a civic duty; he was opposed to directors being paid and looked on in horror at the financial doping that was beginning to creep into the game. When he called it a day, in 1996, a new breed of young, thrusting modernisers were coming through, and the writing was on the wall. 'Now you are talking of millions not making a difference,' he said on his retirement. 'It's time for new blood, people who are more in touch with these new, extraordinary, economic realities.' A year earlier, Brian Winston, after running Orient for twenty-three years, had also stepped down. 'People like Harry, Leslie and me were hungry,' said Winston, 'we had fought for our place. That's the thing that pushes you all the way through. I think getting involved in football was a way for Jews of our generation to say: "Look, we're one of the crowd here."'

· According to Winston, his generation's tough childhoods had motivated their business success. But the new generation suffered similar hardships. David Gold, chairman of Birmingham City before taking over his beloved West Ham with David Sullivan, was born in Stepney a few years before the war and raised in abject poverty; his father, an East End criminal known locally as 'Goldy', spent time in prison during his childhood. This was the era of legendary gangsters like the Richardsons and the Krays, when Cable Street and the Old Kent Road were no-go areas. In his autobiography, Gold admitted he 'was ashamed of being Jewish because of the perception and the insults. It was bad enough being poor, having no shoes and no money, and being cold and hungry, but then to have someone spit on you because you are a Jew is devastating.'

He remembered a friend, Sammy Warzofski, being picked on at school because he looked Jewish and went to *shul* every week. Once, after playing for West Ham boys against Norwich, he decided to eat ham sandwiches so as 'not to stand out from the others'. At his grandmother's house, he looked forward to her 'glorious chicken soup, a fantastic treat . . . [she] would produce huge bowls of his nectar'. Having escaped persecution in Poland, she never talked about her father – who had committed suicide, 'driven to despair by anti-Semitism.'

For the young, football-mad Gold, sport was a way out of the ghetto. 'To be Jewish in the East End of London during and shortly after the war was difficult,' he wrote. 'Football was my escape from the poverty trap . . . sport turned our lives around: [his brother] Ralph with his boxing and me with my football.' He played for West Ham boys and was on the books at Fulham. His father, however, refused to sign the forms that would have turned him into an Upton

Park professional, and he was forced to complete a brickie apprenticeship before building successful businesses in property and porn. Not everybody has been entirely sympathetic to Gold's struggle to transcend his difficult start in life. 'If I see another David Gold interview on the poor East End Jewish boy done good,' the former Crystal Palace Chairman Simon Jordan once declared, 'I'll impale myself on one of his dildos.'

When Alan Sugar took over Spurs, in 1991, his wife Ann, speaking on behalf of many Tottenham fans, asked him: 'Since when have you been interested in football?' Sugar's father and uncle had occasionally taken him to White Hart Lane as a kid, but in building Amstrad into a £308 million-a-year business he had little time to follow his boyhood team. He may not have shared Gold's early enthusiasm for the game but *The Apprentice* star, the son of an East End tailor, also rose from humble beginnings to go on to greater success. Brusque and pugnacious, he grew up on a Hackney council estate 'from a very poor family, where life was all about not having any money, not having anything and working very, very hard. I didn't want to have to live that way. While I was at school, I was making more money, selling bits and pieces, than my father was earning.' It was at school, when not flogging scraps of material out of a pram, that he also first experienced anti-Semitism.

Within minutes [of his first day], I heard racial remarks about Jews. 'Hey, Charlie, tell that bloody Jew to get out my way – he ain't playing with us.' 'The fucking Yids are using the goalposts – tell 'em to piss off.' It was the first time I'd heard the expression 'Yids' and I couldn't quite understand what was going on. When I went home that night . . . I was traumatised . . . The guys with whom I'd joined Joseph Priestley weren't

Jewish, but as time went on they started to recognise the fact that I was, and regrettably some of them became racists.

Although he had saved Spurs from the twin threats of liquidation and Maxwell, his treatment of the club as a business venture alienated many fans. Sacking their idol Venables and then, after a succession of dismal failures, hiring Graham, a star player and former manager of bitter rivals Arsenal, only increased the hostility. 'The thing about football people,' he said, 'is they don't like change. They tend to get stuck in their ways.' In reducing the massive debt and putting Spurs on a sound financial footing, he argued, he had merely applied the nous imbibed from the markets of his childhood. Like Gold, he had never forgotten where he came from: the East End ghetto. It was here, in these noisy, babbling streets, haunted by the synagogues, cemeteries, Russian vapour baths, shops, theatres, markets, tobacconists, bookmakers and jewellers of a vanished community-in-exile, that he learned – like Silver, Zussman, Lazarus, Silkman, Gold and a host of other Jewish boys made good – how to live on his wits, negotiate a good deal and find new ways of generating money. Brought up on the spiel of stall-holders, he could always identify the *kibitzers* at White Hart Lane: 'There's a lot of Jewish supporters and they often curse their own team. You can hear from the tone of their voices that they're Jewish . . . they will be the first to say "waste of money" if, God forbid, a player doesn't perform . . . Jews, bless 'em, are the greatest critics on God's earth.'

10

The Money Men:
When Roman Captured the Holy Grail

CLAVANE'S CIGARETTES

R. ABRAMOVICH (CHELSEA)

'Roman Abramovich has parked his Russian tanks on our lawn and is firing £50 notes at us.'

David Dein

Roman Abramovich: The Accidental Pioneer

In 2012, Chelsea became champions of Europe for the first time in their history after a penalty shoot-out victory over Bayern Munich. Their quest to win the Champions League had begun nine years earlier, when they beat Zilina in the qualifying round, their first European match after Roman Abramovich's takeover. Eight managers, 3,193 days, 101 games and around £600 million later, captain John Terry finally got his hands on the big silver thing, lifting it towards the Munich sky to complete one of the most unlikely triumphs in the history of European football.

*

Whilst watching the Chelsea–Bayern match, a phrase that, as a good, secular, assimilated English Jew I thought I would never hear myself use, suddenly popped out of my subconscious. Would a Chelsea victory, I speculated, be 'good for the Jews'? It was a question my grandparents' generation would frequently ask, eventually to the point of self-parody. Any political, social, cultural or sporting event, from the election of a government to a new scientific discovery, would be judged according to this criterion. I always considered it a nonsense, a product of a narrow-minded, over-anxious, insecure, residual-ghetto mentality. And yet I found myself asking the very same question on the night of 19 May 2012. Like Tebbit's attitude to international cricket matches, it seemed important to take sides.

I had just read an article about how Jews had been written out of Bayern's history and how the club's pre-war past had come to be associated, in the German mind, with beer halls and Brownshirts. Given Chelsea's Jewish ownership, it suddenly dawned on me that I might have to put aside a longstanding loathing, dating back to the 1970 FA Cup final, when the flashy Londoners kicked lumps out of the Mighty Whites – who, admittedly, retaliated in kind – to cheer on Roberto Di Matteo's boys. In pre-Nazi Germany, Bayern had been run by the businessman Kurt Landauer and coached by Dori Kürschner and Kálmán Konrád, all Jews. Richard Dombi, a Viennese Jew who led the club to their first championship in 1932, introduced an innovative youth training system and pushed for professionalism. After Hitler's 'Aryanisation' of the game, Bayern's members, players and administrators were forced to leave; many were later murdered. Landauer was arrested on *Kristallnacht* in 1938 and briefly held in Dachau. In 2001, a journalist asking about Bayern's Jewish history was told by a club press officer: 'We are not interested in these things.'

My reflex action was to support Chelsea anyway, regardless of such a backstory. Although I hate flag-waving, I always, as a rule, cheer on the English team – even Manchester United – against foreign opposition. This unthinking patriotism is, no doubt, a symptom of my own over-anxious, insecure, residual-ghetto mentality. For, as I realised on that night, I might not be a typical English Jew but I am clearly a product of my community's long-standing Anglophilia. I was born in England, as were my parents and all four of my grandparents. Although I take issue with him on the fundamental question of Jewish sportsmanship, a concept he no doubt sees as oxymoronic, I concur with Howard Jacobson's take on national identity. 'When Henry V appeals to "you good yeomen, whose limbs were made in England"', the novelist wrote in an *Independent* column, 'I always think he is addressing me. And when he speaks of "gentlemen in England, now a-bed who will think themselves accursed they were not there upon Saint Crispin's day", I still fancy he is addressing me. Because, though I wasn't in fact there, I'd like to have been.' I would argue that it is precisely this desire to be English, to be more English than the English in fact, that explains the role Jewish outsiders, from Bookman to Abramovich, have played in English football over the past 100 years. From the turn of the twentieth century, when anglicisers set up the Jewish Lads' Brigade, the Brady Street Boys' Club and a Jewish football league to steer potentially disaffected youth on a straight and narrow path, to the turn of the twenty-first century, when Roman invaded Britain, Mr Football Jew has attempted to prove himself both on and off the pitch, at times incorporating discrimination as a kind of incentive.

Besides, the more I read about that Bayern backstory, the more I noticed the intriguing parallels between the Landauer and Abramovich eras. I would never dream of making the case for the latter as a football visionary, but without intending it he has become a pioneer of sorts. Since his helicopter landed in London in 2003, the Premier League has become the envy of the world. And there is no doubt that one of the reasons he spent £600 million on Chelsea was the 'epiphany' he experienced at that year's Champions League quarter final between Manchester United and Real Madrid, a few months before buying the west London club. 'I fell in love with the beautiful game,' he explained, in one of his rare interviews. Landauer had a similar life-changing experience in 1919, watching MTK Budapest, another 'Jewish club', playing stylish, intelligent, quick-passing football. He spent the next decade recruiting as many of that team as possible, all of them Jewish. This 'foreign invasion' helped transform his club into a bastion of enlightened values and good football. Abramovich's relentless pursuit of the European Cup has been well documented, but his other mantra has been: ditch the dull defensive football and start playing the beautiful game.

The Abramovich effect has, understandably given the forces of obscene greed and predatory selfishness it has unleashed, been blamed for many of the ills of the modern game. But it has also helped shatter one of the enduring myths of English football, indeed of Englishness: its insularity. A leitmotif of this book has been the Jewish community's extreme anxiety to win acceptance in its adopted country. It is a theme which has defined all sections of this fractious and unruly tribe, from working-class, East End football fanatics to middle-class, central European football fanatics, from Ashkenazi eastern Europeans to Sephardic Israelis, from the established banking families of the nineteenth century to the foreign investors of the early twenty-first century. At the same time, every successive 'Jewish invasion' has contributed to English football's metamorphosis from a homogenous, working-class game to a global, multicultural entertainment. To adapt Mikes, just as Jews were becoming true Englishmen, the whole country turned alien. In the fifties, the following joke did the rounds in the community:

Two Jewish émigrés bump into each other.
   'How's your health?'
   'Wonderful.'
   'Family?'
   'Thriving.'
   'Business?'
   'Booming.'
   'So why the long face?'
   'I'll never fit in here. I will never be accepted.'
   'So, get some proper English clothes. Go to Savile Row. You'll fit in then.'
   Next time they meet the first man is dressed like an English aristocrat.
   'Well done,' said his friend, 'But why still with the long face? Health all right?'
   'It's good.'

'Family?'

'Fine.'

'Business?'

'Couldn't be better.'

'So, what is it?'

'Well,' said the first man, 'We lost the Empire.'

Abramovich's arrival undoubtedly speeded up this transformation from emblem of Empire to the League of Nations. On 15 August 1992, the first day of the first ever Premier League season, there were only eleven foreign players. Twenty years later there were over 300, representing sixty-six countries. Unsurprisingly for a league televised in 200 countries, half of its clubs are foreign-owned.

I suppose it is one thing to give homegrown Jewish entrepreneurs their due, quite another to justify the obsession of an oligarch who benefited from the wild, unregulated practices of post-communist Russia and bought his way into the football elite. The Roman invasion launched an era of billionaire owners, skyrocketing ticket prices and world domination. I know I should be lamenting the loss of football's soul: spiralling wages, an uncompetitive league and a growing feeling of distance from pampered prima donnas who masquerade as committed footballers. But there has been something about his obsessive quest for the game's Holy Grail – previously considered an illusionary goal, a pursuit doomed to failure – which has appealed to me. And, whether intentional or not, his move to London, in 2003, has helped transform English football into a global proposition. Jewish figures are no longer exotic, mysterious oddities – now they are just one tribe amongst many.

Given Abramovich's key role in Chelsea's emergence as a European superpower, there has – unsurprisingly – been a shift in attitude down west London way. Chelsea fans simply cannot believe their luck. At times, like the rest of the country, they have baulked at his autocratic methods, especially his ruthless disposal of managers. But they remain eternally grateful for his largesse. What, to adapt the famous Monty Python sketch, has Roman ever done for us? Apart from winning club football's most glittering prize – alongside three Premier League titles, three FA Cups and two Carling Cups.

The self-styled 'Roman Army' no longer, at least openly in football grounds, taunts the 'Yid Army' up the road; anti-Semitism has become the exception rather than the rule at the Bridge. In the 1980s, the stadium housed a nasty cadre of racists and was targeted as a recruiting ground by neo-Nazi elements. This was a common occurrence at many football grounds, including my own spiritual home. At Elland Road, it didn't make a blind bit of difference that the club, then the most feared in Europe, had a strong Jewish connection. In fact, when things went belly up after Revie left, there was frequent anti-Semitic chanting in the Kop directed at Cussins. 'I remember Manny getting some anti-Semitic remarks when he wasn't making things happen,' Silver told me. 'I thought that if Leeds weren't successful the Jewish community would get hammered. When we won the championship, I was very popular as a Yorkshireman. But when things went wrong, I was criticised by some fans as a Jew.'

Like Bookman, English football's first Jew, Abramovich was immediately cast as 'the Other' on arrival, a shadowy figure who had emerged from a dark, shady, unknowable east European world. Born in the bleak north Russian town of Syktyvkar, both of Abramovich's parents had died by the time he was three. He was taken in by his father's brother Leib and uncle Abram. His family were proud of their Jewish identity, refusing to follow the example of assimilated co-religionists who had recategorised themselves as Russian. He was brought up in Ukhta, a grim Russian outpost, the product of Stalin's

Gulag, built by – mainly Jewish – dissidents. Ukhta's football team was coached by the former Spartak Moscow star Nikolay Starostin; the reason a player of Starostin's stature had ended up at Dinamo Ukhta was because of his anti-Soviet activities. When Abramovich went to university in 1983, Jews were still unable to enter certain academic institutions, and private enterprise was illegal. But after dropping out of college, and being conscripted into the army, he was demobbed into Mikhail Gorbachev's brave new Russia. Glasnost and perestroika were rapidly transforming society, small businesses were sprouting up all over the country, and there was a mad dash for cash. Abramovich – who had previously outwitted the system by buying cigarettes, perfume, designer jeans and chocolates in Moscow and selling them on to friends in Ukhta – hired a market stall to sell the rubber ducks he made from his small flat. The next few years are a little blurry, but it appears he ended up being ideally placed to make a killing out of the crash privatisation programme that followed the collapse of communism. After becoming part of Yeltsin's inner circle, he joined forces with Boris Berezovsky to take over one of the country's vast oil concerns, Sibneft, and amass the fortune that unleashed English football's own goldrush.

His motives were endlessly discussed: Chelsea was his plaything, his insurance against a political backlash by the Russian government, a way of diverting attention away from his meteoric rise to riches. But, whether it was his intent or not, one of his legacies has been, like the previous Russian-Jewish invasion 100 years earlier, to broaden the game's horizons. Abramovich has never made a big deal of his Jewishness. Indeed, he hasn't made a big deal of anything in his nine years at the club. He has given only a handful of on-the-record interviews, although his inner circle has let it be known that he is proud of his religious heritage and has donated to several worthy charities. It would be ridiculous, of course, to compare

Abramovich's story with the plight of the penniless, Yiddish-speaking Bookmans who fled the pogroms at the turn of the previous century. Yet he and his fellow oligarchs – Mikhail Khodorovsky, Boris Berezovsky, Vladimir Gusinsky and Mikhail Friedman – were part of a generation that survived persecution in a country where anti-Semitism was virtually written into the constitution. Early in their careers, their routes to advancement had been blocked by institutionalised discrimination. In official documents Jews remained the only group to be identified by race rather than nationality. Many of them found ways to work around the system. As the historian Eugene Satanovsky noted, 'even with the lifting of mass political repression, official anti-Semitism as a policy remained in the Eighties, which caused Russian Jews to create their own informal subculture'.

The story goes that, while flying over the River Thames in his private helicopter, Abramovich suddenly spotted a beautiful football stadium. 'Who plays there?' he enquired, completely entranced. 'Chelsea,' the pilot replied. The oligarch liked the view so much he bought the club. 'In fact,' said Keith Harris, who spent the next four days in negotiations with Team Roman, 'the truth is slightly different. The ground he actually saw was Craven Cottage. He said it looked very beautiful, being by the River Thames.' In the fifteen seconds it had taken the pilot to respond to Abramovich's question, the helicopter was already flying over Stamford Bridge. And so it was Chelsea, not Fulham, who were transformed from west London under-achievers into European champions. 'He and his advisers, several of whom were Jewish, weren't different to the businessmen I knew,' reflected Harris. 'I am not Jewish but I have operated for a long time in a world with many Jewish businessmen. And, of course, I tried a bit of chutzpah. Which worked, by the way. I had learned at the feet of masters.' Harris' chutzpah was to get one of the world's richest men to pay well over the price for a club that was £80 million in debt and, it emerged later, on the verge of financial collapse; Abramovich eventually agreed to cover the debt and pay another £60 million.

Chelsea's leverage came from their prospective new owner's desperate need to increase his profile in the West. When Vladimir Putin, a president with old-style Soviet roots, took over from Abramovich's friend Boris Yeltsin he was expected to undo the oligarchs' wealth. Asked what advice he would give to young people aspiring to make money in Russia, Abramovich answered: 'Do not imagine that you will never go to jail.' Once, when he was out shopping in London, the car he was travelling in backfired; he immediately hit the floor, fearful he was being shot at. As Harris says: 'Roman liked London. He had thought about Arsenal – no stadium – and Tottenham – Daniel Levy gave him a crazy price – and so he called Chelsea. I went to see him and his advisers, with Ken Bates and Trevor Birch, on Friday. Chelsea, who I represented, said they'd had this approach from someone they'd never heard of. But they'd checked him out, and he was good for the money. The deal was done on Tuesday after four days of intensive work. Roman never said a word, though. He was completely expressionless throughout.'

Since that United–Real encounter in 2003, Abramovich has been in awe of the Champions League. 'It's the one piece of the jigsaw he doesn't have,' an associate explained before the triumph over Bayern, 'and in his world everything should be complete.' In 2009, on a pre-season tour to the United States, when asked what Abramovich had told him he wanted the team to win that season, Terry replied: 'He wants to win everything.'

In the same way that horse-racing was once the sport of kings, so football is now the sport of oligarchs, sheikhs and poultry giants.

Owning a Premier League club, especially one based in posh west London, with a stadium less than three miles from Buckingham Palace, is the equivalent of owning a good-quality racehorse in the Victorian and Edwardian eras. In 1898, a leading racing writer observed that the Rothschild banking family had adapted 'themselves to the fashions and customs of the land' by cultivating 'the social arts' and extending 'influence in the world of society and sport'. In his analysis of early twenty-first-century Jewish sports moguls, Edward Shapiro noted that 'owning a sports team has become a trophy for wealthy businessmen – self-made individuals who are often psychologically insecure with their status in the social and psychological pecking order. The ownership of a team indicates that one has arrived and is worthy of recognition by peers.' Now worth around £11 billion, Abramovich has sixteen homes, seven cars, six firms, four jets and an armada of luxury yachts – but Chelsea remain his prize possession.

From the Maven to the Mystic

Just before Roman came to Britain, it was predicted that the Premier League bubble was about to burst. Out-of-control wages, and the influx of overseas stars, were beginning to be reined in. Within months, however, his roubles had revitalised – rivals would say distorted – the market. His arrival not only enticed his fellow mega-rich foreign investors into English football, it allowed some of the new industries springing up on the game's periphery – public relations, marketing, kit suppliers, merchandise manufacturers and a huge array of betting companies – to expand, encouraging those middle-men who had previously been on the game's margins to play a more central role. One immediate beneficiary was Pini Zahavi, who, since his button-holing of Robinson at the start of the New Age, had gone on to great things. It was, in fact, the Israeli who introduced Abramovich to Chelsea in the first place and, following a £111 million spending spree on players, picked up a cool £5 million for his troubles.

The rise of the Zahavi-esque middle-man was not to the liking of club owners, many of whom attacked this new breed of agents as mercenary outsiders. Sugar and Gold, themselves once castigated in such terms, railed against the 'predators' and 'vultures' who were putting profit before tradition.

Although Zahavi's ascent preceded the advent of the Premier League – the first transfer he officially oversaw was Barry Silkman's from Manchester City to Maccabi Tel Aviv a year after the Cohen deal – the Chelsea deal confirmed his reputation as one of football's most influential figures.

Silkman says:

Pini was, when I met him, a journalist who had been commandeered by the owner of Maccabi Tel Aviv to find a player who could offer something different. He was told about me being a Jewish player and watched me for a week before signing me up. When I was at Man City, the manager, Malcolm Allison, suddenly called me into his office one day and said there's some bloke who wants to talk to me about a move abroad. I was thinking Spain or Italy, but then here was this guy from Israel offering me three months in Haifa. So I went on loan to Maccabi for three months. After I retired I became an agent. Many of the agents I know like football, but, as I've often said to them, they're clueless. What they do have, of course, is a Jewish head for business. They are very, very good at business. Pini really knows his stuff. He is a maven.

The Cohen transfer was Zahavi's big break, giving him an 'in' at the top English clubs. 'The Liverpool deal was a very important one for me,' he said. 'It was when I discovered the commercial side of football.' The word maven comes from Hebrew, via Yiddish, and was popularised by Malcolm Gladwell in his bestseller *The Tipping Point*. It means, in this context, someone who accumulates knowledge of players, clubs and football markets and passes it on to others. At a Euro '96 game, Zahavi marked Alex Ferguson's card about an unknown Czech Republic player, declaring: 'He's ready for a big performance.' As if on cue, and to Ferguson's great astonishment, Karel Poborsky lobbed Portugal goalkeeper Vitor Baia to score the goal of the tournament. Within a month the winger was at Old Trafford. Zahavi's first major English deal in the big-money era was Berkovic's move from Maccabi Haifa to West Ham United in 1997. On a visit to see Berkovic at Upton Park he bumped into Rio Ferdinand – and moved in to represent the young defender. Two years after being sold to Leeds for £18 million, Ferdinand arrived at Old Trafford in a £30-million move. 'The fact that soccer is a global game now means it is essential clubs have good contacts,' explained United director Maurice Watkins. 'Pini has those contacts. He has correspondents in every major footballing country feeding him information on players and helping fix things.' In Zahavi's own words:

> Souness, Dalglish, Terry Venables, Ron Atkinson – they all became good friends of mine. They saw me as a person who knows football, not as a journalist. I had a deep friendship with the players and some managers. With some I was even soulmates. They saw how much I understand football. In England there were many managers back then who didn't know European players. They didn't even publish the results of

European leagues in English papers. It was an isolated island. They didn't know about European or world football. So managers needed my help with this.

The Israeli super-agent cultivated an extensive network of contacts all over the world – including Moscow, where he befriended Abramovich – setting up some of the biggest transfer fees in football history. He introduced the young French-Israeli Sacha Gaydamak to buy Portsmouth from the previous owner, Milan Mandaric, in 2006. He was involved in bringing Avram Grant to Pompey – and then to Chelsea. One of his best English contacts was the Jewish agent Jonathan Barnett, who introduced him to Chelsea chief executive Trevor Birch. The sale of the club had first been mooted when the three sat down for lunch at Les Ambassadeurs, a swanky restaurant in Mayfair. Two years later, Barnett's role in the Ashley Cole tapping-up affair brought to light the secrecy and skulduggery of the agent's world; he was found guilty of two misconduct charges after Cole, his client, met Chelsea boss José Mourinho while still an Arsenal player. Both Barnett and Zahavi were at the meeting – the latter going unpunished because he is not registered as an agent in England. Since setting up the Stellar Group with the young property developer David Manasseh in 1994, Barnett's business has snowballed; today they have a client base of 500 sportsmen and women and offices in Africa and South America. An aggressive numbers man, who combined driving a hard bargain with a love of the high life, Barnett's client-list has included Glen Johnson, Phil Jagielka, Darren Bent, Peter Crouch, Wayne Bridge, Ledley King and Louis Saha.

When Chelsea chairman Ken Bates was looking for a buyer, Abramovich was almost beaten at the post by another foreign investor. Just before the Barnett–Birch–Zahavi meeting, Bates had been involved in lengthy negotiations with Mel Goldberg, who was acting on behalf of a Venezuelan consortium. Goldberg, an Arsenal season-ticket holder and sports lawyer, had received an introduction fee for bringing Inter Milan star Dennis Bergkamp to Highbury in the 1990s. His claim to fame was his successful defence of Bruce Grobbelaar, John Fashanu and Hans Segers in the 1997 match-fixing trial. Brought up in the East End, he became one of the country's first sports lawyers after inviting some important new friends to his wedding during the 1970 World Cup. As Goldberg says of himself:

I was a decent footballer, I played a lot of sport and I was a sports nut. I still am. When the football season ends I stare at a blank screen, screaming. My father, who was in the *schmatter* business, was fanatically keen on football and a big Chelsea fan and he took me to see them one week and Arsenal the next. I fell in love with the team in red. I can name the great Arsenal teams of 1950 and 1970. I went to Mexico, in 1970, to watch the World Cup and got married in a hotel. It was a total coincidence, but anybody who was anybody in football was there, including the managers of Arsenal and Chelsea, Bertie Mee and Dave Sexton. Bertie Mee gave Isobel, my wife, away. The witnesses were Charlie Cooke, Billy Wright and Danny Blanchflower. Geoff Hurst and his wife were there, as was Bobby Moore and his wife. This is how I got into football professionally. I was now able to pick up a phone and call the managers. I became a friend of Dave Sexton.

In those days, sports law was not a big business. Footballers didn't earn much money, relative to now. They tended to get their dads or brothers to be their agents. I started to specialise in sports law after I worked in America for three years. I could see how the business operated in sport. Sport was big business for lawyers. I knew it would happen here.

One of the first lawyers to be propelled into the public consciousness was Mel Stein, who qualified as a solicitor in 1969 and began representing sportsmen and women eleven years later. He acted for the great Geordie trinity of Chris Waddle, Alan Shearer and Paul Gascoigne. With the accountant Len Lazarus, he masterminded the 'selling' of Gascoigne, one of the most talented players of his generation. After registering the name 'Gazza' as a trademark, the merchandising plan they devised – which included a boot and clothes deal, videos, a record contract, a poster magazine, an autobiography, a Christmas calendar, a computer game and a T-shirt – grossed the Italia '90 golden boy £1 million in one season, a phenomenal amount to earn in the era before all the glitz and wealth that the premiership dragged in its wake.

In elevating Gascoigne into the big time with Spurs and then Lazio, Stein and Lazarus had set the template for propelling future celebrity superstars – like Eric Cantona, David Beckham, Cristiano Ronaldo and Wayne Rooney – into the corporate-marketing stratosphere. Gazza might have got away, but the rest of these players all ended up at the richest club in the world. The catalyst of Manchester United's commercial success was Martin Edwards' appointment of Edward Freedman as managing director in 1992. During a Christmas match between Spurs and United, Irving Scholar had been unable to resist telling his friend Edwards about the Freedman revolution. According to Freedman, 'Irving was quite naive. He was very proud of what we'd achieved. One of his big problems was he always gave out too much information. At times, his heart ruled his head. Martin knew about me, and what we'd done, but not the extent of it. People didn't understand what we were doing.

At the end of the afternoon, Irving says to me: "Edward, how much have we taken this week in the shop?" It was a ridiculous thing to say. I said a figure and it was probably ten times the amount Manchester United had taken. Martin's ears pricked up.'

Over the next six years, with Freedman at the helm as managing director, United became the most powerful brand in world football. He was hailed as 'Manchester United's marketing genius' by *Business Week* and 'football's merchandising guru' by *The Economist*. Freedman recounts:

> With Eric Cantona, that was the first time I saw player power. And what I did was embrace it. I said to Cantona's people: 'If you're going to do a book, come to me first.' They'd ask if they could use the United logo, and I'd say, 'No.' He was our player. So we did a deal. Videos were coming, and they were very popular. We took everyone inside, in house, and we did our own videos and production. Alex [Ferguson] was fantastic. He could see what I was doing. He had a similar sort of background to me. He was quite anti-it to start with – you know 'Don't take the players away from me' – but eventually he'd say to people: 'Edward's a good guy,' which from Alex was really something. The football club used to be run by the managers. They were the guv'nor. And that stopped. Alex looked after his thing, I looked after mine.
>
> I was the highest-paid member of staff at United – apart from the players. Paddy Crerand's son asked Martin Edwards in a pub: 'Who're we going to sign?' And Martin said: 'The best signing I've made is Edward Freedman.' And Crerand's son said: 'Who the fuck does he play for?' Martin meant it.

By dramatically expanding the domestic retail operation and creating new wholesale, mail order, publishing and international networks, Freedman increased the club's annual merchandising turnover from £1.2 million to £28 million in the five years between 1992 and 1997. By 2003, Dein, now in charge of commercial matters at Highbury, was becoming increasingly worried about the spending power of Arsenal's main rivals. Freedman had put United in a different league – and now here was Abramovich, threatening to elevate the west London upstarts into a completely different universe. Something had to be done. When he informed Fiszman about a Chelsea bid for Thierry Henry, then one of the world's best players, Fiszman, who had become the club's leading power-broker, simply said: 'Tell them to fuck off.' The Arsenal board finally agreed to a formal meeting with the Stamford Bridge hierarchy – whereupon Dein strode into the room and calmly announced: 'Thierry Henry is not for sale'. However, displays of unity like this were becoming increasingly rare, and the relationship between the two directors was beginning to fracture. The power in London had clearly shifted from north to west; while the Gunners stayed trophyless, the Blues won two successive titles under José Mourinho and added a third under Carlo Ancelotti. As Alex Fynn observed:

There had always been rich men in football but no one had ever spent so much money so quickly to such effect as Roman Abramovich. It was a financial blue tidal wave that the Arsenal board could not have foreseen as they made their bid to keep up with Manchester United. Arsenal found the task beyond them. Only by also throwing money around did once-profitable Manchester United, now debt-ridden as a consequence of the Glazer takeover, manage to eventually prevent the title going to Chelsea for a third consecutive season.

As Arsenal fell further and further behind their Premiership rivals, Dein and Fiszman clashed repeatedly over various issues. 'Two Jews, three opinions' might be an old saying, but it was particularly pertinent in their fierce argument about a new home for the club. Dein, worried about Wenger having enough money to compete with both the United global brand and the Chelsea nouveau riche, favoured a move to King's Cross or the restored Wembley. He was eventually won round to the £357 million Emirates Stadium, Wenger describing it as the biggest decision in Arsenal's history since Chapman's appointment in 1925. But Fiszman took the credit for the move, and Dein became even more marginalised. In fact, the man who had actually identified the site was Dein's friend Antony Spencer. After Eurostar's bid to incorporate the stadium in their plans for a new station went belly up, Spencer, an Arsenal-supporting land agent and a committed follower of Kabbalah – a Jewish mystical school of thought – came up with an ingenious alternative. 'Why not,' he told Fiszman, 'move Arsenal to Arsenal?' After carefully studying the London A–Z, he had dropped an exact-to-scale footprint of the Wembley site onto a council rubbish dump next to Highbury. It had been a perfect fit. Spencer approached some of the landowners on the site pretending to be a leisure-development planner. 'I spoke to every single owner and told them I'd like to buy an option,' he said. 'A Jewish guy, a printer I think, turned around and said: "It's not every day somebody comes in to buy your property surrounded by two stinking rubbish dumps with rats running round everywhere. You'd better sit down and have a cup of tea." I felt at home. That, to me, was a very Jewish thing to say.'

Spencer met up with all 254 businesses and, one by one, managed to persuade them to sell up. Intrigued, Fiszman asked to come along to one of his negotiations. As they got out of the car, Fiszman said to him, 'Antony, haven't you forgotten something?', meaning his briefcase. 'Oh yes,' said Spencer, who went to the boot and took out a baseball bat. Fiszman blanched, remembering that only the previous week Spencer had given him a DVD of *The Sopranos*. Spencer laughed, put the bat – which belonged to his baseball-playing son and just happened to be in his car that morning – back into the boot, retrieved his briefcase and went to their appointment. According to Spencer:

> You always have to have a laugh, Lots of laughs. Danny and I went to these ultra-*frum* printers. It's like a scene from *Fiddler on the Roof*. We go through the whole procedure, make an offer. So the guy says: 'I want to tell you a story. If I invite you to my house on Friday night and we're sitting and we're having a meal and I give you chicken soup and you sit there and you eat the chicken soup and then you're waiting and waiting . . . and nothing. So your offer is like chicken soup. Where's the dessert?' They're a nightmare to deal with, this very big Jewish family, everyone arguing, everyone with a different point of view. So we make them our final offer. And Danny says: 'You've had your chicken soup. Now I've now brought you dessert.' And they accepted.

One freeholder, a Cypriot garage owner called Jimmy Damianos, stubbornly refused to sell up. Without his site, the project was doomed. After being rebuffed for a third time, a distraught Fiszman exclaimed: 'That's it, the stadium is dead.' Spencer wasn't so sure. Recalling the proverb 'All the wisdom in the world could be disseminated while standing on one leg,' he went back in, stood on one leg and waved a copy of the Kabballah at Damianos. Then he said: 'What the fuck do you want me to do, Jimmy?' It transpired that both men, albeit from different religious perspectives, had studied mysticism. Damianos replied 'What should I do?' 'Let us have what we need,' said Spencer. 'Accept the relocation option and then you still have the opportunity to develop if you want.' The garage owner agreed – and the Emirates was finally given the go-ahead.

Baulking at the whopping costs of the project, and its adverse effect on Wenger's team-building, Dein scoured the world of billionaires and identified American tycoon Stan Kroenke as a potential custodian. 'Why don't we want the Americans at the club? Call me old-fashioned,' said Hill-Wood, 'but we don't need his money and we don't want his sort. Our objective is to keep Arsenal English.' When Dein encouraged Kroenke to buy ITV's 9.9 per cent stake for £65 million, he was brutally dismissed, forced to clear his desk and hand over his mobile phone. By the time of the Gunners' next home game, a month before United were crowned English champions in 2007, Dein was gone, the name-plate below his seat in the directors' box having already been removed. At that year's AGM all shareholders were given a copy of the *Arsenal Opus*, a tome celebrating the club's achievements since its formation in 1886. There was no reference whatsoever to Dein's twenty-four-year involvement. Like so many of the Jewish pioneers featured in this book, he had been written out of the history he had helped to make.

A shocked Henry was one of the first to lament his departure, insisting he might follow suit. Henry's commercial representative was Dein's son Darren, who had been mentored by Jerome Anderson. Anderson had been an agent since the 1980s, when he represented Charlie Nicholas and David Rocastle. He was yet another Jewish rags-to-riches story; in twenty-five years he had gone from reading out the half-time scores at Highbury – being stadium announcer had allowed him to nurture several important contacts – to advising the new billionaire owners of Manchester City and Blackburn. In an echo of Zahavi's role at Chelsea, he helped former Thai prime minister Thaksin Shinawatra bring coach Sven-Göran Eriksson and eight foreign stars to City. He subsequently introduced Venky's, the Indian poultry company, to Blackburn Rovers. Anderson's SEM Group is the largest players' agency in Britain, with more than 150 players on its books. 'Apparently they've taken on an agent to advise them on how to run the club, which players to use and to pick,' Alex Ferguson observed after Blackburn manager Sam Allardyce was sacked in 2010. 'It's unbelievable, very odd. It tells you every-thing about the modern game . . . Jerome Anderson couldn't pick his nose.'

11

The Insiders:
When Bernstein Came of Age

'I feel incredibly lucky. I am part of a lucky generation. I think the generation born at the end of the Second World War were fortunate because we had opportunities to better ourselves. My parents never had the chance that I had. Hard work, intelligence – yes. But also luck.'

David Bernstein

David Bernstein: The New Englishman

In May 1956, in north London, David Bernstein was barmitzvahed. According to his cousin Henry, he was 'on *schpilkas*' throughout the service. After he read the Torah at the synagogue and had, according to Jewish custom, become a man, his thoughts turned to the afternoon's FA Cup final between his beloved Manchester City and Birmingham. In the morning, as the Torah had been lifted up in the air, and then carried around the synagogue on a victory lap – he, his father and his uncles all kissing it with due reverence – he had fantasised about Roy Paul doing the same thing with another sacred object in a few hours' time? As three o'clock approached, however, the rabbi appeared to be in no hurry to leave. He had still to give the traditional barmitzvah blessing. So young David decided to take matters into his own hands. To the rabbi's horror, he left the reception and walked into the front room to watch the match. By the time City goalkeeper Bert Trautmann had been knocked out with fifteen minutes of the match remaining, courageously playing on despite breaking a bone in his neck, the disgruntled rabbi had left and most of the guests had joined Bernstein in front of the television set.

*

Fifty-five years after leaving his barmitzvah to watch City win the FA Cup, Bernstein defied another authority figure, this time in Zurich. His one-man crusade against Sepp Blatter's unopposed re-election as FIFA president almost caused a diplomatic incident. From his boyhood rabbi to Blatter, and from his boyhood hero Francis Lee to Fabio Capello, many a Goliath has made the mistake of underestimating the mild-mannered, affable, former (Bernstein was appointed in 2010 but, as required by the organisation's rules, forced to relinquish the post on reaching the age of 70 three years later) FA chairman. 'David's victory over Goliath,' wrote Malcolm Gladwell, 'is held to be an anomaly. It was not. Davids win all the time.' True, Bernstein's rebellion was spectacularly crushed, a succession of FIFA delegates pouring vitriol on his attempt to postpone the vote until a 'reforming candidate' could be found. But he had won the bigger battle: the battle to belong. 'We English may be priggish and at times hypocritical,' wrote Alexander Chancellor in the *Guardian*, 'but let us be proud of the stance taken by the chairman of the English Football Association, David Bernstein, against the coronation of Sepp Blatter as president of FIFA.'

Born in St Helens, twenty miles from Manchester, Bernstein stayed loyal to City while growing up in north London, despite all his friends being either Spurs or Arsenal fans.

During his five years as Manchester City chairman he took on two star names, Francis Lee and Kevin Keegan. His involvement with the club had begun in the early 1990s, as a plc-experienced chartered accountant – at French Connection he had commissioned their hugely successful 'FCUK' advertisement campaign – when he was recruited to help run Lee's 'Forward with Franny' bid, which led to a takeover. Lee and his fellow investors made personal fortunes from the club's ensuing flotation, but their dream died as the team sank into the third tier. After ruthlessly ousting the City legend, eventually replacing him as chairman in 1998, Bernstein announced that the 'theatre of comedy', as the Maine Road soap opera was colloquially known at the time, would be 'closed down'.

Bernstein recalls:

When I came on to the board I found a vacuum. It was like being in the nineteenth century. The so-called offices were a house in Moss Side somewhere. The club shop was the size of my desk at Wembley. I'm sure it was the same at a lot of clubs. There was a revolution taking place. City, especially compared to Manchester United, were light years behind. During my period on the board I brought in a lot of finance – JD Sports, Sky TV – and raised a lot of money. When we were relegated to the third level of football, I did a double-page 'programme of development' in the local press about how to take the club forward. Fans, to this day, say they were relieved to see someone prepared to take a lead at the worst point in the club's history.

Although he lost his second big battle, with manager Keegan over the £6-million signing of Robbie Fowler, he won a great deal of respect for being the only director to go toe-to-toe with King Kev. 'The only person within the club who was not starry-eyed and affected by Kevin was David Bernstein,' recalled a City official. 'Kevin was well-backed in the transfer market, but Bernstein was very principled, never knee-jerk, and he felt that the Fowler signing was a flawed decision.' Despite presiding over back-to-back promotions and negotiating their occupancy of the state-of-the-art Eastlands stadium – a big draw for Abu Dhabi billionaire Sheikh Mansour when choosing which English club to buy – Bernstein resigned after falling out with the JD Sports executives over Keegan's excessive spending.

The reason I left the club was that Kevin was extremely – well, I'll use the word 'ambitious' for want of a better word – and he managed to seduce the board. The main people with the money, the JD Sports people, fell behind Keegan. After running a very strong show for the first four years, the last year became more difficult. I gradually found myself more isolated. I was very much against the Fowler deal. And I was very upset about selling the club to Thaksin Shinawatra. I thought of trying to block it. I talked to Sky about blocking their shareholding, but I couldn't follow it through.

When the FA's compliance unit demanded to see his bank accounts, in the wake of Lord Stevens' 2006 inquiry into illicit payments, Barry Silkman complained that he and his fellow agents were being victimised. 'It's because we've made a lot of money and we're Jewish,' he told David Conn. 'I'll go on the record with that. You don't see many Jews on the FA, do you?' True, the organisation had, from its formation in 1863 to its support of a breakaway top flight 129 years later, been a bastion of Anglo-Saxon Protestantism. The blazered gentlemen who formed its myriad committees had been drawn from a narrow, elite band of society; the same strata that ran exclusive golf, tennis and jockey clubs. Indeed, four years after the Stevens inquiry, its former chairman, Lord Triesman, told a parliamentary select committee that the lack of diversity within the association represented 'systemic failure'. And yet Triesman, his successor Bernstein – and indeed Dein, the man Bernstein had seen off for the job – were all Jews.

The gates had been opened back in the 1990s, when the legal and commercial expertise of 'outsiders' like Fynn and Lord Justice Taylor, who came from a Leeds Jewish family, was enlisted to drag the blazers into the New Age. It was Fynn who persuaded the FA to back the breakaway Premiership and arguably, without the Taylor Report, which responded to the Hillsborough tragedy by advocating all-seater stadiums, there would have been no commercial revolution. Around a third of clubs have, since its publication, built new stadiums, the rest undergoing major work either to meet all-seater requirements or improve capacity. Twenty-five years after the Hillsborough disaster, the journalist Ian Ridley noted that the demographic of football's audience had changed. 'Of the ninety-six people who died on the Leppings Lane terrace at Hillsborough,' he wrote, 'none was black or Asian, just four were women and only ten of the men were over thirty-five years of age, illustrating that the game's core audience was still the young, white working-class male. [But now there are] more women, more older men, and certainly more younger boys.'

In fact Jewish people have been part of this core audience since the beginning of the century – but Triesman was the first to rise to the top. As he recalls:

In the 1990s, Jewish and other outsiders were finally being invited in to reform the FA. But the paradox is that parts of the FA have changed remarkably little. [When I became chairman] it was a social formation made up of pretty elderly, exclusively white men, who had somehow come to the realisation that they needed to have at least a different appearance to the rest of the world when the rest of the world looked at them, and they'd better have one or two people to do that for them. They thought people like me and David Bernstein would be a bit exotic. David would not welcome anyone saying that, but I'm sure it's true.

Dein had been the first to make the breakthrough. In 1991 Fynn had helped Graham Kelly write the FA's groundbreaking *Blueprint for the Future of Football*. 'The FA are desperate for success,' Fynn observed at the time. 'They are being put under pressure by fans, players, managers and, not least, by the international bodies, UEFA and FIFA, who want a strong England to counter the lobbying of African and Third World nations . . . English football needs a trouble-shooting, John Harvey-Jones type figure.'

Kelly was actually more worried about a Kerry Packer-type figure splitting English football; in the late 1970s, the Australian's World Series had turned the cricketing world inside out. Fearing a Big Five attempt to set up a European, or even world, super-league, he responded positively to Dein's overtures, citing the Lyndon Johnson quotation about it being 'better to have him inside the tent pissing out, than outside the tent pissing in'.

'I was sympathetic to what they were saying,' says Kelly. 'I was writing the FA's blueprint for the future of football and the ideas that David Dein [and the others] were coming forward with for a separate league of eighteen clubs fit ideally into our blueprint. If they'd have had a Kerry Packer they would have been dangerous. It could have been very dangerous [to the whole future of English football].'

To the blazers' great relief, Dein, who had previously been considered a loose cannon, turned out to be a clubbable networker with charisma, energy and political antenna, born, in the *Daily Telegraph*'s words, 'to work a FIFA hotel breakfast room, offering a handshake here, a "how's the family?" there.' He became FA vice-chairman for four years (2000–4) and, at one point, was so powerful the managers of both Manchester United and Chelsea – Alex Ferguson and José Mourinho – combined forces to complain about his influence, arguing he was exercising it on Arsenal's behalf. Dein was behind the appointment of England's first foreign manager, Sven-Göran Eriksson, and his strong UEFA and FIFA connections helped him become president of the G14 group of major European clubs.

In 2008 Triesman was appointed as the FA's first independent chairman by prime minister Tony Blair with a brief to reform the institution and drag it into the twenty-first century. A distinctive feature of the New Age had been the global interaction of football, business and politics – and the good lord ticked all three boxes. A consummate political operator, he was known for his discretion, fine judgement and impeccable connections – and his abiding passion for Tottenham Hotspur. 'I got inside the tent,' he said. 'I think I became a tolerated insider.' Born, like the other two Davids, in 1943, he was brought up in a prefab near White Hart Lane and played amateur football before becoming a senior referee in London and Middlesex for eight years. In his youth, his attitude to the football establishment resembled that of his father's to the golfing fraternity: Mick Triesman, who had grown up in the Brady Street mansions and fought the Mosleyites in Cable Street, had campaigned hard to join a golf club – even though he didn't even play the game. According to David Triesman: 'If you'd have said to him: "Do you know what to do?" he'd have said: "I think you've got to get it up to near that flag and there's a hole up there." But he was absolutely determined to provoke the golf club because they wouldn't let him, or any other Jews, in.' Inverting Groucho Marx's famous quotation, he was desperate to join a club that refused to have people like him for a member. After the Second World War, as Anglo-Jewry became more suburban, and more dispersed across the country, interest had grown in the game. In a 1960 *Jewish Chronicle* investigation, it was found that some clubs were openly anti-Semitic, while others either unofficially blackballed Jews or used official quota systems.

In 1970, Triesman, then a Communist Party member, wrote a seventeen-page introduction to a book called *Football Mania*. Describing footballers as victims of 'ideological oppression' and 'capitalist mass culture', he criticised the game as 'a sport largely paid for by working-class men on the pitch, owned by an exclusive group of capitalists'. He also condemned the FA's ruling council as a bastion of privilege, 'made up of a duke, two earls, a marquis and an assortment of military gentlemen'. He condemned the rising cost of tickets and wrote of 'estrangement' between fans and their clubs. During his subsequent career as head of the AUT lecturers' union, general secretary of the Labour Party and junior Foreign Office minister, his militancy waned; thirty-eight years after his revolutionary manifesto, one newspaper praised him as 'a suit and tie man and a career trades unionist and politician [which] was what the FA wanted after years of scandal and in-fighting'. But his reforming zeal remained intact, and there were great hopes that he would challenge the powerful vested interests that dominated the governing body.

Triesman's period at the Foreign Office might have taught him the virtues of calm negotiation and a level head, but the world's worst hotspots had nothing on English football's shark-infested committee rooms. The Premier League executive, Richard Scudamore, and his chairman, Sir Dave Richards, both savaged him after his attack on football's £3 billion debt mountain. The World Cup bid disintegrated under pressure from internal rivalries. And his attempt to regulate the game, which he viewed as a runaway commercial behemoth, unleashed a ferocious campaign by his enemies. 'He was hounded by the Premier League for warning of clubs' debts and seeking a greater governing role,' wrote David Conn after Triesman, entirely predictably, had fallen on his sword. In 2010 a *Mail on Sunday* reporter had secretly recorded, and subsequently exposed, his views on corruption at a private dinner; he had, in essence, gossiped himself out of a job. In the words of Triesman:

I think all of us underestimate how strong cultural structures are and how hard it is to shift them. One should never underestimate, in my experience, the effectiveness of gatekeeping. You can't have a system based on 'Buggins's turn'. People say: 'What's wrong with Buggins? He put in his time, he did the work. Look at all these youth leagues in, say, Hampshire, they're really good. Why change it?' But it doesn't reflect the sport as a whole and it actively leaves some people out. You never ever change that gradually. It changes because there's a galvanic shock to the bloody system. That shock will be legislation beheading the current system. And then the consequences will go right through the rest of it. It can't go on like that. You can't have a representative group, all of them with locked-in interests in only a particular range of outcomes. You can't have that and expect change. We as a government knew we needed to do it, but didn't have the bottle to do it. We kept being threatened by the Premier League with God knows what consequences – my colleagues didn't want to find them out.

Still, his reign, however short-lived, was a riposte to Silkman's claim that Jews were, and would always be, excluded from the corridors of power.

While Triesman was installed at the FA, Dein was still desperately clinging to the hope of a return. *Persona non grata* at the Emirates, he briefly emerged from the wilderness to join the 2018 World Cup bid. 'I looked around at people who I thought had a very great deal to contribute but had, in the past, been excluded,' said Triesman. 'Which of them [the other board members] would willingly have let David Dein on to the board of the FA? There were big efforts to stop him having the life membership of the FA Council that I think he was entitled to because of the number of years he'd been there. And yet his number of contacts, for example, was absolutely phenomenal.' The bid's failure to secure more than one foreign vote tarnished his reputation – and Dein returned to the wilderness. He was strongly tipped to replace Triesman – but Bernstein, once again the underestimated outsider, got the job. Both contenders had turned their boyhood clubs around by shaking up the status quo – and both had become marginalised figures in their boardrooms.

Significantly, when Bernstein took over from Triesman there was no media discussion about the prominence of Jews in the higher echelons of the game. This was in stark contrast to the reaction provoked by Abramovich's recruitment of Grant four years earlier. I can remember the mutterings in press rooms about a Jewish cabal taking over the Premier League. The *Sun* even ran a column about football's 'kosher nostra'. Martin Samuel wrote in *The Times* that, 'with Roman Abramovich as owner, Grant as manager and Zahavi a trusted confidant of the pair, Chelsea are not so much Russian these days as kosher . . . it is important to acknowledge that the strongest influence on his [Abramovich's] life is not his nationality but his faith.' The former Cabinet minister David Mellor described Abramovich in the London *Evening Standard* as an 'Israel-obsessed Russian'.

In fact, from the moment his appointment was announced Bernstein was presented as the apotheosis of the quintessential Englishman; his successful spell at Wembley Stadium, as director and chairman, had clearly proved his patriotism – not to mention competence. But it was his lone stand at Zurich that indicated the arrival of a rare type of administrator: someone with the nerve to stand up for his beliefs. His refusal to back down against the most powerful man in world football won him many admirers. If he was feeling a little depressed after his FIFA drubbing, Chancellor reassured him, he should 'recall Winston Churchill's remark: "You have enemies? Good. That means you've stood up for something, sometime in your life."'

The FA had, for some time, been shorthand for unprincipled buffoonery, but Bernstein's arrival restored credibility to the organisation, his battle with the game's biggest *machas* winning praise from the normally cynical national press. In February 2012, he stripped John Terry of the England captaincy. As the Chelsea defender had been ordered to stand trial after the European Championship – accused of racial abuse allegations – the FA chairman decided he should, for the duration of the tournament, be relieved of his armband. In a season that had been crying out for leadership over the corrosive issue of racism, the decision – particularly the speed and authority with which it was made – was widely welcomed. Not by England manager Fabio Capello, however, who grumbled about it to one of his country's television presenters. A few days later the Italian resigned. Once again, the resolute, decisive chairman was praised for his handling of a toxic and difficult situation.

Bernstein looked as if he had walked straight out of his home counties' members' club into Wembley Stadium, combining, in classic style, the understated niceties of clubland etiquette with a Churchillian resilience, recalling – for Chancellor at least – the dashing aristocratic heroes played by Leslie Howard in films like *The Scarlet Pimpernel*. The famous scene at the end of that 1935 movie, in which Howard murmurs, 'Look, England!' after spying the white cliffs of Dover, was actually conjured up by three Jewish Hungarians: producer Alexander Korda, writer Lajos Biro and Howard, whose real surname was Steiner. Bernstein's acceptance represents, to my mind, the triumph of integration. His ascent would have delighted the Jewish Lads Brigade commander who, almost a hundred years earlier, hoped that sport would 'instill into the rising generation all that is best in English character, manly independence, honest truth, clean living, love of . . . health-giving pursuits'. It has proved, beyond doubt, that being a Good Sportsman and a Good Jew are not incompatible aspirations, and that Englishness and Jewishness are not mutually contradictory. Bernstein is the classic outsider who has overcome prejudice to become the very model of a thoroughly anglicised Jew. With his identifiably Jewish name, and his ethnic openness, he has also shown just how far Englishness itself has been redefined in the early twenty-first century.

The New Jews

Modern Jewishness is as difficult to define as modern Englishness. My version certainly clashes with the one espoused by a new breed of Jewish owner: the Simon Corney generation. Corney is young, dynamic, ambitious and football-mad. He is also an orthodox Jew. So orthodox, in fact, that he won't watch his team play on Saturday. Tottenham might still be identified as the Jewish Club, but if you are looking for salt beef sandwiches, *menorahs* and *mezuzot* – scrolls of parchment containing the words of the Hebrew prayer 'Shema Israel' – you won't find them at White Hart Lane. You will find them, instead, at an old mill town in Lancashire.

For the past eight years, Boundary Park stadium, renamed Ice Station Zebra on account of it being the coldest ground in the Football League, has been kosher. At one time, as Corney proudly pointed out, he had three Jewish players on Oldham Athletic's books: Dean Furman, Joe Jacobson and Nick Blackman: 'We were pretty close to a *minyan* [a quorum of ten adult Jews required for worship]. At the time we had three directors and three footballers, so we were just four short.'

Spurs chairman Daniel Levy was only thirty-nine when he replaced Alan Sugar, but Corney was seven years younger when he took over the beleaguered Latics with Simon Blitz and Danny Gazal. He attended the Hasmonean school – which serves the orthodox Jewish community of north-west London – with Laurence Bassini, who bought Watford in 2010. And he played in the same Jewish football team as Tony Bloom, the owner of Brighton and Hove Albion and his brother; with Corney and the Blooms in their side, Hillgar

Athletic won the Maccabi Southern Football League and Cup in the late 1990s.

It feels, in a way, as if we have come full circle. Like Louis Bookman's parents, Corney refuses to desecrate the sabbath. Being an owner rather than a player, of course, means he can circumvent this obstacle. But, in January 2012, there was one *shabbat* match he just had to go to. Oldham were playing the mighty Liverpool in the FA Cup third round on a Friday evening. As the Holy Day begins a few minutes before sunset on Friday, he was faced with a huge dilemma. Would he be able to attend the club's biggest game in recent years? He solved the problem by staying with his son at 'Hotel Anfield', 300 yards from the famous ground. By walking to the game they were, he said, 'technically, *halachically*, whatever way you want to put it, not doing anything wrong. It was not in the spirit, but I sure as hell wasn't missing that game. I went to Anfield, said hello to King Kenny and walked the hallowed turf. It was every Jewish boy's dream come true.'

Like the Bookmans, and my old Selig Brodetsky headmaster, Corney firmly believes Saturday should be the Day of Rest not the Day of the Match. 'It's a religious thing but also a family thing,' he explained:

I have three young kids, and that's very important to me. If I didn't have the Saturday off, then I wouldn't see my kids. It's a discipline as much as anything else. And, besides, my kids go to religious schools, and it would be highly frowned upon. But the thing is I live, think, breathe, football.

These days you can do both, be a religious Jew and a football nut. We are definitely living in a more tolerant era, to the point where I don't even think people think about it. America led the way. In many ways I understand why David Pleat, David

Dein and Irving Scholar kept a low profile. They just got on with the job. They did the right thing for them at that time. I go to synagogue every week. I keep kosher. All the festivals I celebrate. I'm very traditional. And it's not affected me in any way in running a football club. There's a small group of us now and we are accepted. When my mate Laurence Bassini heard I was coming to the Watford–Brighton game, he got kosher salt beef sandwiches in for the game. He said: 'What's the point? If I have roasted ham, no one's going to eat it.' I went there with the Blooms and the Bassinis – and it was catered with kosher salt beef. And there are other clubs. I often see a name, a director, like Jeff Mostyn at Bournemouth – and Leyton Orient, QPR, all the London teams have had a Jewish connection somewhere. So no one bats an eyelid. Why should they? We're different, but there are many different cultures in football now, as in society. And we all rub along very well. Of course, it was very different in the beginning. It must have been very difficult. I guess some of the early Jews in football were pioneers.

Conclusion: The Forgotten

'We are masters of forgetting.'

Jonathan Safran Foer *Haggadah*, 2012

In the New Age English football has become, to adopt Philip Roth's assessment of baseball, 'a space where the marginal can become central, where the charges of not really belonging, of not being real men, of being interlopers or cheats can be defeated.' Abramovich's wealth and Bernstein's power have, undoubtedly, insulated them against anti-Semitism. But the fact that the two most influential men in the domestic game refuse to downplay their ethnicity suggests that the epic Anglo-Jewish journey from ghetto outsiders to football insiders is now complete. And that, a hundred years after an Irish-Lithuanian immigrant abandoned his Jewish family for the 'bright lights' of Bradford, we should acknowledge this astonishing success story, and celebrate the gall, brazen nerve, effrontery and incredible guts – the chutzpah – of the mostly forgotten pioneers featured in this journey.

They have been forgotten for three reasons. Firstly, because of the Jewish, and indeed general immigrant, tradition of starting afresh and not looking back. As mountaineers, and upwardly-mobile migrant communities, will tell you, you don't look down when you're climbing.

Secondly, because of Anglo-Jewry's deeply ingrained history of accommodation. In writing this book I have discovered a new appreciation for this strategy. I can understand why centuries, even millennia, of negative stereotypes and images, based on the notion of the Jew as Christ-killer and money-lender, have informed my tribe's self-effacement, why the impulse to lower our voices has always been latent, why tight-lippedness – even in the New Age – has often been advisable. As Naomi Alderman observed in *Disobedience*: 'British Jews cannot speak, cannot be seen, value absolute invisibility above all other virtues.' Our tendency, according to her fellow novelist Linda Grant, has always been 'not to look too Jewy'. We can be 'Jewy' in private, of course, but – from Bookman's outraged parents to Bernstein's outraged rabbi, from Goldberg's disappearing act to Dein's removal from the history books – it makes a kind of sense to keep such stories to ourselves. Like Israeli wine, they don't travel. Far better to confine them to the self-contained, embellished circuit of weddings, barmitzvahs and funerals than give them a public airing and draw attention to our 'Otherness'. That way, anti-Semitism lies.

And yet, in 2003, an influential government report, *Who Are We British?*, concluded that: 'We are a multicultural society . . . made up of a diverse range of cultures and identities, and one that emphasises the need for a continuous process of mutual engagement and learning about each other with respect, understanding and tolerance.' Its author, Sir Bernard Crick, observed: 'Dual identities have been common, even before large-scale immigration.' A historically attenuated Anglo-Jewish identity, which dates all the way back to medieval England, has, in recent years, become more assertive: film festivals, TV documentaries, book weeks, flourishing cultural organisations and publications. In the past, assimilated English Jews rarely wrote or produced work about their own ethnicity, as we know from the careers of Lucian Freud, Peter Brook and Harold Pinter. But a rising generation of writers, artists and critics now seeks to be heard. According to Matthew J. Reisz, editor of the *Jewish Quarterly*, the house journal of Anglo-Jewish intellectual life, they now 'move in and out of Jewish identity as one part of their British identity'. Jewish stories, Reisz observed, are 'being told very well, and unapologetically . . . in a completely unselfconscious way,' as 'part of a wider British conversation'.

So why, then, so few stories about Jews and football? This brings us to the third reason. Could it be that, at some deep-seated level, football is still regarded as an un-Jewish game? Like many Jews of my generation, football provided entry to an English childhood and confirmed my English identity. I loved both its aesthetic beauty and raw physicality. At my Jewish primary school, the playing of it was banned – which made it all the more exotic. But at my synagogue, every Saturday morning, there was a tacit acceptance that most of the congregation would be going to the match in a few hours' time. At my mixed secondary school, I played in Jews v. Christians matches at lunchtime, but soon graduated to the school first team. I often wondered why I was the only Jew in it. There were plenty of other good players, but they were turning out in Jewish leagues on a Sunday. And now, for the last fifteen years, I have been making my living writing about it. This is my second book about football. I have even co-written a play about being a football-obsessed Jew growing up in the 1970s. It was packed out for most nights of its run and received some great reviews. But quite a few of my family disliked it. It was a community play featuring thirty-odd characters, but none of the cast was Jewish. It was staged in Leeds, which still has a community of around 7,000, but I estimated that no more than 100 turned up to watch.

'An age-old question would perplex Jewish circles,' wrote Jeffrey S. Gurock. 'Was it possible for a dedicated player to maintain strong ties to the faith – or at least to continue to ally himself with his people and his past – as he made every effort to emulate the way of the Gentiles in a modern arena?' The conflict between the values of traditional Judaism and athletic competition has not disappeared. When I was a boy, there was a backlash against anglicisation. My headmaster, like many communal leaders, feared it had gone too far. The mission was no longer to make Jews appear and think more English but to Stay Jewish, to make the younger generation more interested in the Jewish aspect of their identity and prevent the further fracturing of the community. But the die had been cast. Our parents and grandparents had been socialised into the English working class through sport. For me, football was a way of transcending the claustrophobic confines of my Jewish suburban existence. It enabled me to become who I wanted to be, to think of myself as English as well as Jewish; to think of my football-mad family as rooted in the life of the country rather than tossed on to its shores by circumstance.

It didn't erase that eternal voice in my head, though. The one that makes me feel guilty for enjoying the pointless spectacle of grown men running around like *meshuga*. For defying the Eleventh Commandment: 'Football is not for a Yiddisher boy!' For shedding a distinctive part of my identity. I used to hear that voice on the terraces, but these days it whispers those six words into my ear every time I get my laptop out at a press box on a Saturday afternoon: 'Does your rabbi know you're here?'

Select Bibliography

Adar, S., *Liverpool: Football, Life and Death,* Glory, 2007

Brenner, M. and Reuveni, G., *Emancipation through Muscles,* University of Nebraska, 2006.

Brook, S., *The Club,* Pan Books, 1990.

Cohen, R., *Tough Jews,* Vintage, 1999.

Conn, D., *Richer Than God,* Quercus, 2012.

Davies, H., *The Glory Game,* Weidenfeld and Nicolson, 1972.

Dee, D., *Jews and British Sport,* Manchester University Press, 2012.

Downing, D., *The Best of Enemies: England v Germany,* Bloomsbury, 2000.

Downs, D. and Edwards, L., *The Definitive Reading FC,* Tony Brown, 1998.

Endelman, T. M., *The Jews of Britain, 1856 to 2000,* University of California Press, 2002.

Feldman, D., *Englishmen and Jew: Social Relations and Political Culture, 1840–1914,* Yale, 1974.

Foer, F., *How Soccer Explains the World,* HarperCollins, 2004.

Fry, B., *Big Fry, Barry Fry: The Autobiography,* HarperCollins, 2001.

Fynn, A. and Whitcher. K., *Arsenal: The Making of a Modern Superclub,* Vision Sports, 2008.

Glanville, B., *The Rise of Gerry Logan,* Secker and Warburg, 1963.

Glanville, B., *Soccer Nemesis,* Secker & Warburg, 1956.

Gold, D., *Pure Gold,* Highdown, 2006.

Jacobson, H., *Coming from Behind,* Vintage, 1983.

Jacobson, H., *The Mighty Walzer*, Jonathan Cape, 1999.

Jacobson, H., *Roots Schmoots*, Viking, 1993.

Keston. M., *Superfan*, Vision Sports, 2010.

Lambert, N. and Mitchell, V., *Jews and Europe in the Twenty-First Century: Thinking Jewish*, Vallentine, 2008.

Lazarus, M., *A Club Called Brady*, New Cavendish Books, 1996.

Mattick, R., *Swindon Town Football Club: 100 Greats*, Tempus, 2002.

McDonald, T., *Leyton Orient: The Untold Story of the Os' Best Ever Team*, Football World, 2006.

Meisl, W., *Soccer Revolution*, The Sportsmans Book Club, 1956.

Midgley, D. and Hutchins. C., *Abramovich: The Billionaire from Nowhere*, HarperCollins, 2004.

Panayi, P., *An Immigration History of Britain*, Pearson, 2010.

Scholar, I. and Bose, M., *Behind Closed Doors*, Andre Deutsch, 1992.

Shindler, C., *Manchester City Ruined My Life*, Headline, 2012.

Shindler, C., *Manchester United Ruined My Life*, Headline, 1998.

Simpson. D., *The Last Champions*, Bantam, 2012.

Sinclair, C., *Blood Libels*, Allison and Busby, 1985.

Sugar, A., *What You See Is What You Get*, Macmillan, 2010.

Taylor, D. J., *On the Corinthian Spirit*, Yellow Jersey, 2006.

Teeman, R., *A Lawyer for All Seasons*, Scratching Shed, 2011.

Wilson, J., *Inverting the Pyramid*, Orion, 2009.

Winder, R., *Bloody Foreigners*, Abacus 2004.

Glossary

Taken from a composite language spoken across much of Europe and beyond and subject to distortion in their passage from the Hebrew alphabet to the Roman one in which they're found here, Yiddish words can be spelt and even interpreted in a multitude of ways. The Yiddish (and Hebrew) definitions included below are intended to help the reader understand the very specific contexts in which the words appear, and as such this glossary makes no claim to be a definitive or comprehensive record of their meaning.

barmitzvah	A ceremony marking the fact that a boy has reached the age of thirteen and is obligated to observe the commandments. The *batmitzvah* is the equivalent rite of passage for girls.
cheder	A traditional elementary school teaching the basics of Judaism and the Hebrew language.
dina de-malchuta	'The law of the land', repeated numerous times in the Talmud, attributed to Samuel.
frummers	Those who are very devout; from the German *fromm*, meaning 'devout' or 'pious'.
gornisch	A corruption of Yiddish words, meaning 'nothing'.

goyim nachas	Dubious pleasure; i.e. pleasure (*nachat*) that non-Jews (*goyim*) experience.
goyishe	Not Jewish, i.e. Gentile.
haftara	Conclusion. A reading from the Prophets, read along with the weekly Torah portion.
halachical	According to Jewish law, based on the Talmud.
heimishe	Homely or warm in an old-fashioned Jewish way.
heym	Home, often referred to as the 'old country' by new immigrants nostalgic for their former lives.
holtzhackers	Literally woodcutters, often used to describe the performance of a task or game with more enthusiasm than finesse.
kibitzers	One who offers (often unwanted) advice or commentary from the sidelines.
kippah	The skullcap worn by Jews during services, and by some Jews at all times, more commonly known as a 'yarmulke'.
lokshen	Yiddish word for 'noodles'.
macha	'Big shot'. Person with access to the authorities.
maftir	Hebrew for 'concluder'; used specifically in relation to the last person called to the Torah on Shabbat and holidays mornings.
maven	A trusted expert in a particular field who seeks to pass knowledge on to others. From Hebrew, via Yiddish, it means one who understands, based on an accumulation of knowledge.

menschilkayt	Properties that make one a 'mensch', a Yiddish word for person of integrity and honour.
menorah	A nine-branched candelabrum used on the Jewish holiday of Hanukkah.
meshuga	Hebrew word meaning 'crazy'.
meshugana	A crazy person.
mezuzot	A small piece of parchment inscribed with biblical passages and marked with the word *Shaddai*, a name of the Almighty, that is rolled up in a container and affixed by many Jewish households to their door frames in conformity with Jewish law.
minhag Anglia	'The English Usage'. A phrase for the essential Englishness of the community, it sums up the characteristic policy of assimilation adopted by British Jewry until at least the late 20th century.
minyan	Refers to the quorum of ten Jewish adults required for certain religious obligations.
moishe gross	Literally 'big Moses'. Refers to small man with a big name. Someone too big for their boots.
musaf	A Jewish prayer.
nachas	Yiddish for joy or blessings; pride especially for one's children.
ostjuden	East European Jews.
peyot	Hebrew word for sidelocks or sidecurls worn by some men and boys in the Orthodox Jewish community.
platz	To burst apart from either an excess of laughter or emotion.

schmatter	Yiddish for clothes, especially the clothing manufacturing industry.
schtarker	A strongman.
schtup	To have sex, to screw.
schpilkas	Nervous energy.
shabbat	Jewish day of rest, observed from just before sunset on Friday evening until the appearance of three stars in the sky on Saturday night.
shiva	The week-long mourning period for first-degree relatives.
shtetl	A small town with a large Jewish population in central and eastern Europe.
shul	Yiddish word for synagogue.
tachlas	Most commonly used to refer to the bottom line, in certain contexts can also denote 'the done thing'.
tallesim	Prayer shawl.
tefillin	Small black leather boxes containing scrolls of parchment inscribed with verses from the Torah. Worn, either on arm or forehead, by observant Jews during weekday morning prayers.
yarmulkahs	Skullcaps worn by Jewish men and boys.
Yom Kippur	The Day of Atonement, the holiest and most solemn day on the Jewish calendar. Observed with a twenty-five-hour period of fasting and intensive prayer.

Picture Credits

Plates

P1

Central Press/Getty Images

From a newspaper in the collection of Joyce Levy

Jewish Museum of London

P2

Jewish Museum of London

Jewish Museum of London

P3

From the personal collection of Peggy Gaunt and Gary Gaunt
From the personal collection of Micky Dulin

P4

William Vanderson/Fox Photos/Getty Images
Popperfoto/Getty Images

P5

Keystone/Hulton Archive/Getty Images
Allsport/Hulton Archive/Getty Images

P6

PA/PA Archive/Press Association Images
Manchester Jewish Museum

P7

From the personal collection of Nick Sonenfield
Popperfoto/Getty Images
Graham Chadwick /Allsport

P8

Bob Thomas/Getty Images
Clint Hughes/Getty Images
Peter Macdiarmid/Getty Images

Index